Production Collaboration in the Theatre

Production Collaboration in the Theatre reveals the ingredients of proven successful collaborations in academic and professional theatre training, where respect, trust, and inclusivity are encouraged and roles are defined with a clear and unified vision.

Garnering research from conversations with over 100 theatre professionals on Broadway and in regional and educational theatre, the authors provide multiple approaches to working together that are designed to help students and teachers of theatre discover and develop the collaborative tools that work best for them. Each chapter offers practical application with discussion prompts from real-life scenarios to practice and develop the critical problem-solving skills necessary for theatre artists to navigate common collaboration challenges. Compelling topical case studies and insightful interviews invite readers to explore the principles of collaboration and inspire them to build joyful, equitable, and collaborative relationships in academic and professional settings.

Production Collaboration in the Theatre offers theatre faculty and students a practical approach to developing the interpersonal skills necessary for a lifetime career in collaboration in the theatre. An ideal resource for actors, directors, designers, and production teams, this book provides theatre artists in training with an opportunity to develop their collaborative style in a way that will guide and support the longevity of a successful career.

Rufus Bonds Jr. (AEA, SDC) is the resident director of *The Lion King* on Broadway and an assistant professor for musical theatre performance in the Syracuse University Department of Drama. He is recognized nationally and internationally as a director, actor, and writer. Productions include: London – Porgy in *Porgy and Bess* at the Regent's Park Open Air Theatre; baritone-soloist for Duke Ellington's *Sacred Music*, Carnegie Hall;

Broadway – *Rent, Once on This Island*, and *Parade* (Drama Desk nomination for Best Supporting Actor); national tours – *The Color Purple* as Mister, *The Lion King* as Mufasa, and *Miss Saigon* as John. Directing projects range from *Lysistrata* to *Into the Woods*. Rufus is a Eugene O'Neill semi-finalist for his play *The Sisters of Rosewall High*.

"Have Faith"

Maria Cominis (AEA, SAG-AFTRA, DG, NAAT) is an actor, playwright, author, and professor of acting at California State University Fullerton Department of Theatre and Dance. She is also a master teacher of the Uta Hagen and Michael Chekhov techniques. Her television credits include *Desperate Housewives, New Girl, All My Children*, and *One Life to Live*, and her theatre credits include *Bernarda Alba, Diviners, Ivanov*, and *Knives are Silent*. For more information, visit www.mariacominis.com.

Mark Ramont is an associate artist at Ford's Theatre. He worked professionally as a director and theatre administrator for over 25 years before becoming head of directing at California State University, Fullerton. He was associate artistic director at New York City's Circle Rep, where he worked with professionals such as Anne Bogart, Paula Vogel, and Joe Mantello. He is the recipient of the Princess Grace Foundation – USA Statuette Award.

Production Collaboration in the Theatre

Guiding Principles

Rufus Bonds Jr., Maria Cominis, and Mark Ramont

Routledge
Taylor & Francis Group

NEW YORK AND LONDON

Cover image: © Getty Images

First published 2022
by Routledge
605 Third Avenue, New York, NY 10158

and by Routledge
2 Park Square, Milton Park, Abingdon, Oxon OX14 4RN

Routledge is an imprint of the Taylor & Francis Group, an informa business

© 2022 Rufus Bonds Jr., Maria Cominis, and Mark Ramont

Library of Congress Cataloging-in-Publication Data
Names: Bonds, Rufus Jr., author. | Cominis, Maria, author. | Ramont, Mark, author.
Title: Production collaboration in the theatre: guiding principles /
Rufus Bonds Jr., Maria Cominis, and Mark Ramont.
Description: [1.] | Abingdon, Oxon; New York: Routledge, 2021. |
Includes bibliographical references and index.
Identifiers: LCCN 2021028416 (print) | LCCN 2021028417 (ebook) |
ISBN 9780367409746 (hardback) | ISBN 9780367409753 (paperback) |
ISBN 9780367810252 (ebook)
Subjects: LCSH: Musicals–Production and direction. |
Theater–Production and direction. | Artistic collaboration.
Classification: LCC MT955 .B615 2021 (print) |
LCC MT955 (ebook) | DDC 792.602/3–dc23
LC record available at https://lccn.loc.gov/2021028416
LC ebook record available at https://lccn.loc.gov/2021028417

ISBN: 978-0-367-40974-6 (hbk)
ISBN: 978-0-367-40975-3 (pbk)
ISBN: 978-0-367-81025-2 (ebk)

DOI: 10.4324/9780367810252

Typeset in Goudy
by Newgen Publishing UK

I dedicate this book to those voices spoken in the shadows, to my family who always lift my words, and to Maria and Mark for our powerful journey toward truth.

Rufus Bonds Jr.

For Charlie: May all your collaborations be filled with love and joy.

Maria Cominis

For Marshall W. Mason and Anne Bogart, who taught me what collaboration and generosity are.

Mark Ramont

Contents

Preface

Maria Cominis

Twyla Tharp said, "In the end, all collaborations are love stories." I'm not sure I would have agreed with her three years ago. I was in the middle of one of the most challenging collaborations of my academic career when Routledge asked me to peer review a colleague's book. At the end of the process, they ask what resources I might like to see available. I mentioned in the peer review survey that someone ought to write a book on production collaboration geared for academia. My colleague, John Kaufmann, and I initiated a panel for ATHE in 2018 called "Fruitful Collaboration with Directors, Production Design Faculty & Students." Based on the interest in participating on the panel, we learned that this was a very hot topic; however, I didn't intend to be the one to write it. My first thought when Routledge reached out was, "I am in no way an expert in collaboration, but I know people who are."

I realized that this was an opportunity to research best practices in order to solve my own collaborative challenges and maybe bring some joy back into my collaborations while inspiring students to find their way through this elusive skill.

I knew I couldn't write this book alone. My collaborative style is thinking out loud – I need someone to jump start me. At the same time, I sent my own son – who was also choosing a life in the arts – to college. One Sunday, he and I walked Del Mar beach on his day off during his first year at UCSD, where he was musical directing his peers. He was so passionate while talking about the challenges of collaboration and what the solutions might be. Who could I interview that might have answers to all his questions? Even though he was new to collaboration, he had some pretty wise solutions. I thought I had better listen.

I reached out to friends who were working on Broadway and they were more than generous when it came to sharing whatever they could to support the next generation of theatre artists. It was clear that this project was to become a bigger conversation, calling for many points of view.

At the same time, Mark Ramont bailed me out on a project by stepping in as dramaturg when the playwright became unavailable. His suggestions were spot on. He had over 30 years of directing experience, and had been an artistic director. He therefore had a very different take on things from my own. Mark challenged my point of view as a true collaborator, and I valued that.

When the COVID-19 pandemic and racial and social reckoning all collided within months of each other, our initial ideas were turned upside down and we took pause and listened. Things were different and we couldn't ignore it. The complexities of racial and social inequities embedded in our institutions sent us to examine our own beliefs and practices, and we asked, 'What must we do to become part of the solution and change?'

We realized that we needed another voice. I listened to panels and webinars, and I found myself returning to Rufus Bonds Jr.'s inspiring talk on culture and collaborating in the classroom to seek understanding. When Mark and I hit a brick wall, he said, "I think we need another author and I think it should be Rufus." Rufus had graduated from CSUF with an MFA in directing under Mark's tutelage. Before Rufus came to us, he had a prolific Broadway career, originating the role of Jim Conley in *Parade* under the direction of Hal Prince and performing in multiple Broadway shows and national tours. Not only was he born to sing, he was also born to teach. Before I could take a breath, I said "Yes!" and by the next Sunday writers' meeting, Rufus was on board.

What I didn't notice before taking on this book is that *fun* collaboration is a lot of messing around. Talking around the topic. Making each other laugh. Sharing, supporting, agreeing, disagreeing, getting frustrated at times, but at the end of the day, listening and expanding our limited points of view to learn from each other. Out of that comes understanding and compassion, two necessary blessings for successful collaboration.

I am so grateful for the contribution Mark and Rufus have made as co-authors and for their compassion as human beings. I am also grateful for my guys at home: my husband John, who believes in me more than he should, and for Charlie, but for whom this book would not exist if he hadn't nudged me and told me he would definitely read it if I wrote it.

I hope you find the guiding principles helpful in navigating your collaborations, both in life and in the theatre. Above all, I agree with Twyla Tharp: at the core, what we do comes from love. We come to the theatre because we love it. We love telling the story, sharing the connection with one another and with the audience because if it is not born out of love, then why do it?

Maria Cominis
March 2021

Acknowledgments

The authors wish to thank every person who engaged in conversation with us. Your input and point of view, whether it aligned with our own or not, informed us and widened our lens as we examined these tenets for successful and joyful collaboration. We look forward to our next collaboration with you.

Thank you Stacey Walker and Lucia Accorsi at Routledge Publishing; Sue Berkompas from Vanguard University; Scott Bolman and Sarah Ripper from CSUF; and John Kaufmann from Evergreen Valley College.

Contributors

The following people contributed through lengthy interviews and ongoing discussion.

Lynn Ahrens, lyricist, librettist, and composer**

Brooke Aston Harper, educator, actor, and activist

Alexandra Billings

David Bridel, director, playwright, educator, performer, and writer

Stephen Flaherty, composer and lyricist **

Jill Gold, production stage manager

John Gromada, sound designer **

Kimberly Harris, actor

Kari Hayter, director and educator

Celise Hicks, choreographer

Arianna Huhn, anthropologist

Toni-Leslie James, costume designer, and educator*

John Kaufmann, director and educator, Evergreen Valley College

Ron Kellum, artistic director

Ben Krywosz, director and artistic director

Kecia Lewis, actress

Stanley Wayne Mathis, actor

Heather McDonald, playwright

Tracey Moore, actor, author and educator

Mariel Mulet, Esq., Labor and Employment Law Section of the California Bar, AWI

Cricket S. Myers, sound designer*

Chelsea Pace, author, intimacy choreographer and coordinator, and educator

Michele Patsakis, DM, educator and singer

Danny Pelzig, director, choreographer, and educator

Jim Pentecost, producer, stage manager, and director

Lora K. Powell, stage manager, and educator

Clint Ramos, costume designer**

Kelvin Rhodes, actor, educator, and activist

Laura Rikard, professor, intimacy choreographer and coordinator, director, and actor

Rui Rita, lighting designer

Susan Sampliner, company manager

Ann Sheffield, set designer and educator

Amber Snead, casting director and actor

Cheryl Thomas, hair and makeup supervisor

Salisha Thomas, actor

Daryl Waters, composer, arranger, orchestrator, and conductor**

Ralph Zito, dialect coach and educator

The Collective

The following people contributed through conversations, questions and surveys.

Mary Baird, actor

Paul Barnes, director and educator

Ron Bashford, director and educator

Jim Bracchitta, actor

Kye Bracket, performer

Lise Bruneau, actor

Rob Bundy, artistic director, director, and educator

Jeff Calhoun, director and choreographer*

Tony Cisek, set designer

Kyle Cooper, director

Sheldon Epps, artistic director, director, and director of diversity programs

Jonathan Fielding, actor

Kenny Finkle, playwright and educator

David Friedman, composer, musical director, and arranger

Sue Frost, commercial producer**

Gene Gillette, actor

Josh Grisetti, actor, director, and educator

Adam Gwon, composer and lyricist

Jef Hall-Flavin, director and educator

Richard Hellesen, playwright and educator

Takeshi Kata, set designer and educator

Thomas Keegan, actor

Steven Kemp, set designer

Lily Knight, actor

Kellee Knighten Hough, actor

James Kronzer, set designer

Marcus Kyd, actor

Steven Landau, music director

Matthew Lopez, playwright**

Craig McDonald, actor

Timothy Mackabee, set designer

Robert Mammana, actor

Donna Migliaccio, actor

Carine Montbertrand, actor

Colby Nordberg, lights and projections designer

Geoff Packard, actor and educator

Michele Pawk, actor and educator**

Kenneth Posner, lighting designer**

J.T. Rogers, playwright**

Erhard Rom, set designer

Jay Russell, actor and filmmaker

Andrew Samonsky, actor

Lane Savadove, artistic director, director, and educator

Eric Schaeffer, artistic director and director

Kim Scharnberg, music director, conductor, and orchestrator

Kimberly Schraf, actor

David Selby, actor

Cotter Smith, actor

Leigh Strimbeck, actor, director, and educator

Mary Hall Surface, director

Jeff Talbot, playwright and actor

Paul Tetreault, not-for-profit producer

Justin Townsend, lighting designer and educator**

Delicia Turner Sonnenberg, artistic director and director

Holly Twyford, actor and director

John Thomas Waite, actor

Nick Van Houten, lighting designer

Kay Walbye, actor

Court Watson, set designer

Jeremy Webb, actor

Tyrone Wilson, actor and educator

Christopher Youstra, musical director and conductor

** Tony Award

* Tony nomination

Introduction

Librettist John Weidman says the secret or mystery about collaboration "is the ability to find the third solution. One collaborator says blue. One says red and after you talk, we say, purple and everybody is happy. And that's what a good collaboration is … and purple is not satisfying because it's a compromise, it's satisfying because it's something that could not have been arrived at without those two minds having that conversation and when it happens, it's thrilling."[1] His collaborator, Stephen Sondheim, concurs: "It usually ends up richer than what you started with."[2]

Learning to collaborate is an essential skill for any theatre artist. It is also a viable life skill that informs every relationship. The ultimate goal of collaboration in the theatre is to provide space for *everyone* to be able to bring their best work to a given production so we can collectively provide the most impactful experience for our audiences – who, it must be argued, are our most important collaborators. When we succeed, we have built a community, a chosen family that shares a common bond and a common philosophy driven by the story of the playwright with the potential to change the world.

In this book, we hope to provide the reader with insights into successful, exciting, and prolific collaborations. To do this, the authors will articulate some guiding principles of collaboration, and apply these principles to real-world experiences that will help the reader to develop a practical approach to their own collaborations. These guiding principles were developed from interviews, email exchanges, and many conversations with each other and with practicing theatre artists and educators, as well as from our own decades of experience as theatre professionals and educators. The guiding principles are time-tested, with their proven value evidenced by successful productions in the past and at the present time of writing this book. But as with everything, change is inevitable even before the ink can dry. Whether these

DOI: 10.4324/9780367810252-1

principles continue to guide future collaborations will remain to be seen by you, the next generation of artists.

The theatre is created by people from an astonishing array of cultures, races, gender identities, and beliefs; these differences are what make it a uniquely powerful and accessible medium like no other. It therefore seemed intuitive to reach out to a diverse and broad pool of experts and practicing professionals to gain a wider perspective. From Broadway to regional theatre to professors who teach in the trenches, we reached out to colleagues from a wide variety of backgrounds and experiences, who assisted us in real life research on this vast topic. We will refer to our esteemed research contributors on various topics of this book as "The Collective." The Collective allowed us to gather and synthesize the most current information on best practices, recurring challenges, and professional preferences in today's professional theatre. Within The Collective, we have also identified "Contributors," who provided expanded insights into collaboration through interviews and extended conversations about their personal joys and challenges within their professional collaborations. Their generosity extended to sharing failures as well as successes, and as learning comes from mistakes as much as it comes from success, we share both while respecting anonymity.

None of the information here is intended to be prescriptive. Instead, we offer the reader a guide to seeking their own style of collaboration as they carve out their unique path on their journey in the life of a theatre professional. No production is ever the same, and we share the belief that each participant involved is significant to the final outcome, while also acknowledging that in theatre, no one achieves success on their own. This is why collaboration is so important to the theatre. It is our hope that this book helps to lead you towards the true joys and rewards the theatre offers through collaboration.

Scenarios

One of the wonderful things about working in the theatre is that every show is its own work and comes with its own challenges. The answers to the same problems will change from company to company, and over time. On one hand, this is why we like to work with people we know; on the other hand, few things are more exciting than working with people we don't know for the first time. What worked on one project might fail abysmally on the next.

Still, we believe we can learn from each other's experiences, and the choices one artist makes can inform the choices we make in similar situations.

Scenarios ask us to walk in each other's shoes, to recognize ourselves in each other and, because they don't provide the ultimate outcome, ask us to think long and hard about how *we* might react in a similar situation. They can help us prepare for eventual situations – and maybe avoid the pitfalls experienced by others before us.

The scenarios at the end of each chapter (except Chapter 4) are taken from real-life experiences in the professional and academic worlds and are conversation starters. They are a means of sharing experiences that can be discussed in a safe environment without the high stakes that existed in the actual situations. They are based on truthful events experienced by one of the authors and/or our colleagues, but the names and shows have been changed to protect the privacy of all involved. At the end of each study, you will find questions that pertain to our collaborative principles. We encourage you to discuss these with your peers and collaborators. In case you are curious about the actual outcome of the problems we present and the authors' different takes (what *they* would have done), we have provided Appendix 4: What Would We Do? (The Scenarios).

The challenge of collaboration is essentially the challenge of working with people. With each new project, we have to learn new rules of collaboration: a new vocabulary, a new way of working, new tools to work with, new ideas, new forms, new ideas. We can – and must learn from the past – but we must also constantly understand and embrace the fact that change is inevitable. People change. Constantly. It never gets easy, but it can get better. Hopefully, by thinking about these – and discussing them with *your* collaborators – you'll see how the principles of collaboration can be put to work, ensuring that the excitement and joy of collaboration always outweigh the frustrations that are inevitable when people try to work together.

Notes

1 Broadway World TV, "BWW TV Exclusive: Stephen Sondheim & John Weidman Tell the Story of ROAD SHOW at Encores! Talkback." Accessed February 24, 2021 from www.broadwayworld.com/article/BWW-TV-Exclusive-Stephen-Sondheim-John-Weidman-Tell-the-Story-of-ROAD-SHOW-at-Encores-Talkback-20190804.
2 Broadway World TV, "BWW TV Exclusive."

1
Challenges and Guiding Principles
Seeking Common Ground

A University College London Division of Psychological and Language Sciences (UCL-PaLS) November 2017 study found that watching a live theatre performance can synchronize the audience's heartbeat. The team monitored the heart rates and electro dermal activity of 12 audience members at a live performance of the West End musical *Dreamgirls*. The team found not only that individuals' emotional responses were mirrored, but the audience members' hearts were also beating in unison, with their pulses changing in relationship to what was happening on stage. This continued throughout the intermission. Study leader Dr. Devlin said, "Experiencing the live theatre performance was extraordinary enough to overcome group differences and produce a common physiological experience in the audience members."[1] This experiment suggests the performance of *Dreamgirls* touched the audience with the universal chord of needing to belong to something bigger, and that theatre has the power to bring people together as a community – and indeed community is at the root of theatre's origins.

In ancient Greece, theatre was created to honor the gods, funded by the city and voted by judges chosen by the people. It was based in ritual and culture. In Africa and Asia, theatre was rooted in myths, rites, and folk celebrations. These traditions externalized the beliefs of society. Our theatre today, at its fundamental level, inherits these characteristics. The difference is that we have more elements, more collaborators, and many different points of view. Lastly, our theatre has many different purposes. Whether the goal is profit, not-for-profit, education, cultural expression, entertainment, or to promote change, theatre is social and creates community because in theatre we unite in our differences.

Much like the *Dreamgirls* audience, theatre-makers bring their individual experiences, culture, education, opportunities, values, opinions, and biases into their work, which makes collaborating interesting but also offers

DOI: 10.4324/9780367810252-2

challenges. These challenges are what make theatre unique because theatre widens the lens of humanity, enabling us to see the world from many different perspectives.

Do you think each of the 12 audience members involved in the experiment shared the same point of view about what they saw? It would have been interesting to follow up this experience with a post-show discussion to see what the audience thought and whether their opinions aligned. Since it was not included in the study, allow us to speculate.

Each person in the *Dreamgirls* audience might have had a slightly different intellectual and visceral response to the musical, even though their physiological data shows them synchronized. An individual's intellectual response is put into context by their "point of view," driven by preference, aesthetic, and life experience.

This is true for a company when mounting a production. A variety of perspectives is essential in collaboration because it gives each production its identity and allows everyone to share their area of expertise. Differing points of view contain exciting opportunities, but how we navigate those different points of views can sometimes present challenges. A company shares many different points of view. When putting up a production, this can make collaboration challenging but also essential because it gives each production identity and purpose.

What Makes Collaboration Challenging?

Tracey Moore, actor, educator and author, talked about her time working with Ben Krywosz and Roger Ames in the Composer/Librettist Studio at New Dramatists, in which she participated as an actor. Five librettists, five composers, and five actors practice collaboration by exploring different ways of telling stories through music. Tracey shared that it was one of the most life-changing experiences of her career. She felt she had a real impact on creating new musical theatre works, and gained a better understanding of what collaboration entails.

Tracey discussed a concept developed by Ben Krywosz, co-founder and artistic director of Nautilus Music-Theater in Minneapolis, about the dynamic between the collaboration and the product:

> Ben uses an axis graph to illustrate his point. One axis of the graph indicates the perceived value of the relationship (very important, not

important) and the other indicates the perceived value of the product (very important, not important). One collaborator might value the relationship over the product and one might value the product over the relationship. Ben illustrates: "There's this interplay between the valuation of the relationship and the product and that in itself – that negotiation for value – is the collaboration. Some partnerships may have a diagonal graph line that goes right up the middle where both parties value the relationship and value the product in the same way. But it is more likely that you have one person more invested in the relationship and another person more invested in the product, or that these things fluctuate over time. Occasionally, those two dots end up so far apart on the graph that the collaboration falls apart.

Tracey used Jerome Robbins, choreographer/director, as an example:

The history of Jerome Robbins is that everyone despised him, but to me it was just a question of where he was on this graph. He only cared about the product. He didn't give a damn if anyone liked him. We could consider him a bad collaborator, but look at the shows: *West Side Story, Gypsy, Fiddler on the Roof*. Then you look at Lynn Ahrens and Steve Flaherty, or Kander and Ebb: it appears that these are more balanced collaborations that value both strong relationships and strong products. So the idea is that you don't necessarily want to dictate what a collaboration looks like, but it might help if both parties understand where the other is coming from.

Since 1986, Nautilus Music-Theater has been a collaborator's heaven for composer/librettist teams, and it is one of the best-kept secrets in the collaborative world. While Ben's work with collaborators is specific to co-authors/co-creators, we can use his axis graph (Figure 1.1) to view why we might collaborate better with one person over another and why some collaborations just will not work.

Ben Krywosz defines collaboration:

Authentic collaboration is a state of grace whose entry we have no control over; it occurs organically when circumstances and participants are ripe. We can cultivate that ripeness by following easily identifiable principles, but a healthy collaboration can't be forced.

One mental model for taking a "snapshot" of any one moment in time during a collaborative process involves tracking the importance and quality of both the relationship and the project. This concept, borrowed from the world of progressive team-building, allows the participants to develop the interactive strategies of compromise (blending), domination (leading), accommodation (following), and resignation (letting go).

Interactive strategies

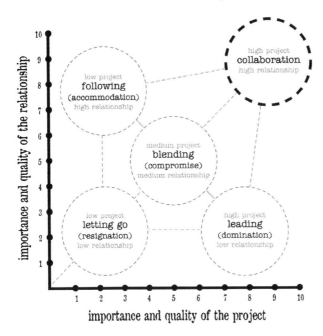

Figure 1.1 Nautilus Music-Theater interactive strategies

Skilled collaborations have learned how to actively dance elegantly through all these strategies, moving cooperatively in response to each other like the choreographic wizardry of Fred Astaire and Ginger Rogers. Over time, the sum total and net result is authentic collaboration, even if at no point during the process did that state of grace actually occur. The collaborative process requires an intentional exercise of collaborative skills, a clear awareness of one's values, and a committed confidence in the benefits of working together.

What makes production collaboration challenging is the varying points of view unique to each collaborator within a production. However, this is why great plays get produced over and over again. Why are productions of *Hamlet*, *Death of a Salesman* or *Romeo and Juliet* – or any popular play – produced each year? Are all productions the same? Of course not!

Each production is unique to the company that produces it, the collaborators within it and its audience base. Point of view leads to unique insights and interpretations, and while we will not all agree, this is what keeps theatre constantly changing, growing, and challenging the status quo.

Our Research

The data gathered in this chapter were harvested from the survey administered to a number of theatre professionals, referred to here as "The Collective." The authors distilled the information from the survey, which addresses primary challenges in theatre collaborations that prohibit a creative atmosphere and healthy working relationships. We have boiled down these challenges into five categories: inflated ego, lack of time, poor communication, inequities and lack of a clear vision.

A *healthy ego* is seen in a person's confidence, sense of self, resilience, the ability to solve problems, the ability to develop meaningful relationships, and a sense of meaning in their life. An *inflated ego* is seen in the rehearsal space as dismissing ideas before they are considered. It involves not fully listening to one another; communication breaks down, misunderstandings occur, feelings are hurt, blame is cast, and there is an overall lack of trust and safety. It is seen in power plays through domineering, over-controlling, dictating, belittling, and intimidating behavior. It emerges in personality conflicts and the desire to be right over compromising. It is visible in pursuing one's own personal agenda over the greater good for the whole project. It can be seen in a pre-conceived vision of a performance, design, or directorial concept, which does not allow for other contributions or expansion. Ego is also heard in negative, overly harsh statements used to instill fear and doubt, and to create factions. It reveals itself through being closed off, a lack of humility, defensiveness, no objectivity, obstinance, and refusal to engage in discussion. It is the virtuoso impulse.

Anyone can be guilty of having an inflated ego, which can destroy a collaborative, safe, and equitable environment; this compromises the work as well as the overall joy in creating a piece of theatre. Former university student, Broadway actor, Salisha Thomas shared that in her experience, the higher the level of the work, the fewer inflated egos she found in her collaborations:

> Every room I have walked into [Broadway experiences] it has been everyone's listening and whoever has the best idea, that's the one we're gonna go with. I mean there is the director, who says, "I'm the director but your idea is way better, let's do that." That kind of environment feels like, let's put this thing on together. Because the whole point is that the product on stage is bomb. It's not about any one person. What better way than to actually love each other in the process.

> A lot of times it [school] was the push I needed. It really did prepare me. I would say moving to New York, or doing theatre outside of any

academic setting, I may have been spoiled. But everybody I have worked with there is zero ego, which is like wait, what? I mean, you're working on Broadway and you're so humble and so nice. It feels like, I feel safe to make choices. I feel encouraged to be myself, especially if I've gotten the job. They let me know, we want you, what would you do? It makes me feel like I can just play and if something doesn't work, it's okay, we'll laugh it off and try something else.[2]

Lack of time is another challenge faced by collaborators today. Time is an extremely precious commodity in the production process. Creating under pressure does not serve the work but it is a harsh reality, and with each passing day of rehearsal it becomes more precious. Rehearsal time can be the first item to be cut from the budget when a producer is looking to reduce their overheads.

There is a real tension between the artist's need for time to create and the ability of budgets to meet that need. The largest part of any professional production budget is personnel, so time really does equate with money. In regional theatre, producers often hire non-union performers who can rehearse before the union performers arrive. The question becomes: How do we keep the spirit of collaboration alive when time is short and these inequities become the norm?

Working under this pressure can make people short-tempered and impatient, and can sometimes lead them to behave unprofessionally. Impatience might be seen as an "I need it now" mandate or "too much to do, no time for you" attitude, or mean "the answer is no" without consideration. These responses can compromise collaborative relationships as well as the overall positive working environment.

On the other hand, a great director can create the illusion of time when there is none. The director can hide this stressor from the cast and designers by somehow covering all their bases (table work, discussions) with ease, knowing that the clock is still ticking while prioritizing. It can be tough, but many directors make this happen without anyone knowing it.

On the other hand, when the "time is money" pressure pervades the atmosphere, it can squelch creativity and performance. Broadway actor Salisha Thomas shared that during a performance in a workshop for donors, the composer came up to the lead who had been nailing every rehearsal up to this point and told her, with others an earshot away, "Don't mess this up. There's a lot of money out there." Salisha said, "I saw first-hand how he put this unnecessary pressure on her. She was perfect every rehearsal and in the performance she cracked."[3]

Another challenge is *poor communication*, which can result from time constraints or over-committed theatre artists who are juggling many projects. Ego can also lead to communication breaking down.

Lack of *a clear vision* was another challenge expressed by The Collective. Clear vision does not mean the director single-handedly envisions the play into life. The playwright/author creates the play and the *vision* of a particular production begins with the director. A clear vision is the unifying thread that the director uses to guide, lead and galvanize everyone's choices towards the story being told.

The last major challenge to collaboration, which our theatre makers believed to be most pressing today, is *inequities*. Opportunity is a pathway to success. The primary goal of theatre is to tell the human story, and if we are excluding any group – whether by way of the stories we tell or the participants within a production – we are not supporting theatre's basic goal of community, which includes a diverse and constantly diversifying artistic population that reflects and/or expands its audience.

These inequities can be seen in dismissing, rejecting, and excluding voices that are not being heard. Rigid hierarchy is one of the ways inequity is maintained: "I am senior rank. You can't do this project because I choose to and my choice trumps yours."

> I feel it's my social responsibility to shine a light on areas that don't get seen. My personal feeling is that it's an artist's responsibility to be engaged with the culture. And when the culture is going through turmoil, I think an artist can't ignore that. I don't feel every artist has to be politically engaged, but I can't imagine that you can be an active participant in this culture and not in some way reflect that in the work you are creating.[4]
>
> – Lynn Nottage, playwright

The Guiding Principles

Are there guiding principles we can identify that will help us to achieve a successful, rewarding collaboration? We believe there are, and we have narrowed them down to four. We began by embracing some accepted beliefs created by model artists who have achieved one of the most collaborative productions in history. Composer and star of *Hamilton* Lin-Manuel Miranda, director Thomas Kail, choreographer Andy Blankenbuehler, and music director Alex Lacamoire share their golden rules for collaboration:

1. Have trust and faith in your team. Give trust to get trust.
2. Over-communicate.
3. Be vulnerable: be the first to give away credit and the first to take blame.
4. Keep your word on things – both big and small.
5. Everyone is responsible for their area of expertise.[5]

We then turned to our "Collective" to refine and narrow these principles. The four guiding principles that we present in the remainder of this chapter were created by synthesizing the primary concerns and barriers to success of The Collective with the wisdom of the *Hamilton* team. Their purpose is to provide antidotes to the barriers of successful collaboration in the hope of achieving more inclusive collaboration in the theatre. While they are not a "cure all," they do provide a template for best practice in collaboration.

Guiding Principle #1: Practice Trust, Respect, and Inclusivity

In our survey, the word "trust" appeared in the responses 20 times; the word "respect" appeared 30 times. Trust is earned when we know someone will follow through with what they say they are going to do. Respect comes from knowing they have the skills to do it and have proven to do it well. Once these two essential elements – trust and respect – are demonstrated, generosity can be a mutual gift. The alignment of these principles in a collaboration is perhaps why you might see people working together over and over again, and following one another from project to project. The greatest collaborations can attest to this.

Cultivating an inclusive environment where trust and respect are a mutual gift will only contribute to the success of a production and improve the overall experience. This responsibility to set the tone of collaboration lies initially in the hands of the producer and then, once the production is set in motion, the director.

There are as many directing styles as there are directors, from the auteur at one end to the lack of a director on the other; however, trust, respect, and inclusivity are determined by the leader of any production. The authors support the most collaborative position on this wide spectrum.

If trust depends on being given the opportunity to show potential, then this requires a path free from barriers. Learning about our collaborators can help us navigate these relationships. Each member of the company has something to contribute in their area of expertise.

Cultivating an inclusive theatre where trust and respect are a mutual gift is the first step in clearing a path for opportunity and success for all theatre-makers. The road is paved by acknowledging differences and embracing the community it serves.

> The commonality [in a great collaboration] is everyone engages in radical empathy. For me that's the number one thing that needs to happen. Folks that engage in it need to deploy radical empathy and adopt it as a baseline rule. You diverge in your beliefs, everyone ought to be able to look at the other person's position. Everyone should not be collaborating with everybody. I think it's a myth to say that everyone is like-minded. I tell my students: Find your tribe, find your like-minded people, find the folks who are passionate about the same things. The primary ingredient is radical empathy.
>
> I work with Liesel Tommy a lot. We've known each other for a long time and we share similar lived experiences, being immigrants, coming from developing countries and looking at having learned in America, and [learned] American history through non-traditional avenues. I col-laborate with a lot of directors who care about the same things I do. I feel there is a wide breadth of like-minded empathetic people that I grew up with. I take it for granted that over the years I subconsciously persisted ... I don't think collaboration can be perfected overnight. It requires long-term trust, as a system of trust.[6]
>
> – Clint Ramos, Tony Award-winning costume designer and set designer

Guiding Principle #2: Maintain Constant and Open Communication

The word "communication" appeared in The Collective survey almost 50 times. Clear communication is a perpetual exchange of sending and receiving where intent matters. Our words matter. Our silence matters. What we say to whom and when matters. The theatre is a community, and a very small world. It is social. If it is to be a place where we create (which is a vulnerable act), then successful, clear, honest communication is the bedrock of the process. Passionate disagreement is also part of the process, but if couched with professionalism and kindness, free from hostility, the relationship will be more likely to support the best product.

Communication is about listening – really listening to understand, not to reply. It is challenging on many levels because smart people are always thinking and creating, and the wheels are always turning. This can be seen when the receiver is formulating an answer before the sender is even finished and fully heard. You might have been on the receiving end of this, where there is a disconnect and you know the person didn't even hear you and the person is formulating their next punch before you're done speaking. Or you may be guilty of not listening. Everyone is guilty of this. It's human. It's called subtext in acting. The first step in communicating more effectively is if everyone is speaking the same language. Tony-nominated sound designer Cricket Myers gives a great example of what this means:

> Every other element in the theatre is visual except for sound. They [other artistic collaborators] don't speak in terms of sound and are frequently intimidated by the idea of sound. One of the things Cal Arts taught me how to do really well was how to talk about sound in a visual way. You talk about the story, you talk about the themes, you talk about ideas and I'll translate that into sound. One of the most important parts of collaboration is getting on the same page with terminology and language. If I notice the director uses the term "texture" a lot or uses the term "patterns" or uses the term "thematic" or whatever language they use, I tend to pick up on that and start using that same language. So when I talk about music I talk about the textures in music or the patterns in music so I'm using the same words that the rest of the design team is using even if they don't directly relate to sound but it lets all [of us] be on the same page. We're all talking the same language. Tony-nominated sound designer Cricket Myers gives a great example of what this means:

> There was a show early in my career where the LD [Lighting Designer] wants the act to end this way and the Director says, "No. I want it to end this way." And the two of them are arguing back and forth and I kind of stepped in between and said why don't we take a breath and let the lighting designer build what he envisions because I actually think you both want the same thing but you're describing it in different ways. I'm hearing the same thing out of both of you guys but you're saying it different. So why don't we show instead of tell? It's funny because the LD built exactly what the Director wanted but they were using different languages and so they just never got along or they never felt they understood each other. It's something I picked up really early in my career. They have to understand each other's language.[7]

Great communication demands that we define clear expectations of what needs to be accomplished by who and when. Assumptions cause problems, so getting the facts from the source can prevent communication from breaking down.

Technology: The Necessity and Mother of Collaboration

Before our virtual life, collaboration used to be second nature. Before FaceTime, Skype, and Zoom, and all the other social media applications, one-on-one meetings in homes, restaurants, and studios were filled with banter, sparring, debates, problem-solving, and socializing. We worked together. Sweated together. Had meals together. Argued, debated. Disagreements can be and should be part of theatre-making. These disagreements are fueled by passion and meant to happen face to face. Live. In the moment. That is where theatre was born and where it lives its most authentic life.

Not everyone is going to respond in the same timeline, but responding in a timely manner is professional protocol and expected. Every collaborator has a different style and different preferences. Some thrive on facts and concrete, committed deadlines; others need flexibility within the concrete world and may need a sounding board to "talk out their ideas." Sharing important information in a timely fashion is key to the production's non-negotiable deadline: opening night. Knowing how your collaborator communicates is essential – ideally, it's a mutual understanding.

Today, with most communication being virtual, this allows for more work to be done in a shorter amount of time all over the world. It is practical and it is the way we work now, but it can also compromise the humanity in the work. Theatre by nature is social and collectively we must protect its function, which is to exist with one another in the moment as often as we can and whenever it is possible.

Being Heard

The consensus from The Collective is that if everyone has a stake in the production, they will invest fully and give the best of themselves and their expertise as artists. It is therefore to the director's benefit to ensure that all points of view are valued. If an idea is not of service to the story or the vision agreed upon, then it is unlikely to work. The collaborative process requires tension and disagreement, but conversation can be fruitful when it is an exchange of ideas, both sides are being heard, and all suggestions are considered if they are on topic and within the context of what is being discussed. At some point, time becomes a priority and it is then that the director's responsibility is to make the final call on whether the choice is in or out.

Author Sidebar (Rufus)

There is a scene when Mufasa discovers his son is in danger of death. My reaction to the scene is informed by being a father and being a Black man. How can we be in Africa, portraying a lion, and dismiss the Black man underneath the costume? If we are to be true to our craft, how do I dismiss myself? At the time the resident director came to my dressing room to give me a note regarding how to talk to Simba in that particular scene. The note was to be gentle with him. I informed the assistant director that this would not happen with a Black father. In silence, he turned and departed the room. Where there is no conversation or motion to understand, collaboration is not possible. When a person of color feels unseen, ignored, and disrespected, collaboration is not possible.

Hard of Hearing

Feedback is sometimes hard to hear, but it is part of the process in creating the best work in service to a production. If all members of the company are speaking the same language, then feedback is more easily seen as being in support of the whole enterprise and not viewed as a personal affront. Feedback is one of the most essential elements in communication in the theatre, and when met with objectivity, it can be a game changer in your work both on the receiving end and in the sending. Coupled with generosity, it can single-handedly change your relationships for the better. When giving and receiving feedback, putting Principle #3: Generosity into practice can be extremely helpful.

Author Sidebar (Maria)

After ten years of being a teaching artist at conservatories in New York City, I took a teaching job in Southern California, which included directing a small musical. I had performed in musicals most of my life, but had changed direction and chosen to focus on straight plays. I was green to the politics inherent in an educational institution, both from students and faculty. It seemed that I was going through a sort of hazing by both. I found such resistance from students during notes. The cast gathered in the theatre following run-throughs. Half the students would sit slumped in the theatre seat, some with note pads and some without. A few key players would not give me their attention as I gave notes. My notes were from an acting perspective: "I'm not seeing this. Can you explore this?" They were not well received by a few of the principal players, but it was the overall negativity that stopped this project moving forward. I didn't know what it was that was not allowing them to receive my notes to better the show. So I asked them to choose a deputy, like we do in professional theatre, to field complaints. They did just that. They asked me to give notes to the ensemble first so they could leave and focus on the principals afterwards. I did just that. I never heard another complaint again. The few who were not taking notes didn't start taking notes, but the overall vibe improved. I've often thought about this over the years. The only thing that changed was that they had a place to go to channel their frustration, their inequities. They were heard and a change was made.

Principle #3: Encourage Generosity in Yourself and Others

Collaboration thrives on generosity, but under the stressful circumstances of production and fatigue, the fundamentals of interpersonal relationships and civility can sometimes be forgotten.

Generosity is seen in many ways. It is seen in giving your colleagues' idea a chance before it is dismissed. It is seen in asking, 'Do you need anything from me to help you move forward?' It is sometimes staying out of the way and sometimes it is intervening. It is actively being engaged with one another in pursuit of the greater good: the production.

Generosity is not seen when there is resistance – when it is my way or the highway. It is practiced through flexibility and the willingness to try to test things out in real time together.

Author Sidebar (Maria)

When I was directing *The Cherry Orchard*, Ann Sheffield was my scenic designer. She had created the most beautiful paintings of trees with various blossoms, depicting the seasons and the symbolic loss throughout the play. The problem was that the thrust stage on which we were working had little to no space, so we had to turn to projections to show the passage of time using her artwork. Unfortunately, the projections did not do the artwork justice. Ann spent so much time testing and finessing to make the images clear. She had the projector moved and she spent hours in the theatre making it right. She narrowed down the best options for me to view. Her generosity of time and attention to detail still amazes me. She is one of the most generous collaborators I have had the pleasure of working with.

Sometimes in technical rehearsal, fuses run short – not electrical fuses but human ones – and things can be said out loud for all to hear that perhaps are better discussed in private. Calling people out might be necessary, but it can be communicated in the spirit of generosity. We may not see things the same way, but learning from each other and engaging with one another are essential to the growth of collaboration and the theatre in general. Sometimes these conversations are uncomfortable, but success is found in having them and getting to the other side.

Professor Loretta J. Ross, author, activist, and educator, asks, "Why are you making choices to make the world crueler than it needs to be and calling that being 'woke'?"

The antidote to that outrage cycle, Professor Ross believes, is "calling in." Calling in is like calling out, but done privately and with respect. "It's a call out done with love," she said. That may mean simply sending someone a private message, or even ringing them on the telephone (!) to discuss the matter, or simply taking a breath before commenting, screen-shotting, or demanding that one "do better" without explaining how.[8]

Everyone in a collaboration has a job to do. Generosity is seen when each participant knows their job and stays in their lane. This means not directing another actor – that's the director's job. If someone asks for your opinion, that's different, but focus on your responsibility and in that you're practicing generosity and trusting and respecting your colleagues to do the same. If you see something that needs attention, it is likely that someone else will see it too and it will be addressed. If it isn't addressed, then share it with whoever you answer to.

Guiding Principle #4: Pursue a Clear, Unified Vision

The word "vision" was used 20 times by The Collective. As a cautionary reminder, however, the word "ego" appeared an unlucky 13 times. The role of the director has changed over time, and will continue to evolve at a pace that will be informed by society. A production helmed by George Abbott (*Pajama Game, Damn Yankees, Once Upon a Mattress*) is quite a different kind of collaborating than that of George C. Wolf (*Angels in America, Take Me Out, Bring in da Noise, Bring in da Funk, The Iceman Cometh*) or Anne Bogart (*The Baltimore Waltz, Dead Man's Cell Phone*) or Liesl Tommy (*Eclipsed*). If you don't know these directors, look them up. They have all made important contributions the theatre. Learning from the past informs the future.

A clear vision begins with the director in most productions. They are the touchstone keeping the creative decisions pointing in the same direction, focused on the story, and unified in the purpose behind the story.

A clear, unified vision begins with the director, but then it must – in a collaborative environment – evolve. Once a company is established, designers, actors, and the director will collaborate and the vision will be developed through the rehearsal process and design meetings. It is in these weeks of development the vision becomes truly unified, with all key players making contributions.

In a cohesive collaboration, no one will measure who contributed what idea and where. An open door to creativity allows every person involved to have a stake in the game, making them proud to be a part of the production, which supports an equitable creative atmosphere.

Using that power with great care, respect and collaborative leadership has been shown to be more productive, and those who practice in this way are more in demand. When a company is creating under a clear unified vision, there is a universal language, a common mission, and shared investment. It gives everyone involved a connection to why they are here and invested in the project.

Each artist contributes to the vision, but if a choice does not align with the director's overall vision or is not justified in relation to the vision, then the choice won't work for the final outcome and reasonably cannot be included.

Another caveat is that decisions can also be determined by "the muscle" of the show. William Goldman in *The Season* describes what is meant by "the muscle":

> The Muscle is chiefly responsible for what finally does or does not get on stage. Sometimes the Muscle can be a star, *viz* Sandy Dennis. Sometimes it is the director. It can be the writer, if the writer is Arthur Miller (without Kazan) or Neil Simon (without Nichols). There are occasions – almost always disastrous, when the general manager or even the set designer can be the person who shapes things. If the Muscle is properly placed, the show has a chance for success: if not, not.[9]

On the other side of this spectrum is devised work, where there is no leader but a set of agreements made by the ensemble. However, if at a standstill, it is the person who brought in the project who will make the call if a collective agreement is not found.

I was involved at the creation and subsequent production of two major Broadway musicals, one a huge success, and the other a huge failure. The difference: one pursued a unified vision and the other didn't.

Everyone has to be writing the same show. In the case of the success, the writers and director all agreed that the show was about tolerance and acceptance. It was written at the speed of lightning and hardly a thing was changed. Once written, the director decided the design should be lavish and colorful, the cake with all the icing. One of the writers thought the show should be smaller and more realistic, but deferred to the overall vision, thus resulting in a unified collaboration.

On the second musical, the authors could never agree on both what the show was about and its tone. In this situation, the writer was also the director. The book writer/director was more interested in the supporting characters than the two main characters. This created a problem for the composer and lyricist, who ended up having great difficulty writing songs for the main characters. The book had a vulgar tone, which contrasted with both the songs and the design, which had more style and class. The result was a confused and unsuccessful show.

Sometimes the vision is defined at the beginning, and at other times it becomes clear as the work progresses. Either way it is essential to the success of the project.

— Jim Pentecost, Producer/stage manager/director

Final Thoughts

Consider the job before signing the contract

Different individual purposes can interfere with the ability to establish a unified vision. One person's purpose in accepting a production might be to create their best work, to grow artistically and share a memorable and moving experience for the audience. Another person's purpose might be self-promotion, money or a credit. Or it could be some combination of these, but the question each individual must ask is: "Does the production's potential align with my values and my time?" If it doesn't, can you successfully participate as a collaborator on the project? It is important to consider these questions before you take the job, and also to ask all the necessary questions about subject matter, pay, and time commitment. Otherwise, once you are involved, it is more of a burden to back out and your decisions can impact everyone involved.

Theatre artists might accept a project for little to no money in order to work with someone they respect and admire. Knowing that someone's artistic values align with yours, you may be more inclined to trust that the project will be worth your time and effort, and cultivate a relationship that may provide opportunities later.

Twyla Tharpe, award-winning Broadway choreographer and director, has achieved a prolific body of work and describes herself as a career collaborator. To this point, Tharpe defines collaboration as a habit, and habits are practiced. She defines the process as:

People working together. Sometimes by choice. Sometimes not. Sometimes we collaborate to jumpstart each other. Other times focus is simply on getting things done. In each case, people in a good collaboration accomplish more than the group's most talented member could achieve on their own.[10]

Tharpe holds all collaborators accountable for the success and the failure because:

People are people. And people are problems. But – this is a very big but – people who are practiced in collaboration will do better than those who insist on their individuality. It's a way of working in harmony with others but it begins as a point of view. You might be the problem or a big part of it.[11]

The guiding principles are intended to help you to achieve harmony in your collaborations. There may be discord, and we may step out of rhythm with one another, but ultimately once the principles are put into practice you might find your exchanges become easier and you may even find you begin to finish each other's sentences. When a company becomes divided, gossiping, and back biting, this will ruin creativity and although the product may ultimately survive, the joy in the work is often lost and the production will be remembered in this way. This is why artists choose each other time and time again. There is a reassurance that, as collaborators, we know how to work together, which includes all the guiding principles that allow everyone to achieve their best work.

> I have learned because I have worked with him [choreographer]. My first show with him was 2005. I know what his counts of eight are so when he says to me "it's six counts of eight", I know how much time he needs [laughing] and I find a piece of music to fit that, that rhythmically fits that. I laugh because anyone else, if he said six counts of eight, they'd be like, that doesn't mean anything unless there's music. I find music to fit his counts of eight because I just know what he wants.[12]
>
> – Cricket Myers, Tony-nominated and Drama Desk Award-winning sound designer

Scenarios for Discussion

Scenario 1: Building trust – a summer production

Trust is essential to collaboration – without it, communication breaks down. When I began in the theatre, actors automatically gave their trust to directors. Today, I find that, more often than not, directors have to earn an actor's trust. There are two reasons for this: actor training has become very good, producing highly skilled actors who are less reliant on directors for basic coaching; and actors work more than directors – and a lot of them have become impatient with directors who don't treat them with the respect such experience is due. I learned a huge lesson about trust while directing a summer theatre production of a contemporary play with three extraordinary actresses. Two were quite young, but would go on to extremely successful careers in television; the third was a highly experienced, wonderful actress of the theatre. I was still pretty green, but getting my sea legs. Here is what happened:

Cast

The director: Mark (me)
The lead actress: Brooke (not her real name)

This is really just about the two of us.

If you have ever worked on a summer production, you know it goes quickly: two and a half weeks, including techs, then two weekends of runs and it's over. There's no time to monkey around. I used – and still use – a process that I adapted from Anne Bogart, which my students have come to call "journaling." It's a process that allows the actors to express their characters' journeys, and to have a voice in shaping the story of the play, while also deepening their understanding of the play. It's always one of my favorite parts of rehearsals, and no matter how short my rehearsal period, I give at least two days – and usually a week – to this process, even in summer theatre.

Our table work session was as delightful and wonderful as any I've had. The actresses were excited and hungry, and we all seemed to get along extremely well – until we started to get on our feet. At that point, anytime I would make a suggestion (not a direction, mind you – just a suggestion), Brooke would stop me with, "Let me figure it out." I initially got frustrated, then depressed. I wasn't necessary to her process; she didn't need me in the collaboration. Her work was great, her choices wonderful, but I wasn't part of the team.

One day, however, she got into a very challenging part of the play – and couldn't figure it out. When she turned to me for help, I was ready – and we worked it out together. From that point on, we worked together wonderfully and it became one of the best collaborations I've ever had. I realized later that she hadn't trusted me; I learned she'd been wounded by other directors, so I had to earn her trust.

In the other scenarios, we haven't given the endings – we want you to figure it out. In this case, however, the ending is central to understanding the importance of this story. It's not about the director – it's about the story, and what the actor needs to bring it to life. If they need nothing to do their job, then so be it. But chances are they will need the director; all you have to do is be ready. Luckily, it was a happy ending. The actress and I remained friends for years, and I always looked for (although never found) other opportunities to work with her.

The endings aren't always happy, unfortunately. Twice in my career, I wasn't able to gain an actor's trust – and both times it was devastating. The first time, I lost the actor's trust somewhere along the way, but I couldn't figure out what I did wrong. About the time we went into techs, he shut down and wouldn't communicate with me at all. He simply nodded his head and that was all I ever got from him again. I tried to get him to talk with me, but nothing. It was a two-hander, so I asked the other actor what happened, but he had no idea. I had obviously done something to destroy his trust in me – and it was so bad that healthy communication ended. To this day, I have no idea what I did. I would never have fired him; he was simply too good and time was too short. It would have destroyed my confidence if I hadn't jumped right into rehearsals for another show.

The second time, I didn't have the actress's trust from the beginning and never was able to gain it. She resisted my concept (even though we discussed it prior to casting) and direction every step of the way. Even the day of our first preview, she fought a very simple adjustment I asked her to make. Again, I wouldn't have considered firing her for a second: she was brilliant in the role. But without trust, healthy communication is impossible; and without healthy communication, there can be no real collaboration; and without collaboration, the joy goes out of the work. Every time.

Questions

1. Discuss the times that you've been successful or unsuccessful in earning your collaborators' trust. What makes the difference? What did failure/ success feel like? How did you overcome it? *Did* you overcome it?
2. What are ways that you can build trust with your collaborators?
3. What are some of the things that are barriers to trust?
4. What are some of the things that can destroy trust?
5. If trust is lost, how do you rebuild it?
6. How easily do you give trust to others? What allows you to give your trust?

These questions have no easy answers, but require a lot of thought and self-reflection. They aren't problems you can solve theoretically, but only in the moment. Hopefully, however, you can prepare yourself for the inevitable moment when you will lose that most valuable commodity: trust.

Scenario #2: How do you maintain unity?

People in a long-running show become territorial. They find people who are like-minded and build their inner circle of friends for comfort and community. They develop relationships for support while they sacrifice being away from their family and loved ones to perform eight shows a week. These relationships sometimes become the source that assists the actors to balance their lives. At some point, the inner circle is broken. An actor may leave for another show, they may decide to take a different career path, and sometimes actors are released. In either of these situations, when someone departs the circle, it can be a tremendous loss. There are feelings of being alone, isolated, and abandoned. Sometimes people can work through these emotions and sometimes they can't. The reaction sometimes creates resentment, negativity, and conflict in the company. Unfortunately, there are cases where this resentment is directed towards the newest cast member, who has entered the company excited, eager, and appreciative of being cast in a hit show, not expecting anything other than acceptance.

Questions

1. How do you address the morale of the cast?
2. How do you deflect the resentful actions?
3. How do you support those experiencing loss?
4. What activities or events do you create to maintain the unity of the company?

Notes

1   UCL, "Audience Members' Hearts Beat Together at the Theatre," University of London Division of Psychological Sciences (PaLS), November 2017. Accessed February 20, 2021 from www.ucl.ac.uk/pals/news/2017/nov/audience-members-hearts-beat-together-theatre.
2   Salisha Thomas, interview with Maria Cominis, Orange County, California, November 20, 2020.
3   Salisha, interview with Maria Cominis, November 20, 2020.
4   Anne Sachs, "Words. Words. Words: Playwrights on Playwriting," *Theatrical Intelligence* (Blog). Accessed February 21, 2021 from http://theatricalintelligence.com/tag/theresa-rebeck.
5   Scott Mautz, "The Creative Geniuses Behind *Hamilton* Just Shared the Secrets to World-Class Team Collaboration," Magazine. Inc.com, December 2018. Accessed February 21, 2021 from www.inc.com/scott-mautz/the-creative-geniuses-behind-hamilton-just-shared-secrets-to-world-class-team-collaboration.html.
6   Clint Ramos, interview with Maria Cominis, Orange County, CA and New York, October 27, 2020.
7   Cricket Myers, interview with Maria Cominis, Orange County, CA and Los Angeles, June 19, 2020.

8 Jessica Bennett, "What if Instead of Calling People Out, We Called Them In?" *New York Times*, November 19, 2020.

9 William Goldman, *The Season: A Candid Look at Broadway* (Harcourt Brace, New York, 1969), p. 285.

10 Twyla Tharp, *The Collaborative Habit* (Simon and Schuster, New York, 2009), p. 4.

11 Tharp, *The Collaborative Habit*, p. 14.

12 Cricket Myers, interview with Maria Cominis, June 19, 2020.

2
Defining Roles

Roles and Responsibilities

A key factor in engaging in a successful collaboration is understanding – and respecting – the role that each collaborator plays in the creation of the final project. This is perhaps easiest to understand by using the analogy of a large cast in a play: there are lead roles, supporting roles, bit parts, and supernumeraries (extras). Not every role has the same responsibility, but all roles are significant in creating a first-class work of art. Each actor must feel that their character is an essential part of the story, yet understand their role's unique contribution to the telling of the story. They all must understand that they are a part of something greater than any individual, and bring their complete passion and focus to the project, whether they are on stage for three hours or 30 seconds.

In the first half of this chapter, we will look at the roles and responsibilities of each of the creative collaborators and discuss how these roles intersect. While everyone in a production is a member of the collaboration, we will focus on the major artistic collaborators in the theatrical production of plays. We have divided the collaborators into four teams for the purpose of identifying relationships as they exist in the professional world: the creative team (producer, playwright, director); the design team (sets, costumes, lights, sound, projections); the production team (stage managers, production manager, technical director, master electrician, etc.); and actors.

The majority of the work currently achieved in theatre training programs is divided into this conventional structure, so we will present the definitions of roles and responsibilities (job expectations) from this traditional perspective. However, not all theatre is created within this traditional structure. We will point to those artists who specialize in other ways to collaborate later in the book.

DOI: 10.4324/9780367810252-3

The Creative Team

Producer

The producer is the person, organization, or institution that chooses a project to produce. They are responsible for securing the funds for the production, hiring the collaborative team, providing rehearsal space and performance venue, and overseeing the entire process from the selection of the play all the way through the load-out following the final performance. They oversee marketing, ticket sales, front-of-house – virtually every aspect of the production.

In the not-for-profit theatre, the producers take the form of an artistic director/managing director team or any number of other leadership structures: producing artistic director, executive director, etc. As a not-for-profit organization, they have legal responsibility to produce work that is for the benefit of the community and accessible to that community. Because the costs of producing theatre under this model are prohibitively expensive, these organizations must raise money through means other than ticket sales. Even the most successful productions cannot pay for themselves, so the producers must raise money through fundraising and other sources of revenue. In not-for-profit theatres, ticket sales can account for as little as 50 per cent of an institution's necessary income and will rarely exceed 85 per cent of an institution's budget needs.

While making money may be a motive for producing commercial theatre – Broadway being the most visible of commercial ventures – it is a very risky business, and very few actually make money at it. Harold Prince, one of the most successful producers of all time, once said that (prior to *The Phantom of the Opera*) all of his funders were his friends, none of whom were wealthy – and he himself never considered himself to be wealthy. Why on earth, then, would a producer invest time, energy, and resources into producing theatre? For the same reasons as an artist: they feel compelled to bring a work of art to life.

A producer – whether commercial or not-for-profit – has opinions, aesthetic/artistic values, tastes, and passions. They choose projects that they feel compelled to share with their audience; their belief in and passion for that material is *essential*. Many tend not to think of themselves as artists, but that doesn't minimize their investment in the production. They are essential participants in the collaboration, and should be welcomed into the collaborative process.

Producers tend to be very involved in hiring the creative team, casting and pre-production. Often when a play goes into rehearsal, they will start to become more distant, allowing the artists room to create. They will show up for run-throughs and will give praise or express concern. While absent from the rehearsal room, they keep a strong eye on rehearsal reports and on preparing the production for load-in and technical rehearsals. The producer's presence generally begins to be felt increasingly from the time of the final dress rehearsal. Their visible involvement really kicks into high gear with the first performances in front of audiences. It is at this point that they can become really engaged in the artistic product, and it is not unusual for them to give all kinds of notes, including (in the case of new work) suggestions for cuts and rewrites.

There are, of course, intrusive producers who can get in the way of the art and make the artists' lives difficult. But the majority of producers want what everyone on the team wants: a successful production. The smart producer hires the best people they can – then gets out of their way. Conversely, the smart artist knows that the producer is the production's greatest friend, an essential resource, and an indispensable member of the collaborative team.

> It's a brutal business, it's a harsh business. It's the kind of business that unless you love a project or love the show you're not going to get involved with it because the risk of reward, frankly, is terrible.[1]
> – Rocco Landesman, theatre owner and producer

Author/playwright

The only artist who invests more in a project than the producer is the author. Even in devised work, there is always a legal author. That author may be an ensemble, a director, or anyone else, but there is always an author. The contents of this section will refer to the traditional form of author in the theatre: the playwright.

The playwright creates the story, which they express through the written word. The playwright determines what happens – the events – and the order in which they happen – the plot. They create the characters that the story is about, give them language and actions to propel them on their journey, and through those words and actions express the ideas that the story is about. They provide the stage directions for what the audience sees and lay the foundation for what the audience will hear. They create a unique and special world, imbuing it with facts and details that we call given circumstances – essential building blocks to a specific and unique work of art.

In the theatre, the playwright is the primary artist. No part of the text may be altered without the playwright's approval. In the case of an original production, playwrights even have approval of director, designers, and casting. While they cannot make the decisions, their approval is essential. All artists in the theatre must respect the primacy of the playwright by thoroughly analyzing the play and bringing their best efforts to express the play through their specific craft and point of view.

The playwright can live with a play inside them for years before committing their story to paper, and many of our greatest plays are born from the life experiences of the playwright. It took Paula Vogel two weeks to write her Pulitzer Prize-winning play *How I Learned to Drive*, but it was born from experiences that occurred decades earlier. Once written, it can take as little as a year, but more often several years, to go from script to production. Many plays spend years in "development" before getting a first production. During this process, the playwright is the one constant presence, and their investment in the final product is *huge*. It is important to remember this. An actor will play many, many roles in their lifetime; the most successful directors and designers will work on hundreds of productions in their career. Our best playwrights are having extraordinary careers if they see *ten* of their plays produced in their lifetimes. For example, August Wilson, our most prolific African-American playwright, had ten plays produced on Broadway – two after his death in 2005.

What this means is that the playwright is often the least experienced collaborator on a team, yet has the most personally at stake. Many have invested *years* of their lives into a single play, while their collaborators' encounter with the material will be shorter – as long as a year or as little as two months in the case of a world premiere production at a regional theatre. It is little wonder that the playwright is usually the most nervous person in the theatre, especially during previews up to opening night. The collaborative process with directors and actors during rehearsals can prove tremendously frustrating for the playwright. As Heather McDonald, a nationally produced playwright, put it:

> When I've spent a long time with a piece, sometimes over years, to have an actor or a director say things like, "Oh, I don't know that I'd say this, how about this instead?" I can want to strangle them. I appreciate collaborators who bring a lot to the process, and I do rewrite a ton in the first production, but I expect a respect for the text and images and an effort to try to make sense of the world that's there.[2]

How they interact

The director/playwright relationship can be the most challenging – and rewarding – in the theatre. A successful production of a world premiere in New York City can catapult the careers of both playwright and director – or sink them. This can cause *enormous* tension in the relationship, and even the best relationships will have their ups and downs. Think of it as a good marriage: one of the best things life has to offer, but it takes a lot of work!

Author Sidebar (Mark)

One of the most successful director/playwright collaborations in New York theatre was between playwright Craig Lucas (*Reckless*, *Prelude to a Kiss*, and *Light in the Piazza*) and Norman Rene, who directed most of Craig's plays and films (*Longtime Companion*, *Prelude to a Kiss*) until Norman's untimely death from AIDS in 1996. Craig was often asked what the key to their successful collaboration was. Craig's reply was deceptively simple: "Norman directs, and I write." They understood their roles, and respected each other tremendously. Norman knew it was his job to tell the story using the tools at his disposal, *not* to write (or rewrite) the play; and Craig understood that it was Norman's job to make the final choices in the rehearsal room and in technical rehearsals when it came to actors and the design elements. This didn't mean they didn't talk to each other throughout the process – indeed, quite the contrary: they were extraordinarily good at communicating with each other, and trusted each other implicitly.

Director

The theatre existed without a director as we know it today for close to 2500 years. What changed? Realism entered the picture, creating the need for ensemble acting – the idea that all actors in a production need to inhabit the same world from the same point of view. At the same time, the audience began to demand verisimilitude, which affected all areas of design. This, in turn, was affected by developing theatre technologies that greatly increased our visual and aural choices when telling a story on stage. The theatre developed a need for someone to *unify* all these elements into a single vision, and that unifier emerged as the director. Bringing unity to all elements of a production is what brought the director into existence, and it remains the director's number one job. *No other artist can take responsibility for this task.*

The director of a production is ultimately responsible for ensuring that everything the audience sees contributes to the total experience of the story. *Everything* must come together into one unified story. It can be helpful to think of the director as the lead collaborator with the power to make decisions that they feel will best result in a unified production. Some people believe the director has too much power, but that power is really commensurate with the director's responsibility. They have the power they need to fulfill the responsibilities of their job. They – and they alone – are responsible for delivering a production that meets the standards of the producer. To put it another way, if a production fails, the responsibility will fall squarely on the director.

If the playwright determines *what* the story is, the director determines *how* it will be told. The director determines the initial concept – the way that *this* production will tell *this* story. This is essentially the framework within which all choices must be made. Sometimes this concept is created with the design team; sometimes it is developed before the designers ever meet with the director. What is true is that this initial concept is developed over the course of pre-production and rehearsal as a collaboration with all the artists. However, for better or worse, it is ultimately the director who must choose which ideas fit within the frame of their vision – and which do not. This means that potentially a lot of good – even brilliant – ideas may fall by the wayside, but not every idea belongs in every production; it is the director's responsibility to determine which of them do.

The director collaborates with two distinct groups in two distinctly different processes (which will be discussed in greater detail in the next chapter). The first group is the design team: sets, lights, costumes, sound, and projections. This group begins the collaborative process, and often its decisions are made well before actors are even cast. It is this group's task to determine the physical world – visual and aural – within which the story will take place. The second group comprises the actors. This group gives life to the playwright's actions, and it is this group that takes most of the director's time and attention. As Lifetime Achievement Tony Award Recipient Marshall W. Mason says, "The director's most important function is to lure believable performances from actors."[3] Both groups come together in technical rehearsal, and it is at this point that the work for unification is approached in great detail. If the foundational work of both groups is strong, then technical rehearsals will be relatively easy; if not, it can be a slow, painstaking experience that leaves everyone exhausted and rudderless.

The director is responsible for setting the collaborative tone and guidelines for the process of both groups of artists. It is through the director that the principles of collaboration are set, pursued, and enforced. Each director sets their own principles, and each director's process is unique. There are no rights or wrongs here, but each member of the team will adapt to or rebel against these principles, and any challenges that arise from a difficult collaborative process will eventually have to be dealt with by the director and/ or producer. This can take the form of compromise, capitulation, embracing difference or, in extreme cases, dismissal (including possible dismissal of the director).

How they interact

- The best relationships between a director and producer are true partnerships, with clear communication of expectations set by both parties. The director must be sensitive to the producer's personal investment in the project and accommodate the producer's ideas when possible; the producer must trust the director to do their job – even if it ultimately means the final product isn't the production the producer envisioned.
- The relationship between director and playwright hinges on understanding the full extent of the playwright's investment. Playwright Heather McDonald who is also a director, has a unique understanding of this.

When you come into the rehearsal room, the person who has spent the longest with the play is the playwright. And then the next person is the director. And the playwright is there to learn about what their play is now through the voices and hearts and gifts of good collaborators.

I've learned that my best artistic partnerships are ones where a director and I bring rather different things to the table. That I don't necessarily need someone who has the same sensibility I do or who even relates to the play in the same way I do. I just need them to be passionate about it for some reason and have it resonate with them in some deep way. It's a more interesting "marriage" if we're different. I already bring what I bring. Sometimes friends who I really click with have done rather uninteresting productions and someone that has a pricklier relationship to the play brings something rather stunning.

One time I was directing a new play that I quite loved by a very smart playwright. And there was a very big section near the end – it was five pages long – and I had a sense that once we had all the visuals and the actors, that the image might do what the words had already done, and that the words had led me to that image. I thought deeply about it before asking him to cut five pages that were beautifully written. And when I did talk with him about it, I explained my thinking and asked if he thought that what was happening now visually and with the actors was too much and if he had another idea about it, or whether we might look at it in a run without those five pages, keeping in mind what was best for the play and the story he was trying to tell. He was at first kind of upset, and went away and thought about it and in the end we did go without those five pages.[4]

The Design Team

Set designer

The set designer is responsible for creating the physical environment in which the story of the play unfolds. They determine how the space is carved out of the empty stage. In essence, they create a playground map in which the actors and directors "play", and out of which the story can organically unfold. Their choices must provide enough flexibility and neutrality to make sense for every moment of the story, but still provide a specific visual world that can evoke mood and express themes. They have a lot of say in how realistic, expressionistic, impressionistic or theatrical (you get the picture) the audience perceives the story. The set designer is responsible for approving the furniture, props, lighting fixtures, set decorations – basically any item that is neither costume nor lighting that ends up on the stage. In the same way as the director is responsible for unifying the elements into a cohesive whole, the set designer is responsible for making sure everything looks like it belongs there.

The director's collaboration with a design team almost always begins with the set designer. In a perfect world, the ideal situation is to have all the designers initially meet together to share research and ideas. These days, this goal is more difficult to achieve. If by some miracle all the designers are free and in the same city at the same time, there is still a chance that at least one of the creative team will virtually participate in the meeting. Nevertheless, most regional theatres try to make this first meeting of the *team as a whole* happen.

The director may then meet individually with the designers, and the first of these break-out meetings is most often with the set designer. The set design thus often provides the foundation for the visual elements of the production, and guides the costumes, lights, and projections in terms of color, style, period, and movement.

How they interact

- The ground plan is the most crucial intersection between the director and the set designer. It holds in it the *potential* for *all* the play's images and movement – in other words, the staging – which is the primary and most visual expression of the director's art and craft. No director should relinquish their responsibility to stage the story to any other artist. Interestingly, the set designer must also learn to *think* as a director, able to envision potential staging opportunities and the geography of entrances and exits. Collaboration on the ground plan between the director and set designer is therefore *essential*. They must agree on the major events of the story and where they take place on the stage. They must determine together what furniture/set pieces/props are essential to the telling of the story, and their placement in the environment.

- Along with the ground plan is the issue of how the story moves from location to location. Many, if not most, of today's plays tell their story in a variety of places and times. How these changes occur without slowing the story down or doing serious damage to the play's rhythms is a conversation the set designer and director must have before the set is finalized. Optimally, a wide variety of tools are available to the director and designer – automation, turntables, platforms, wagons, technicians, actors, and so on – each with their pros and cons, each taking time, and each impacting the budget and technical rehearsal schedule. The more quickly a story moves in time and space, the more important it is for *all* designers to participate in the decision-making process. Sound, lights and, if used, projections all allow for the swift movement of time and location, while costumes can either slow down or quickly allow for these changes. The set designer and director would be really unwise to decide how the story will unfold without consulting the team, and then turn to that team – the other designers – and say, "Okay, your turn!"

- It is interesting to note that musicals are generally planned within an inch of their lives before the first day of rehearsal, while the creative teams of plays will sometimes leave much until the tech rehearsals, thinking there will be time to "figure it out." But as the demands of plays become more and more complex, as they become more and more fluid regarding location and time, design teams and directors might be wise to look to the planning of musicals as a model to be replicated. However, musicals, like plays, evolve in the process and although planning is essential for staying on task, we must always allow for the flexibility needed to make room for new discoveries.

A lot of people don't think about inviting the lighting designer into the conversation in the beginning, which is funny because, I mean a lot of people are like, "Oh, you know – lighting. Once we get the set then we'll know what the lighting can be" or, "Once we get the costumes, we'll know what the lighting can be." For me, the most rewarding situations are always when I can get into those first conversations about the overall feeling we're trying to achieve, the overall story that we're going to tell, and establishing what the language is going to be – that is really important. And I don't always get that. It's great to know it does happen.[5]

– Rui Rita, lighting designer

Costume designer

The costume designer is responsible for creating the visual representation of character. This includes clothes, hair, makeup, and accessories. Their role is about the *total* creation of character.

Author Sidebar (Mark)

One of the most vivid examples that first brought this home to me was the character of Grizabella in the original production of *Cats*. Every square inch of the actor was covered in a way that visually communicated who Grizabella was and her role in the story. The costume – in its *entirety* – allowed for the actor to express the character through movement and facial expression to a point where the actor and character were seamless. It was pure theatre magic that needed no CGI.

In some educational institutions, hair and makeup are assigned to a separate designer who acts, to a degree, autonomously from the costume designer. In most professional theatre situations, however, hair and makeup personnel collaborate directly with the costume designer, who is ultimately responsible for hair and makeup research and choices.

How they interact

- After the director, the costume designer's most important collaboration is with the actors – the people wearing the clothing and bringing the characters to life. The designer and actor must be on the same page as to the story being told and the character's role or function in the story. The wise costume designer will have conversations with the actor about character, and will use the actor's physical attributes as the foundation for their costume choices. Unfortunately, this isn't always possible. Actors are often the last ones brought into the process, and often the costume designer won't even see the actor until shop deadlines for purchasing materials are due. Therefore, it is imperative that the director and the costume designer converse about the motivation and essence of each character during the design phase. Once the actor is part of the equation, it is often still possible to make slight adjustments.

> I think it begins and ends with the actor. They are the vessel. I always think of costuming as a sociological, emotional, and psychological dig. The vessel of the character is really the actor. Many of my considerations depend on what the actor feels. A lot of young designers think it's what looks good on an actor and what we teach is prescribing collections to the actor's body. And I feel to me it's really that costuming needs to be a platform for the actor to find the character and that means constantly checking in with the actors about how they feel. The big question I ask at a costume fitting is: "How does it feel? Stare at yourself. Look at yourself in the mirror and how does that feel? Does that sit right?" I think for me it has to come from an emotional point of view. Design has to be found in an emotional response to the material, the play. The design itself is a manifestation of that emotional response.[6]
>
> – Clint Ramos, Tony Award-winning costume designer

Lighting designer

The lighting designer, in the simplest of terms, allows the audience to see the story of the play. But their work can have tremendous impact on how the audience perceives the show emotionally, and their choices of focus, direction of light, intensity, and texture can enhance the style or genre of the play, and play an integral part in the unfolding of the story. Lights help to establish time, place, mood, and atmosphere. The impact of movement of light on the rhythm and emotional power of a dramatic story is enormous. Lights also act as a kind of visual glue, cohesively unifying sets, costumes, and staging. It is a powerful medium that can enhance, obscure, diminish, or excite the work of the entire team – designers, directors and actors. It can clarify or confuse a story, and heighten or destroy a key moment.

How they interact

- One of the director's most important tools is focus: attracting the audience's eye to where it needs to be to experience the fullest impact of the story. In effectively using this tool, the director has no greater collaborator than the lighting designer who, even more than the director, can focus the audience's visual attention. Lighting designers aren't just lighting a set or costumes; they aren't just creating an atmosphere or mood; they are illuminating and enhancing the director's staging of the story. Their most important responsibility is to make sure that the audience *sees* what it *must* see in order to understand and experience the story. Like the director and the set designer, the director and the lighting designer must be on the same page regarding what the major events of the story are, where they take place, and the desired impact of the image on the audience.
- The other area of essential collaboration between director and lighting designer is the movement of lights; as mentioned above, this can have a tremendous impact on the overall rhythm of the production and on the emotional impact of key moments. If a light cue is too quick or too slow – or in the wrong place – it can diminish the impact of that moment. This is why it is so imperative that lighting designers attend as many rehearsals in advance of the technical rehearsals as possible.

Author Sidebar (Mark)

Too many times, I've been aware of lights starting to move, drawing my eye away from the story for some reason known only to the lighting designer. The disconnect comes when the lighting designer interprets the play alone at home, seemingly ignoring the interpretation created in the rehearsal room and theatrical space – which is ultimately what they *must* light, or risk doing irreparable damage to the production.

It would be worth mentioning here that it behooves the lighting designer and the set designer to collaborate well in advance of the set designer's final due dates so that any accommodations required regarding the set and lights may be integrated, and therefore offer the best environment with which to achieve the lighting design.

Sound design

As plays have become more "cinematic" in nature, requiring minimal representations of specific environments, sound design has become key, along with lights, in establishing location. Sound exists on many levels. Certain sound effects are key to the action of the play – a gunshot heard off stage in *The Seagull*, for example. Ambient sounds can establish mood and environment, as in the sounds of jiggers and crickets, or a band playing in the distance in Lanford Wilson's *Talley's Folly*. It can cinematically underscore a scene in the form of music, strengthening the emotional context of a particular scene.

Author Sidebar (Mark)

My earliest encounter with the power of sound design came on Anne Bogart's production of Paula Vogel's *The Baltimore Waltz* at Circle Rep. (I was Anne's assistant director.) John Gromada, at the time a very young designer, now one of Broadway and regional theatre's most sought-after designers, was the sound designer on the production. He spent more time in rehearsals than any sound designer I'd encountered – before or since – testing music choices, working with Anne to integrate sound into the story well in advance of tech rehearsals. The staging of one entire sequence was inspired by John's brilliant choice of music for the scene. It heightened the impact of the scene and allowed for the scene's humor to come through. It also clarified the style of the production for all of us, including Anne, and informed a lot of the choices in the rehearsal room from that moment forward. Overall, the success of the OBIE Award-winning production was due, in no small part, to John's work and his deep collaboration with Anne. It remains, for me, a shining example of collaboration at its best and most creative.

Many sound designers, including John Gromada, are excellent composers in their own right. The addition of a composer to the collaborative team is heaven, and brings with it a specificity to the design (and production) that is tailor-made to the needs of the dramatic story. I had the joy of working with John on a production of *The Glass Menagerie* at Ford's Theatre in Washington, DC several years ago. We determined early on that music would be an integral part of the story, and John wrote some of the most haunting, beautiful music I've had in a production. Once again, John, who lives in New York and travels constantly for work, was in rehearsals in DC an extraordinary amount of time. When he couldn't be there, he would send us revisions of sound cues, working with me and the actors to make sure the length and arc of the cues were perfectly timed for the story we were telling.

Projection designer

The projection designer is one of the newest additions to the creative team. Initially, they came under the jurisdiction of the lighting designer, but they are now fully fledged members of the collaborative team. The images they produce can be profoundly moving. The flexibility they provide the director and playwright gives almost unlimited possibilities to the way stories can be told. Sir Andrew Lloyd Webber's *The Woman in White* was written to be in constant motion, with the projections joining with moving set pieces to give an almost cinematic movement to the story.

I have a really good relationship with projection designer Aaron Rhyne, who I've worked with a lot – and he's also a good friend. In a production, projection and lighting obviously have to work hand in hand because we're both vying for the same lumens. And so often it's a balance of, you know, who can tell the story better in this moment. And I find the most effective collaborations are where you don't see where light, scenery and video projections begin and end.

Aaron sort of thinks more dramaturgically. He thinks like a director. It's not gear driven. It's based on the story that we're trying to tell. And it's not lumen driven. It's who can handle this moment better. And Aaron and I really get that. Our long-term relationship means something because there is a short-hand and there's a confidence where I can say to him, "That video doesn't work" and he can say to me, "Take that light off. It just doesn't, you know, doesn't work." And we usually have each other's backs as well. I think that's really important, especially with video.[7]

– Rui Rita, lighting designer

The Production Team

Production manager

In regional theatre, this position is closely aligned with the artistic director, and acts as a liaison between the production design team, the technical support crew, stage management and actors, and the director. They have oversight of the production budgets and are charged with making sure production areas stay within budgetary constraints. Perhaps more importantly, they make sure everyone is communicating and information is flowing to the people who need to receive it in a timely manner.

Stage manager

The stage manager is the key link between the rehearsal room and the production team. The person in this role is vital to the running of a smooth technical rehearsal period and the maintenance of production values through the run of the show.

> Professional collaborator! That is the stage manager's job. It's facilitating, overseeing, and coordinating everybody else's collaboration. As that point person, it's your job to make sure that people are succeeding in collaboration so things don't fall between the cracks or there aren't misunderstandings or ill will because something was misinterpreted or someone misspoke. It's what a stage manager does.[8]
>
> – Jill Gold, stage manager and author

Technical director

Technical directors (TD) are partnered closely to set designers in that they help bring the design vision to reality via the carpentry shop and careful budget estimates and tracking.

Master electrician

The master electrician (ME) works closely with the lighting designer. They advise on lighting inventory, and coordinate light hangs and focus calls. They may also be called upon to work with the design team and other technicians regarding any required special effects.

Costume shop manager

Costume shop managers and costume designers work closely with each other and the actors to bring the designs to life. The costume shop manager also works with a crew of drapers, cutters, and stitchers throughout the build and technical rehearsal process, facilitating fittings, shopping trips, and alterations.

Company manager

The company manager is the point person, running the day-to-day business of the show. Their work is administrative. They are also the liaison between management (the producer/general manager) and the company.

Susan Sampliner, a freelance theatre artist, has been the company manager on *Wicked* since 2003 – it is very unusual to be on one show for so long. Susan is the point person, running the day-to-day business of the show from an office during the day, and being the eyes and ears of the general manager and producer at the theatre at night, after opening.

She sees the pitfalls in collaboration happening when communication breaks down:

> It happens when people are not listening to each other. People get stuck in their own needs and own camps and they stop listening to those people with whom they are collaborating. The best thing is if you've got a director who really sets the tone with their creative team and both respects and listens to them, and a producer and general manager who realize they hired the best in the business and let them do their jobs. If you let the experts do their jobs and you listen to them, the collaboration is going to be awesome. If you don't let them do their jobs, or don't listen to what they tell you when they have the expertise, that's going to lead to problems.[9]

Actors

The actors are the artists who embody the story. If the actors fail to do their job well, the rest of it doesn't matter. A set can't tell the story on its own; it can only provide the environment in which it can to take place. Costumes can help an actor *look* the part, but they can't act the role. Directors can act out the role for an actor in rehearsal (as Moss Hart did with Julie Andrews in *My Fair Lady*), but they can't perform it. It is therefore *essential* that every person in the collaboration understand that everything they do is to support the work of the actor. The ultimate goal of the collaborative team, of course, is to tell the story as impactfully as we can, so we are all (including the author and the actors) in service of the audience's experience of the story, *but* the best way to achieve that goal is through the actors.

Author Sidebar (Mark)

When talking about collaboration, we tend to think in terms of equality of all members of the team. This is a pleasant way to look at it, but it can also get us into a great deal of trouble if we don't recognize that within equity, there are still roles, status, and value. Not everyone's role on the collaborative team is of equal status or value. The great theatre director Peter Brook boils theatre down to three essentials: actor, author, and audience. The author creates the story, the audience receives the story, and the actor is the conduit through which that story flows from author to audience. It's important that we all understand where the focus needs to go. Note that directors are NOT essential; designers are NOT essential. Remembering this keeps me humble in the rehearsal room and keeps my focus where it needs to be. I grew up learning – and believing – that the work of the best directors and designers is invisible, allowing the *story* as told by the actors to shine through with the *support* of all of the other elements. I still believe this.

How they interact

- Marshall Mason's assertion that "a director's most important function is to lure believable performances from the cast"[10] recognizes the primacy of the actor in communicating the story and establishes the collaborative relationship between the actor and director as the most essential to the success of any given production. As in all collaborative relationships, this does not mean it will be free of disagreement or even battles, but it does mean that the director who acknowledges actors as their artistic equal will more likely earn the respect and trust necessary for both director and actor to function at their best. As Academy Award-winning director Sydney Pollack (*Out of Africa*) said, "A director can't force an actor to do what they don't want to do. It just doesn't work that way."[11]

- Acting requires a tremendous amount of courage, and it is essential for the director – in fact, everyone on the production – to understand and support this. Acting is an act of courage. The director, therefore, must provide a space where actors can feel safe to be courageous. No one is more responsible for creating a safe and creative environment for the actor than the director. This environment must also be the space where the director ensures that major tenets of collaboration be practiced constantly and consistently: #1 trust, respect and inclusivity; #2 constant and open communication; #3 generosity; and #4 a clear, unified vision.

Building the Team

The success of any collaboration will, to a great extent, depend on the specific artists who fulfill the responsibilities of the above roles as members of the collaborative team. But who decides who has a place at the creative table?

Artists are hired and teams are gathered through any number of means, but production always begins with a producer – a commercial producer, an artistic director, an executive director, a department chair – determining that they want to produce a particular work or property. It is important to note that there is a difference between creating and producing. Many, many works are created that never see the light of day because the authors/creators cannot find a producer or producing organization with the desire to present the work in front of an audience.

If the project is an original play, the playwright immediately becomes a central part of the collaborative team; if it is a previously produced project, then the producer must secure the rights for that property. If the venue is a commercial or high-profile theatre, the author may want to participate in the selection of the creative team and/or other aspects of the production – or they may simply take the royalty check and let the producer alone.

With the production of an original play or musical, the author has a lot of say. They have the right to approve the director, designers, and actors. They may also have input into the creation of the designs. No changes in the property can be made without the author's consent. (This is also true of published plays.) Their presence in the collaboration is significant. Terrence

McNally once said in a question-and-answer session at an open forum at the University of Texas that, as the playwright, he "abdicates nothing." He is involved in every step of the production.

After the rights to the property have been secured by the producer, which team member comes next? The answer will/can vary widely. Sometimes a property is brought to a producer by a director who hopes to become attached to the project – which may or may not happen. If the producer is an artistic director, they may have chosen the project because they wanted to direct it. If it is an original piece, the producer and playwright may start meeting with potential directors, starting at the top of the A-List and working their way down.

Is the director always the first hire? Often they are not. In a commercial venture or even in a major repertory company with a pool of actors and designers associated with it, an actor (typically, a lead) or actors may be brought on first and/or designers assigned. When a director is eventually chosen, they will be in the position of having to agree to the team or not take the offered job.

In some ways, making the director the second, third, or even later hire creates challenges for the director, which can work against a successful collaboration. More than any other artist, a director relies on other artists to realize their vision. The other artists bring the director's vision to life, so the success of any production will depend heavily on the director's ability to get all of the artists to work together collaboratively. Remember that delivering a successful production to the producer is ultimately the responsibility of the director. This is the main reason why most directors like to work with designers and actors with whom they have worked before. They not only have confidence in the quality of their collaborators' work but, as a team, they have had successful and enjoyable collaborations in the past.

Most producers are wise enough to choose a director early and to allow them the primary say in the choice of the creative team. In the not-for-profit institutions, designers are often chosen from a pool of designers who have successful track records with that institution, or from resident designers. Designers who work consistently in regional theatre venues are often chosen for their perceived proclivity for a particular style. These companies may also be open to a collaborator outside of their pool if the director is insistent enough, or if the designer's profile is high enough. Occasionally, top choices from the director or producer may not be available, in which case a search begins. Résumés are solicited, interviews are held, and a final selection is made.

The selection of actors – or casting – also varies greatly. If the theatre has a company of actors, the producer will usually begin there. If a director is a guest artist, they may be invited in to read, audition, and/or interview the actors. If the director has worked with the company before, then casting may occur through a conversation between the producer and director, without any formal auditions. In the case of a very large company such as the Oregon Shakespeare Theatre Festival, casting of the company may not even involve the director, but may be determined by the artistic director, who has to balance the needs of everyone – and the budget of the theatre.

Commercial ventures almost always begin casting with a search for recognizable stars, which may or may not involve the director. Stars draw investors, who ultimately make the productions possible. A name director's track record can also draw investors, but most producers recognize that the audiences come to see actors, not directors. If a star is chosen before the director, the star most likely will have some say, if not final approval, of the director.

Once all the known actors are cast, the search begins for those roles left uncast. These searches usually take the form of auditions organized and run by casting directors, who solicit agent submissions and pull from their own vast pools of actors. With regional theatres, this may begin with auditions for local actors, as it often does in Washington, DC. Ultimately, companies may find themselves going to larger casting sources – New York City, Los Angeles, Chicago – to cast unfilled roles.

The above avenues for choosing the collaborative team don't by any means represent an exhaustive list. There are as many ways of pulling teams together as there are producers and institutions. What should be clear – and can't be overstated – is that the producer has the largest voice in the room, followed by the playwright (in the case of a previously unproduced work), and then by the director. It is with these three that the collaborative process begins, and their ability to work as a team will set the tone for the remainder of the collaboration. Their shared vision, passion, skill, and artistry will determine the success of final product.

Scenarios for Discussion

Scenario 1: Changing the schedule

You're the director and you have notified the stage manager of when you want to stage the bows. You come to rehearsal and realize the stage manager has changed the schedule without your knowledge or permission to change it. The dialect coach could only come on Monday and asked for the change so the stage manager went ahead with it without consulting you.

What do you do if you are the director? Do you generously adapt or do you let the stage manager know you were not aware of this change so the dialect coach will need to wait until after you stage the bows and you have completed your rehearsal.

What do you do if you are the stage manager and the dialect coach asks for the change?

What guiding principles could have been utilized?

Scenario 2: Colliding roles – the artistic director's dilemma

Artistic directors are a bit of an odd duck when it comes to the rehearsal process. They choose the material, they pick the director, they work with the director to pull together the strongest design team possible, and they sit by the director during final casting sessions, offering their insights and, ultimately, their approval. In some ways, the artistic director is like the patriarch or matriarch of a family. When you direct at their theatre, you are in their home, and you are expected to treat them with the respect and dignity that comes with the position.

The artistic director is almost always at the first rehearsal, welcoming all the guests into their home, offering them support, and laying the expectations for a superb production. From then until opening, the presence of the artistic director becomes a very tricky balancing act. If you are too involved, you risk stifling creativity; if you aren't involved enough, you risk upsetting the collaboration at a critical moment in the process. This is the story of a production where the latter was the case.

Cast

Artistic director – Rob
Director – Mary
Supporting characters: The design team
The production was a world premiere of a play with a very challenging design problem.

Rob had approved the solution, acknowledging with Mary and the set designer that it wasn't ideal, but it fit the budget.

Rehearsals with the actors went very well, but Rob never came to rehearsals – not even to see a run-through in the rehearsal room, which is typically the first time an artistic director attends after the first rehearsal. When the company moved into the theatre for techs, Rob kept saying he would stop by to watch, but he never did. He would always send word that he wasn't able to make it, but he never made it. Mary had been in touch with Rob during the entire rehearsal period, and was frankly getting worried. This was only Mary's second production with the company, and Rob's approval was important to her.

When the team got to the challenging part – the end of the play and the problem with only an okay solution – they tried many options before running out of time before a scheduled run through. This time, Rob attended and watched with delight – until the end, when everything fell apart. This was Mary and her team's first time seeing their final choice – and watching it not work was excruciating. When the rehearsal ended and the actors were released, Rob pulled the design team together – *without Mary* – and the first words out of Rob's mouth were, "We have a real problem here." He then went on to the design team about every that was wrong, asking for solutions to the problem without once involving Mary or asking for her input. Rob then left the theatre without a word to Mary.

Questions

FROM MARY'S PERSPECTIVE
How should she move forward with her design team? Or should she withdraw from the production?

FROM THE DESIGN TEAM'S PERSPECTIVE
How do they move forward to a solution that will make Rob happy? He is, after all, the person who will most likely hire them again at this theatre; he is their boss.

How do they move forward with Mary? Do they include her in the conversations about the problems?

FROM ROB'S PERSPECTIVE
He is responsible for ensuring the production works. The first performance is in two days. Does he replace the director with one of his company directors?

Does he ask the director to step aside and ask one of the designers to lead the search for a solution? Or does Rob ask Mary to meet with him the next day with a list of solutions? What if Rob thinks none of them will work?

FROM YOUR (THE STUDENT'S) PERSPECTIVE

1. What does each artist's role in the collaboration allow them to do?
2. Do you see a way to rebuild the collaboration with everyone, including the artistic director?
3. Could Mary or Rob have done anything differently?
4.. What could have been done early that might have prevented the situation from reaching this point of crisis?
5. What do you see as the most problematic aspects of this scenario?
6. Who ultimately has the responsibility for:
   • solving the problem
   • ensuring that the production is successful
   • keeping the team working as a team?

Scenario 3: Staying in your lane

The power play between characters can be dangerous, damaging, disrespectful, and sometimes downright cruel.

Cast

Actor – Able
Director – Bob
Sound designer – Carl
Artistic director – Dean
The show was a musical.

At the beginning of tech rehearsal, Abel, an established actor of many years in the business, spoke with Carl about his voice. Abel was seeking a path to collaborating, a way to ensure the protection of his instrument. Able also informed Bob, the director, of his communication with Carl, and he supported the collaboration. As Able and Carl began to work, Carl became aware of how in tune Able was with his instrument and how the art of sound affected his voice. The collaboration was working. Seeing Able converse with Carl, the artistic director, Dean, became livid. He rushed to the director to tell him an actor had no right to speak with the sound designer and to stop it right away. The director, having worked with the actor, expressed that the actor was of a particular pedigree, that he understood what he needed to be successful, and that he would always engage in a conversation respectfully.

The show opened, and the actor and the sound designer were pleased. When the director departed, the artistic director communicated to the sound designer to change the sound and compress the actor's voice. With this action, the actor could feel the change and approached the sound designer. He denied that anything was different. The actor began to lose his voice.

What should the actor do? Should the actor confront the artistic director? Should the actor inform the director?

Notes

1 Rocco Landesman (theatre owner, producer), *Show Business: The Road to Broadway*, directed by Dori Berinstein (Liberation Entertainment, October 16, 2017, DVD).
2 Heather McDonald, email message to Mark Ramont, January 14, 2020.
3 Marshall W. Mason, *Creating Life on Stage: A Director's Approach to Working with Actors* (Heinemann, Portsmouth, NH, 2007), p. 3.
4 Heather McDonald, email message to Mark Ramont, January 15, 2020.
5 Rui Rita (lighting designer), interview with Mark Ramont, February 23, 2020.
6 Clint Ramos (costume designer), interview with Maria Cominis, October 27, 2020.
7 Rui Rita (lighting designer), interview with Mark Ramont, February 23, 2020.
8 Jill Gold (stage manager), interview with Maria Cominis, June 22, 2020.
9 Susan Sampliner (company manager, *Wicked*), interview with Maria Cominis, April 13, 2020.
10 Mason, *Creating Life on Stage*, 3.
11 Sydney Pollak, interview in special edition features, *Tootsie*, directed by Sydney Pollak, 1982 (The Criterion Collection, 2014, Blu-Ray).

3
Putting the Guidelines into Practice on a Production Timeline

As a theatre community brings a plethora of diverse choices to the table, offering many points of view, there will be challenges. In this chapter, we suggest how the guiding principles might work in practice within the traditional structure of a production timeline. These guiding principles in application provide a path to navigating the pressures you might find when working on a production and will also help you to find joy in the process. There are many paths to successful collaborations. As you begin your journey as an artist, you will come to develop your personal style.

Much of what theatre artists achieve is motivated by interpretation and aesthetic. The artist brings their story, their life experiences, and their unique individuality to a production, but the culmination of the production depends on how everyone's singularity can unite. Widening our perspective provides a lens of understanding for each person who contributes to the success of a production. Theatre is never made by one, but by all and ideally for all.

The following timeline is geared towards an academic structure, which serves anywhere between two and ten productions a semester. It is in these stages of production that challenges present themselves. Each stage of a production will have its own level of pressure, where communication, professionalism, and morale may be put to the test under the production calendar microscope.

Twyla Tharpe, choreographer and author of *The Collaborative Habit*, describes herself as a "career collaborator." She says, "Everybody pitched in and got it done. In sports, it's always about the team."[1]

In the spirit of collaboration, and following Chapter 2, we will refer to each group or production area as a team. There is the creative team (producer, playwright, director); the design team (sets, costumes, lights, sound,

DOI: 10.4324/9780367810252-4

projections); the production team (stage managers, production manager, technical director, master electrician, etc.); and the actors. All teams contribute to the creation of a production and are part of the larger team, which together makes up the entire company. Within each area are numerous individuals who specialize in doing a specific job with a designated timeline and support staff to assist.

For each area of a production, the needs and timelines are different. For the first few weeks, each area will create in its own bubble. Awareness of the other areas' needs and timelines can inform decisions that will impact a production creatively, and can also prevent costly mistakes down the line.

The various parts of the company achieve their different tasks in smaller collaborations until everyone converges to bring the production together during technical rehearsals (tech week). Clear lines of communication support the most updated information possible, which keeps progress moving towards opening night. This means questions are answered in a timely manner by email, text or phone. One area's decisions can impact those of another, and if not responded to can hold up progress. It is important that these lines do not break down. Once they do it can be hard to get them back on track, which can have a domino effect.

The Production Process

The stages of production in a traditional season are:

- pre-production
- rehearsals
- previews
- performance run
- post-production.

There are different models of production schedules, and how the collaboration works in each is different. This includes regional theatre, Broadway, off Broadway, national tours, higher education, theatre companies, and community theatre. Although the stages are the same, the timelines are different. Original works are different from already produced works. They often have preview performances, with rehearsals during the day, which allow for revisions before an official opening. In educational theatre, it is rare to have a preview period.

Pre-production

Pre-production is the period between the moment a production is given the go-ahead until the first rehearsal with actors. This period consists of budgeting, the hiring/determination of key production personnel (including the director and designers), and design, casting, and production meetings. Often when companies are creating a season, preliminary design deadlines are due way before rehearsals begin. Pre-production meetings allow design and production staff to discuss the framework of the production, such as concept, budget, casting needs, and limitations. This is a time to lay out expectations in all areas. Preliminary designs are just that: preliminary. changes are inevitable and necessary, and can be motivated by aesthetic, concept, budget, and/or learning curve.

During pre-production there will be many meetings. The difference between the two are; design meetings are conceptual and production meetings are technical.

Design meetings

Usually, design meetings will start long before the first full production meeting and the first rehearsal. The design meetings are smaller meetings between one or more of the designers and the director. This is a development meeting where the vision or concept is introduced by the director and the designer(s) contribute their ideas, thoughts, and the beginning stages of their design. Typically, this is a conversation where there is listening to, and receiving of, each other's point of view about the play and the overall concept.

Whatever you name it – vision, concept, or approach – it answers why the play is being done today, and belongs at the center of all conversations. What is the play's relevance to now? If it is an antiquated piece, is it being updated? What is the context and what is the historical and cultural framework? What is the question being proposed by doing this piece? What is the emotional journey? What is the social impact on the community? Is it purely to entertain and, if so, is it connected to something now that will help it resonate a bit more deeply? What are the elements that will initiate and justify the vision?

These initial design meetings are crucial for establishing a professional working relationship where ideas are considered. If it is a newly formed relationship, then the meetings provide a chance to learn about the person as well. How do they work? What are their artistic values and sensibilities? Ideally, it is a creative and reciprocal conversation, both remaining open to "what ifs" and allowing the director to steer the direction the design will take. (I may have just lost a few designers.) Bear in mind that this is a traditional schedule. Directors conceptualize and they galvanize. They might even give you suggestions on the design, but designers design and directors direct and in a great production the lines are blurred. Sometimes the collaborative process requires tension and disagreement, but conversation can be fruitful when it is an exchange of ideas, both sides are being heard, and all suggestions are considered. The desired outcome of design meetings is to find that co-investment in decision-making.

Conversation over ground plans with other designers generates insights, which can deepen and develop ideas, strengthening the overall design and bringing clarity to the overall concept. Sound and lights can see how their designs will assimilate in relationship to the space, both aurally and visually. Costumes will get a sense of color, and see how other elements might affect their design choices, such as a raked stage or changes in elevation. Once decisions about the set are clear, the model is created to give a three-dimensional perspective so all can visualize the movement of the piece as a whole. At this point, the set designer begins work on preliminary designs, which are necessary to determine whether the ideas fall within the allotted budget. These preliminaries are important to all areas so they can see where their element fits in or where they might need to speak up before everything is set in stone. Scenic and costumes and lighting will need to discuss the color palate; the sound designer will need to identify speaker placement and location of power sources to avoid collision later on.

PUTTING GENEROSITY INTO PRACTICE

The antithesis to generosity is resistance. It can be seen when a collaborator has fallen in love with an idea and can't see it any other way. They may want to protect their idea even though it has been advised that it will not work for one reason or another. This can be seen when someone holds on to their choice even if does not serve the bigger picture or if it is physically impossible, sometimes digging in their heels all the way to technical rehearsals. This is risky.

Resistance can be seen in collaboration by an unwillingness to find other solutions or the inability to try alternative choices. Sometimes it is the language used. "No" might be the first impulse. Director Kari Hayter provides a valuable perspective on resistance.

As a director, I have experienced creative resistance from both actors and collaborators. It is very challenging to have actors who trust neither you nor themselves. The most challenging actor is the one who isn't aware of *how* their insecurities or hesitancy affects the entire process of exploring creatively. They may feel generous and ready to work without realizing that particular vocabulary and/or behavior can subconsciously create a resistance that makes exploring and communication quite challenging.

I have been hired as a director where conceptual ideas for a production have already been solidified as the basis for a very specific vision. My ideas were welcome; however, there seemed to be a confused and timid resistance from the whole creative team since the production wasn't initially conceived with a unified, collaborative effort from the entire team. From my experience, the danger of this subconscious resistance from the team ultimately confused and inhibited the actors and the audience, stopping them from fully embracing one cohesive, creative idea.

Production meetings

A production meeting is a group meeting involving all areas of production and design. They do not include actors or administrative personnel. The purpose of these meetings are threefold: (1) to update everyone on the progress of the production; (2) to identify problems that need the attention of multiple production areas; and (3) to set schedules for tech week and other events that involve more than one area. These meetings are generally held at regular intervals and continue into tech week, where they generally are held at the end of every rehearsal until opening.

The production staff ask: How do we technically make this all happen on stage in the designated timeline? These individuals are schooled in rules, regulations and skilled to think of every possible contingency. Their job is to look ahead. Production staff are also working on multiple projects. Production is the practical side of the process – which is not to say it is not creative. Much of production problem-solving is logistical, and requires a very creative mind that can foresee the future. Sometimes these colleagues get a reputation for saying "no," but they have the knowledge about logistics and "how" things happen, and often will suggest the most efficient path to get there.

The production meetings are led by the production manager, who will sometimes defer to the director to initiate the conversation, starting with the priorities on the agenda. Each area will have representation in attendance. The topics should involve everyone. If one area gets stuck, side bars can hold up the agenda. Protocol is to take another smaller meeting afterwards so as not to hold up the meeting. Depending on the institution, there can be months of production meetings or just a handful. It largely depends on the timeline of the individual production and the institution. The conversation will include, but not be limited to, scheduling on build, load-in, hang, and focus – and often budget. There will be problems to solve for each area.

It is also an opportunity for each area to address concerns to the director that might impact another area. If the scenic choice is to paint the floor cool and the costume designer is leading in the same direction, this could be a problem, since it may wash out the actors. The director has an opportunity to address problems that involve everyone, so as to take full advantage of the time before technical rehearsals begin.

Production meetings are not the place to have conversations about the creative elements of the designs, but rather to discuss how the designs will be executed. If a fundamental problem with a design emerges in a production meeting, then the director and the designer should probably set up a separate breakout meeting.

When there is a standstill, the questions to ask are: Is it a test of wills or really a creative necessity that should be given a chance? What is the creative justification for the impossible choice?

This is where ego might be rearing its head, and a dose of generosity in the form of compromise might solve the conflict. At the end of the day, it is the director's job to make the call – but what if the director is the one who is stuck on a choice that is seemingly impossible? The design and production team may have to troubleshoot and offer alternative solutions. These moments of disagreement are when returning to the initial vision may lead the team to a solution and where the guiding principles can be practiced.

THE REALITY

Next time you enter a production meeting, take a moment to take in the room. Observe body language, expression, conversation or lack thereof. What do you see? What's the social temperature in the room? Is the energy bouncing off the walls with chaotic and enthusiastic activity, or is it subdued? Maybe colleagues are engaged in intense conversation before the meeting begins. Maybe there are clusters of laughter or thoughtful exchanges while sharing nosh and lukewarm coffee. Maybe what you see are indirect conversations as laptops boot up and distracted theatre-makers fiddle with models and ground plans. Maybe designers are frantically preparing and looking for renderings, sleep deprived and operating on their third Rockstar before noon. Maybe you engage with an old friend with whom you worked a long time ago and enjoy a mini-reunion, excited to work together again. Or maybe you see someone you worked with in the past where the experience was not positive, and both of you dodge each other, dreading the possibility of having to work together again. But you both know the theatre world is small, so you politely acknowledge each other's existence. It is likely your experience will be unique and different for every production on which you work.

On one hand, production meetings can be a stimulating time to engage in a larger conversation about how all the elements will come together and on the other hand they can sometimes bring out the middle schooler in the best of us, attempting to prove our work, hoping our ideas are accepted.

Meetings can be crammed in between jam-packed schedules and busy lives. There is always an agenda, most often against the clock with not enough time allotted to attend to every item fairly.

In a perfect world, ideas merge into the whole, which supports a clear and unified vision. When there are questions, the choices will be put to the test to see whether they support the vision and the story being told. When all this aligns, it is synchronicity, and can feel like a third entity – as if creativity itself has intervened.

Preparing is the most important part of your role as a collaborator. Here are a few things that can help you to prepare for these encounters, to ensure meetings are fruitful. They may seem obvious, but one can never underestimate the power of preparation.

Preparation questions for design and production meetings

WHAT DOES THE PLAY MEAN TO ME?
Have you read the play? In an academic setting, my guess is that at least half the people around the table in a production meeting have not read the play. Is that a surprise? It should be, because if there is one thing that is a given in any situation you may find yourself in within the theatre is that you *must* read the play – more than once. There are few "musts" in this book, but this is definitely a "must." There is nothing worse than watching someone pretend they have read the play when they have not. Never show up to a meeting not having read the play. It seems obvious, but it is imperative. This is expected at every level of creating in the theatre. You must read the play.

End of discussion. If you do not read the play, what can you contribute? And research the period and history of the production. The more you know, the more inspired your choices will be. This preparation will be expected of you and duly noted.

WHAT IS THE LIST OF INFORMATION THAT YOU "NEED TO KNOW"?

As you begin your process, there may be important facts that are necessary, which inform your design/directing decisions. Make your list and listen attentively in the meeting. Some of what is on your list will be answered. If it is not answered in the meeting, then reach out to the people who can answer these questions so you can move forward with your process. Ask. If you get brushed aside, it is sometimes the nature of the distracted beast. Seek out the best time to make contact.

"People are people. And people are problems. But – and this is a very big but – people who are practiced in collaboration will do better than those who insist on their individuality."[2] The creative mode can bring out the best or the worst. Creative people can be intense, passionate, impatient, and distracted, as they multi-task down a chaotic hallway or busy New York City street – wherever the collaboration may be. Intense people are often lost in deep thought. The director holds many of the answers to your questions. If they are bombarded after meetings, reach out to the stage manager to see when would be a good time to talk.

When you have the ear of the director, use your time wisely. Trust that your work will speak for itself. If you present yourself prepared, with a point of view and a willingness to listen, and with an intent to add to the conversation in support of the vision, you will contribute to the production's success and be doing your job.

Below is a list from each area and what they need to know to do their job. It's not comprehensive by any means, but it will offer a wider perspective on how many people are involved in one production and the important information they need to do their job.

- *Director needs to know:* ground plan; entrances and exits; how doors open; size, shape and strength of furniture and props; how costumes, hair, accessories, and shoes affect movement; how sets move; lighting practicals and how they work; how special effects will be executed and by whom; anything that concerns actor safety; regulations (fire and building codes, etc.) that might impact staging.

- *Scenic needs to know:* budget, period, style – is it abstract, realistic, magical realism, period, absurd, linear, non-linear world? scene breakdowns – interior, exterior; how many different locations; seasons – visuals help to place the tone, atmosphere, and color choices.
- *Lighting needs to know:* set design, scene breakdown, transitions, how many instruments, how many electrical circuits are available for lighting instruments? A list of equipment is helpful so newcomers can easily be assimilated. Do we need to work with a rep plot (standardized lighting system) or can we adjust the lighting? Realistic or surreal world? Day or night? Time period which will inform type of lighting. What is the color palate of set and costumes?
- *Sound needs to know:* equipment inventory; scene breakdown. Is there a budget for sound, including to obtain rights to songs or other music? Sound system and programs used. What is set up and what can be added? Does the director already have ideas about the sound source material? Speaker location sourced. Who will do the routing? Who will program? Are there assistants? Will there be live music? What amplification is provided in theatre? Will I work with a composer?
- *Costumes needs to know:* Scene breakdown; budget; period; how many characters; how many costumes; who the actors are and their measurements; stock or build options; double casting needs. Do actors play multiple characters? Will there be a raked stage that will impact movement and type of shoes? What is the color palate of the set design?
- *Property masters needs to know:* Budget, beyond what is on the property list; period; how close the prop will be to the audience; realistic or stylized. Are their consumables? Weapons that need special care and handling? Special effects, such as blood packs? What will need to be built or rented?
- *Production stage manager (head of stage management team) needs to know:* How many characters? How many cast members? How many equity and non-equity? Rehearsals: where, when and for how long? Union rules. Who will be on the stage management team? Is there a need for special skills artist dialect coach, fight choreographer or intimacy director that may need to be hired? Identifying trigger warnings. Signs to be put up front of house, which means contact marketing.

WHAT IS THE BUDGET?

Each area will need to know their budget. Budget can be the linchpin that bursts the creative balloon and dashes dreams or brings out one's creative genius. Unfortunately, it is the reality at every level of production, but budget doesn't have to impale creativity. It can actually do the opposite. Lower budgets help to distill the design ideas to the essentials of the story being told. Getting creative on a shoestring might inspire some to listen more acutely to other points of view, sometimes creating something that is even groundbreaking.

> Collaboration is what makes it work. Even in a musical. You need that collaboration; you need that support. I did a prod of Cabaret – in a tiny, tiny little house but wanted to put effects on certain voices in certain moments so I collaborated with the director and with scenic designer [about] where we could hide mics and then I worked with the choreographer to block the people I needed closest to the mics on the stage. At this point, I need this person's voice to reverberate. She (the choreographer) said, "I will choregraph her right here so she can land in right in front of the hidden shotgun." The smaller the budget, the bigger the collaboration needs to be. I only have four mics guys, let's work together to get everybody heard as opposed to I have a massive budget and you're all on wireless.
>
> – Cricket Myers, sound design Tony Award nominee for
> *Benghal Tiger at the Baghdad Zoo*, 2011

Author Sidebar (Mark)

It can be really tricky when confronted with the realities of budget to figure out whether you should stay with the original concept, or change it to fit the parameters of a theatre's resources. I remember getting a call from the artistic director a couple of weeks before I was to start rehearsing a new play, telling me that the set design was way over budget and that the designer and I had to reconceive the set. I was lucky enough to be working with a terrific collaborator – Tom Kamm – who was a great problem-solver. Whereas I was completely flummoxed by the idea that we had to scrap a design we had worked so hard on, he calmly said, "I had an idea earlier that I discarded that I think will work to get us where we needed to be." What he came up with was far more theatrical, imaginative, and pared down to the essentials. It really helped us tell the story in a much more interesting way.

A couple of decades later, I was associate producer on a project where the design was way over budget and we had to ask the designer to reconceive the set to bring it within our financial resources. This time, the designer withdrew from the project. It was a new musical that had taken a ton of work to get it ready for budgeting, and I can't blame him.

The replacement designer actually had a better grasp of the style of production, and as with the earlier case, really worked with the director to pare choices down to the essentials of what was needed. The result was a set that better reflected the spirit for the production that the director had envisioned.

Sometimes, a director and designer will make budget by cutting elements out of the design. This happened with one of my last professional productions. Rather than reconceive when we were told the design was way over budget, we worked together to pare down the set to its essentials. Unfortunately, this time the result was a set design that maintained the idea, but looked bare-boned. I've never quite figured out if we would have been better off reconceiving the production. The production looked great, but I couldn't shake the feeling that I knew how it *could* have looked with the cut elements reinstalled.

Theatre promises to keep us connected, and putting up a show will always rely on individuals gathering in the same room to make the magic happen. Sometimes meetings happen virtually out of necessity. The director's responsibility is to unite all areas with the same information, guiding how all parts will eventually work and function in accordance with the vision of the play.

Rehearsals

After pre-production, rehearsals begin. Rehearsals consist of the period of time generally spent in the rehearsal room from the first day of rehearsals until the last day in the room before moving into the theatre and beginning the process of integrating design, technical elements, and the actors. The focus of rehearsal during this period is on the actor-and-director collaboration, and the goal is to discover the most effective way to tell the playwright's story. Even on a new play, where the playwright is often a collaborator in the room, the primary focus is still on the director/actor process.

The director determines the structure of the rehearsal process. While this is different for every director and every project, there are some basic phases that are common to most rehearsals:

- *Table work.* This is where the company sits around a table and reads and discusses the play. Questions are asked, although not necessarily answered immediately, and the focus is on understanding what is in the text and the overall story that is being told.
- *Research.* This is a period in which the actors and director work to develop a deeper understanding of the play. It can include academic research (often presented by the dramaturge) or creative research, such as improvisations and exercises.
- *Staging.* This is the period where the play is given its initial physical life, determining basic movement and work with props. Is there fight choreography or intimacy that may require specialized directors for these specific areas?
- *Enrichment.* This is a period of time where the director and actors work through the text, focusing on the details of each moment. This can be very painstaking, but incredibly rewarding, and it is generally here that the story starts to come to life.
- *Run-throughs.* Sections of the play – or the entire play – are rehearsed without stopping. It is here that the director and actor discover and or understand the arc of the play. The focus is on character journeys and the momentum that the urgency of the story generates.
- *Refinement.* This final stage of rehearsals prior to techs is where the actors and directors start focusing on the communication of the performance to an audience. It usually focuses on pacing and rhythm, and can consist of exercises that encourage developing the energy required to reach an audience. These exercises can include Italian runs, sing-throughs, and whisper-throughs, depending on the needs of the company.

While the above phases can be found in almost every rehearsal room, the ways in which they are executed vary widely, with some practices being highly collaborative and some not. If our goal is to foster the most collaborative environment, what are some of the principles that we can bring to bear?

Fostering a collaborative environment

A few guiding thoughts to foster a collaborative environment:

FOR THE ENTIRE COMPANY
- *Be generous with your trust and respect.* If someone breaches your trust or disrespects you, talk to them. If you feel like you can't do that safely,

then ask the stage manager to be present. Don't assume anyone can read your mind. Establish clear boundaries so trust and respect can live in the environment. Never forget that we are all on the same team and the entire company wants the same thing: a successful production created through a process that is enjoyable and productive.

- *Know your job and stay in your lane.* If there is something that you notice is out of your job description, take it to the head of the area.
- *Choose your battles wisely.* Not every choice is a matter of life or death; save your energy for the fights that really matter. Being combative will add unnecessary tension to the rehearsal room and will inhibit collaboration within the cast.

FOR THE DIRECTOR:

- *Establish trust and identify boundaries with regards to the material and the company.* Introducing the company and identifying job descriptions, so everyone knows who does what, supports everyone's expertise. Identify professional protocol with respect to the material if there is sensitive or intimacy involved. Knowing the leader has a plan will put everyone at ease.
- *Establish a rehearsal structure that promotes collaboration.*
- *Ensure everyone is heard.* All choices need to be explored fully. The theatre is an art form in which the only way you can tell whether something works is to *see* it. There's a big caveat here for the actor: your ideas need to be articulated in such a way that they do not force a choice on another actor. In other words, your idea needs to come from a place of what *you* can do in a moment, not how you want another actor to react to what you do.

When I was working on a production of *The Glass Menagerie*, the actress playing Laura asked the actor playing Jim to tear off a small piece of the gum before handing it to her. This may seem like a simple, collaborative request – and the actor was certainly willing to comply – but it asked Jim *the actor* to help, rather than Jim *the character*. In real life, we find ways to get someone to do what we want, so I stopped them, and asked the actress the "magic if" question: "if you were Laura in these circumstances, how would you communicate what you want from him?" (Williams gives you no line for this action, and it goes against Jim's generosity to offer only a piece of the gum.) The actress found a beautiful moment where she took the whole piece of gum, tore off a tiny piece, and gave the rest of it back to "Jim". The point here is that you're stepping outside of your character and asking the other actor to do something that solves the problem for you, rather than working through the problem within the circumstances of your character. Working *through* something almost always results in interesting choices.

- *Be clear about your expectations*, whether practical (come to rehearsal on time, be off book by the due dates, etc.) or aspirational (strive for the highest stakes possible, don't settle on choices too early, etc.). Clear expectations promote trust and communication.

- *Talk less, listen more.* Lots of directors love to talk, and in doing so often miss golden opportunities that the actor discovers in the moment. A lot of times, what they say winds up being unnecessary. If you hear a read-through where the story comes out clearly, you don't need to spend an hour telling the cast what the story is; they get it. Train yourself to listen with your whole being: your ears, your eyes, your soul. You will save a lot of time, and you'll discover that listening promotes generosity.

- *The more you tell an actor what to do, the more you diminish their desire to collaborate.* They will stop thinking and will start waiting for you to tell them what to do. This will make the director's job much harder, and it will kill the collaborative spirit.

- *Actors need to try things – even choices that they know won't work.* Learning that a choice doesn't work gives an actor greater confidence in the choice that *does* work. Treat all choices as valuable learning opportunities. The truism that we learn more from our failures needs to be embraced in the rehearsal room.

- *Actors function best when they feel a sense of ownership.* Encourage participation from everyone in the ensemble and at every level. Seek their opinions, and receive them with an open mind.

- *Be respectful of an actor's time by planning ahead.* If you need an actor at rehearsal, then you have to feel free to call them in, even if you wind up not using them. However, if you call an actor and then don't use them, you start to build resentment. At the very least, acknowledge the fact that you didn't use them, and apologize – even if they're being paid to be there. No one likes their time to be wasted.

- *Try to create an atmosphere where an actor never feels like they have to make you happy.* Actors like to please people, and praise from a director can be gold to them. It can also stifle creativity and divert focus from making honest, truthful choices. Keep the work focused on the work, *never* on you.
- *Never forget that you are on the same team as the actors* – and that you both ultimately want the same thing: a successful production.

FOR THE ACTOR

- *Do your homework.* Your analysis of the text and your role is essential work. Don't wait for a director tell you what the text means.
- *Come to rehearsal prepared.* This includes coming warmed up and ready to work. It means knowing your lines. It means bringing choices to the table. If you aren't prepared, you can't be an effective collaborator.
- *Treat rehearsals as a period of exploration and discovery*, not as a time to "get it right." Encourage exploration of your impulses.
- *Work towards an attitude of "yes, and"* rather than "my character wouldn't." The hardest thing for a director is a resistant actor – the actor whose first impulse is to say no or challenge a direction. This will eventually damage the collaborative spirit in the room.
- *Talk less, act more.* You may be an actor who needs to talk through choices before giving them a try, and that's okay, but be sensitive to how you are using everyone else's time – even if you have a lead role.

> As a director, I generally need to see an actor's choice before I can truly understand what they want to make happen, and I generally find that *working* through an idea is more productive than *talking* through an idea.

- *Keep your personal problems outside the rehearsal room.* Professional protocol is to leave personal baggage outside the rehearsal door. Sometimes this is unavoidable, for one reason or another. If it creeps in, as sometimes it can, avoid holding up the rehearsal from progressing. Channel your depth as an artist and use it. If you need to step away, ask for what you need.
- *Remember that the most important thing going on in the rehearsal room happens in the space where people are working.* This work – as you know – takes enormous concentration, so be respectful and try to do nothing to distract from that work.

- *Not all choices will serve the story that is being told.* The director will help guide those decisions so all choices serve the vision.
- *Feedback is given to improve the quality of the work and move the story forward.* There is a difference between taking feedback personally and personalizing the character. Feedback is never a personal attack. When you can look at feedback as an act of generosity rather than personal criticism, you will welcome it rather than dread it. Personalization comes when an actor particularizes the character's journey through specific choices, inspired by their own experiences. It can feel personal. There is no wonder that actors can get defensive about the character. It is important to acknowledge that the actor is playing a character and, although it may feel personal, feedback is about being in service to the character and the story. If it is seen this way, feedback can be viewed as a gift.

FOR THE DESIGN TEAMS
- *How does your design fit into the whole?* The Collective suggests attending rehearsals, especially run-throughs, as soon as you can, which will help preempt problems later. At the production meetings, ask the director how they feel about you attending rehearsal. It is in their best interest to have you observe. If it is okay, it is best to coordinate an optimal time to attend with the stage manager. It shows you are sensitive to the production needs and that you are investing your time into the pro-duction and taking ownership of your work. Creating in a bubble can only happen up to a point. You may have been designing for weeks at home, but you need to see whether what you have will work in reality. If everyone is to have a "co-investment," your initiative to attend rehearsal reveals that you value everyone else's contribution, not just your own, which is working not only collaboratively but cooperatively.

These suggestions are a start, as they encourage communication, gen-erosity, trust, and respect. At the very least, they can help to diminish misunderstandings, hurt feelings, and breakdowns in communication.

Tech rehearsal – where the rubber meets the road

The culmination of weeks of independent creation comes together during tech week. Tech week is the most stressful time of any production. Finally, the director and the entire company converge to bring what has been abstract concept into a concrete theatrical event that communicates dynamically with an audience. It is where the vision is fully realized and where the conversations now become realities – or not. You cannot over-prepare for tech week. Everything is now put to the test.

The stages in the birth of a production require the entire company to be aware that each part of this whole is working towards a clear and unified vision and, as we head into tech week, generosity of spirit could not be more important. Everyone involved, once divided and having conquered their area of expertise, is where theory is put into practice and all is revealed.

The role of the production stage manager is crucial at this stage of the process. It is important throughout, as they are the glue that holds the enterprise together, but even more so during tech week. Even the simple placement of tech tables is essential. Broadway composer and sound designer John Gromada (*Proof, A Few Good Men, Clybourne Park*) shared that he requests a sound tech table within the reach of the other collaborators. Discussion has to be accessible for all areas. Location helps to simplify. Each area will request its tech needs. Sound will require quiet time to tune the space and equalize the room. Scenic will need to approve placement of the furniture and scene shifts will be coordinated by the stage manager. Props will address where and when props are available and safety issues will be announced. During tech week, the director, design teams, and actors will become familiar with everything, so changes will be made. Nothing is set in stone until it is.

In universities and in professional situations such as summer stock, where tech time is short, it is common that, sometime prior to tech week, the director, stage manager and designers might schedule a paper tech or dry tech. This is where they talk through the play, cue by cue, outside of the theatre. Dry tech is where the director and designers set initial cues in the theatre without actors present.

Once tech rehearsals begin, the stage manager and director align their goals, procedures and pace of the day, then the stage manager becomes responsible for keeping everything on target. The stage manager decides where the cues will be called, what line will initiate the "go." It is taken from a specific line in which scenic, lighting, and or actors will transition. There are big changes and small changes. The stage manager is like a conductor, and tells the running crew when to make the change. There are anywhere between 50 and 200 cues in a show.

The decision of the timing of cues is a collaborative process between director and designers. Creating the timing of the cues is related to the timing and rhythm of the play, and is guided by the director and in a professional setting finessed by the designer. These rehearsals are about setting starting points for the coordination of the cues that will be refined once actors are introduced into the process, and will likely change during the tech process until the actors have assimilated all the added technical elements.

In a professional setting, most experienced designers have been through the process hundreds of time. This is one of the fundamental elements to learn as a designer, especially for sound and lighting. Transitions are crucial to sustain an audience's attention. The moments in the darkness or near-darkness are when the audience either digests what they watching or they look at their phone and secretly text their babysitter. It really depends on how a show is paced, so the calling of cues and the execution of it make a vitally important contribution. Experience teaches timing – it is part of the sixth sense of the artist. Usually, but not always, lights and sound will move together, and if the cues are not timed out correctly it can destroy the pace of a show.

Designers are artists in their own right, with an ability to visualize and conceptualize dramatic material that is equal to – or even greater than – that of the director. Designers work on far more productions than a director possibly can, and as a result their knowledge of their own craft (design) exceeds that of the director. This valuable experience can be a boon to a director, but it can also lead to a clash of egos or competing visions in design meetings. Here is where guiding principle #1– trust and respect – comes into play, with the caveat that collaboration is not structureless.

> Collaboration is not the same thing as liberty, equality and fraternity. It's not about having everyone having an equal voice but it's about co-investment in a [shared] mission for a production which everyone understands. I think as with most things we have to start with this healthy tension that exists in all of our disciplines. There is a sweet spot … between pursuing a vision, which comes from the leader of the production (in many cases it's the director), on the one hand, and also successfully delegating the roles and responsibilities on the other. And I think that the most successful version of collaboration comes when those two things are co-existing synergistically.
> – David Bridel, director, playwright, educator, performer, and writer

Dress rehearsals

Each night of technical rehearsals, the machine gets more efficient. Each part works more cohesively and the human parts operate more cooperatively. Everyone begins to take ownership of their role in the success of the production. Start time mirrors the performance schedule. The director may choose to work the acts on two different nights in order to problem solve and address details. In a perfect world, by the third dress rehearsal there are no stops and the inherent audience, the company, begins to get pulled away from their work and hear the show as an audience member. Dress rehearsals dictate what the show will become. The goal is to run the show with all moving parts together with no stops. The director will give notes to area heads after the rehearsal and then, if time permits, give notes to the actors. There is usually a short production meeting as the actors are changing out of costume. It is where the designers can meet with the stage manager and director to give short notes about calls of cues, or any last-minute technical problems to be solved.

Previews

The preview period is important because now the audience will weigh in. After hearing the audience response, the director is likely to give adjustments to tighten the pace and clarify story. Most universities don't have preview periods because their production run is not long enough. However, a good practice is to use the opening weekend as a preview and then integrate adjustments. Subtle changes can take a show from ordinary to extraordinary.

Previews are an important time and, sadly, not enough time is spent on assimilating the audience's role in the educational theatre process. On Broadway or in regional productions, original works rely on previews to get to the next step, and this will inform whether or not the production will have a life after its opening. Previews in the professional world carry a lot of weight when it comes to the success of a production.

Previews were created for new works in order to test material on audiences. Changes made in rehearsal during the day are implemented in the evening performances. The audience response informs the creators about whether the changes worked. The creative team decides when to "freeze" the show, so no other changes are made. Nothing is set in stone until it is. If it is an original work, it is usually is a collaborative decision between the creative team and playwright to decide when to freeze the show. If it is a licensed production, it is the decision of the director and sometimes the producer.

In an academic setting, students have class during the day, making it impossible to integrate more rehearsals. However, the process can be utilized through implementing director's notes. Whether you are a designer, actor or running crew, notes are part of the development process. An experienced director can teach you much about the process from opening weekend to Week 2. They are seasoned with experience and knowledge, and can provide minor adjustments that can send the performance soaring to another level.

But often in an academic setting, everyone is worn out after opening night. They have been doing double duty for weeks and often just want to be left alone. The sign of a true artist and professional in the making is one who seeks out the feedback despite all of that.

Performance run

Opening night

Opening night has arrived. Opening nights are exciting – it's a launch, a ribbon cutting, a first. The air is buzzing, actors are nervous, designers are relieved, the director is anticipating the initiation of the new partner, the audience and the actors are jittery and excited to share their work. The birth of a production is exciting, grueling, frustrating, and euphoric. It is an amazing feat when it all comes together. Everyone has their doubts along the way, but somehow with opening night adrenaline, like magic everyone pulls it off. Nothing replaces live entertainment. As we sit here in Week 10 of sheltering in place of COVID-19, our collective souls are chomping at the bit to get back into the theatre. The theatre fuels our souls, and opening night is like no other experience.

Usually, the director will stay through previews, and give notes to both the cast and design team. When the director leaves after opening, the responsibility goes to the stage manager, who will maintain the integrity of the show and see it through closing and strike. In professional scenarios, directors and designers are not contractually obligated to remain after opening, and many in demand are on to their next job.

In a professional setting, actors rarely get notes from the director after they leave – unless, in some cases, it is an open-ended run, or replacement or multiple cast show. Performance is where a lot of the learning can happen.

As students of the theatre, you are developing your craft at a deeper level in order to prepare for the profession. You are creating a piece of living art. Finessing changes may lead a performance from ordinary to extraordinary. Sometimes, finessing involves both the technical side of the production and the actor's timing, a shift that can take a performance to new heights. Sometimes it is a simple energy change in a scene shift that can pick up the pace. Or an actor can bring on their own prop to assist with the lag time. Simple nuances that may not have been dealt with in the process can inform the success of the production, making a huge difference. Added up, these small adjustments can make a world of difference to an audience. They won't know, but you will know because that is what a professional does: they notice the details.

> To make a show go from good to very good, it's very easy. It's a series of bold, smart things that you have to do. But to make a show go from very good to brilliant, it's an endless series of details, and endless series of unbelievable details that lift it.[3]
>
> George C. Wolf, Tony Award winning Director

Post-production

In educational theatre, there is the tradition of strike. The set comes down. The costumes get returned or stored. The experience of telling this story ends so a new one can begin. Usually there is a party to mark the ending and to celebrate the achievements of all. Theatre is social, and this is important.

Shows open and shows close, but because they consist of living, breathing humans, no two shows will ever be the same. When the curtain comes down and all those people whose hearts synchronized in the audience of *Dreamgirls* get up to leave the theatre and go home, they will take something from the event. They are changed by art. The art of the theatre is unique: it is personal and visceral, and often will remain with audiences for a very long time.

> I will never forget when I saw Mary Zimmerman's *Metamorphosis* at Circle in the Square in New York City in 2002. I had standing room tickets and went alone, shortly after I had my son. It was one of my first outings since becoming a mother. I was changed. Ironically, I will never forget, the first line of the play was, "Bodies, I have in mind, and how they can change to assume new shapes."

I laughed so deeply because I felt I was home. In the theatre. They understood. All of them, they must have known I was coming and they were talking to me. And of course, as I left the theatre intoxicated by the blissful beauty that was this show, I was deeply moved, thinking of the last line of the show, which echoed as I walked down 8th Avenue on my way home to the Upper West Side.

"Walking down the street at night, when you're all alone, you can still hear stirring in the intermingled branches of the trees above, the ardent prayer of Baucus and Philemon. They whisper: Let me die the moment my love dies. They whisper. Let me outlive my own capacity to love. They whisper: Let me die still loving, and so, never die."[4]

I walked out of the theatre changed by this show. A meaning that connected me deeply to humanity.

Many of you might be thinking of your own unforgettable moments in the theatre, which may have led you to this place, embarking on creating theatre yourself. The theatre is representative of who we are, and embracing this aspect brings vitality to the production. It is where we learn about one another. What are your collaborators' areas of expertise, interests, and goals? Knowing someone's individual strengths can be an asset to the production. Who am I going to spend every day with for the next few months? Are we going to tolerate each other or actually enjoy the process that benefits everyone – especially the audience? The audience subliminally feels when a company is cohesive and when there is a unified vision.

The show closes, the people go home, the ghost light lives on. And it will start again. Another production will begin soon enough and you will begin the process all over again. But each time, a little wiser, a little more prepared, a little more experienced. Knowing that you may have an impact on someone's life in the work we do as theatre-makers together and never alone.

Scenarios for Discussion

Scenario 1: Parting company (when a collaboration isn't working) – the play that goes wrong

Sometimes, despite everyone's best intentions, collaborations don't work. Do you push through to that immovable opening night? Do you shut down the production? Do you replace team members? When a collaboration fails, it is probably one of the most painful moments a director – or anyone, for that matter – can face.

For much of my career, I was not a believer in firing actors. Directors cast the show, often knowing what the challenges are. In casting, they put their faith in an actor, often without having worked with that actor before. Yet directors have to take responsibility for their decisions, and it is my personal belief that firing an actor is a very last resort. Fortunately, in my 30+ years as a professional director, artistic director, and associate artistic director, it has only happened a handful of times. Every time I have been faced with the possibility, I have resisted it with every fiber of my being, yet every time it came to making that decision, the result was an extraordinary release of tension. Sometimes, it is the best thing you can do – for everyone.

I learned this hard lesson on one of the most challenging productions I have ever worked on. I was an early career director getting ready to direct a new play that I was extremely excited about. The playwright and I had collaborated before, and even though that experience had been really rocky at times, we both respected each other and felt we made a great team. We had an incredible team of designers, all of whom have gone on to win or be nominated for Tony Awards. With a great team, a great play, exciting pre-production work, we were ready.

The first day was a disaster for a variety of reasons. The lead actress demanded rewrites that would totally change the story. A young actor withdrew from the discussions, making it known that he was unhappy – but for reasons that were baffling to me, and that I couldn't fix. By the end of the day, the playwright said, "I want her gone." I replied, "I want him gone." Playwright: "But we need him." Me: "But we need her." And so we came to a stalemate and agreed to move forward with things as they stood.

For three weeks, things went from bad to worse. The company of eight actors was fraying. A faction of three actors (ironically, all with the same agent) separated from the group and distanced themselves from the rest of us. Finally, it came to a head. One actor threw a fit, and another actor said "enough!" We convened a company meeting: me, the playwright, eight actors and the stage managers.

Those first three weeks were the hardest of my career. (One of the actors who remained in the production went on to become a Tony Award-winning director, said in the 30+ intervening years, he has never encountered anything even close to this again.) Something happened at that meeting that turned the boat around. The next three weeks – which consisted primarily of techs and previews – were among the happiest of my career. What happened?

I'm not going to tell you. Instead, I'll ask you to think about and discuss the following:

1. What were my options? Nothing is off the table.
2. Should we (the playwright and I) have fired one or both of the actors after the first rehearsal?
3. Shared vision became an issue here: the actress had a vision that was different from that of the playwright. Should the play change in the spirit of collaboration? Why or why not?
4. What could have occurred that first day of rehearsals that might have gotten off to a better start? What about the second day?
5. Could something have been done in casting to ensure a more collaborative company?
6. If we were going to replace one or more of the actors, what are the criteria for who goes and who stays?
7. When is it okay to part company? What does that conversation sound like? Whose decision is it? Is it a decision that can be made collaboratively?

Scenario 2: Collaborating in techs – the rogue artist

Ten-out-of-twelves are tech days that span ten hours over a 12-hour period. They are allotted to producing organizations depending on the contract with Actors' Equity Association (AEA), the actors' union. A Broadway production, for example, has an unlimited number of these days, which are grueling. Most not-for-profit companies get a maximum of two. I once worked for a theatre company as an associate producer that was allowed five ten-out-of-twelves.

My first production with this company was a deeply complicated production helmed by a young director and with an extremely experienced lighting designer. By the end of the second day, they hadn't made it out of the first scene. The production stage manager couldn't keep the rehearsal moving, so we replaced him. I started sitting in on rehearsals to try to help where I could. At one point, the lighting designer stopped the rehearsal and said to the director, "You have no idea what this scene is about. I can't light it until you figure out what is really happening here."

In this scenario – as in all collaborations – there are many perspectives and points of view. Consider each:

1. *The director*: You are a young director working with a Broadway lighting designer – that you have chosen. You are on stage and in techs, so you have in fact staged the show. What do you do now? Do you re-block the scene? Fight it out with the lighting designer? How do you feel about being called out in front of the entire company?
2. *The production stage manager*: You've just replaced the previous production stage manager. You've never worked with this company before, but you want to continue working with them in the future. You know you were hired because the previous production stage manager couldn't keep the rehearsal moving. What do you do?
3. *The lighting designer*: You've designed hundreds of shows in your career. You know when a scene isn't working. You also know the amount of time you have to get the show up and running, and you know how to get there – experience has taught you this. Do you push on for excellence, or do you settle for mediocrity and move on?
4. *The associate producer*: As the producer's representative, you have to make sure this production – the company's big money-maker – makes it to opening night a week away. You know the dilemma the production stage manager faces, and you want to support this person. You don't want to interfere in the artistic collaboration, but you are also responsible for keeping things moving. What do you do?

Notes

1 Twyla Tharp, *The Collaborative Habit* (Simon and Schuster, New York, 2009), p. 10.
2 Tharp, *The Collaborative Habit*, p. 11.
3 George C. Wolfe (director), *Show Business: The Road to Broadway*, directed by Dori Berinstein (Liberation Entertainment, October 16, 20017, DVD).
4 Mary Zimmerman, *Metamorphoses* (Northwestern University Press, Evanston, IL, 2002), p. 83.

4
Case Studies
Spiderman: Turn Off the Dark and *Ragtime*

Mounting a production is a huge feat, and mounting an original production is even more so. Mounting a production of an original musical on Broadway is perhaps the largest feat of all. Sometimes seeing an original production to opening night seems like nothing short of a miracle when considering all that can go wrong. Why *does* a collaboration work repeatedly, and why do some never find a flow? This is the age-old question of the theatre artist. It can be asked of any of the areas: acting, directing, designing, producing, and writing.

Musicals are complex, and offer more potential challenges than a play due to the mere fact they generally have more moving parts, more technical elements and, more often than not, more cooks in the kitchen, making them excellent case studies.

In this chapter, we will look at two productions by two different teams who mounted original Broadway musicals: *Spider-Man: Turn Off the Dark* and *Ragtime*. The professional teams that created these musicals provide case studies that illustrate the principles of collaboration at work – or *not* at work.

Case Study 1: *Spider-Man: Turn Off the Dark* (2005–14)

The musical *Spider-Man: Turn Off the Dark* had iconic source material, an award-winning director, Julie Taymor (*Lion King*, Tony Award for Best Musical and Best Director, 1990), and legendary pop icons Bono and The Edge writing the score. What could go wrong?

Hello Entertainment producer Tony Adams got wind of the project and, despite minimal producing experience, won the opportunity to produce. Many say it was his charm that got him the job. But as contracts were about to

DOI: 10.4324/9780367810252-5

be signed, he gathered the creative team together and, before the deal was sealed, Tony was found on the floor, unresponsive due to a stroke at 52 years of age. The Edge was literally looking for a pen in the other room and when he returned he found his collaborator gone before the project even had a chance to begin. It was an unfortunate omen that began this team's process, a foreshadowing of the challenges that lay ahead.

How does a production with a collaborative team of artists at the top of their field, $65 million in funding, and six years of development not succeed? How does a producer continue to keep the ship from sinking despite key replacements, including the director, choreographer, book writer, celebrity leads, and producing teams? How can a production that delayed opening night six times not get it right? After scathing reviews, gossip, and internet hate blogs, it still opened on Broadway as perhaps a sort of spite to show the world, "See, we got there!" and to rub it in, then ran for three years and 1066 performances with consistent tickets sales. At the end of it all, was it a failure or simply an extremely difficult collaboration?

Clear and unified vision

If a production is the sum of all its parts, it is helpful to see what sparked each member of the team to take on the project and how each individual found their way onto the team. It also provides an important perspective on the art of networking, and how it can influence who eventually becomes a part of that team.

Marvel Entertainment saw an opportunity with the movie's success to capitalize on family entertainment on Broadway. With the success of the *Spiderman* movie, Michael Parker – who worked in the licensing department at Marvel Entertainment – got wind of the Broadway project and reached out to his friend, Irish film producer Tony Adams. Despite no real Broadway producing credits, Adams and his partner David Garfinkle won the chance to produce the musical on Broadway.

Tony Adams contacted his friend Paul McGuinness, who managed the rock band U2. Bono and The Edge were hired to write the score even though they hadn't done such a thing before. In their unofficial faxed over "yes" to Adams, they suggested that their neighbor, Irish filmmaker Neil Jordan, write the book. His films were scored by Elliot Goldenthal, domestic and artistic partner to Julie Taymor. You're beginning to see how quickly networking happens. Then Bono suggested Julie Taymor should direct. Taymor didn't say yes immediately, but she found her way into the story through her interest in the myth of Arachne, Marvel's Greek mythical spider who is brought down by her own hubris, originally found in the first issue of the Marvel Comic Book series.

After the first reading of Jordan's treatment, it became clear he was not the right match for the job as book writer, so he was let go. After that, Taymor decided to hold onto control of the book and sought out a co-writer. Glen Berger, who was introduced to Taymor by her then-assistant, came onto the project to co-write the book. At this point he had no Broadway credits, but had earned an Emmy Award for 20th Century Fox Television's animated program *King of the Hill* (1999). Thus began their complex six-year working relationship. During the height of their challenges, Berger recalls, Bono told him, "Your problem, meanwhile is that you're too bashful."[1]

Taymor's interest in the myth of Arachne led her to bring world theatre forms and myth onto the stage. Her vision was dark, brooding, and mythical. Marvel is based on a superhero and family entertainment.

Bono and The Edge sustained their touring and recording careers, and dropped in and out of rehearsals. Seldom did all of them collaborate in the same room – or on the same page, for that matter. Taymor's dual role as co-book writer and director proved to be a conflict of interest. Her role as director had vision, but when the vision was not working and given fair consideration – which included going way over budget – she was not interested in collaborating to make changes.

Berger brought forward suggestions to improve the book and clarify the story, but they were not received by Taymor. In an email, Bono wrote to Berger:

> I am going to speak to JT about bad behavior. A) shooting ideas down before taking time to understand them; B) threatening to throw the toys out of the cot when confronted with problems … We need to support the director's vision up to but not beyond the point of stopping truthful introspection … We'll get there. What is already amazing is way harder to accomplish than fixing what is not.[2]

After Adams' unfortunate passing, the enterprise forever lacked a clear vision. Adams' partner, David Garfinkle, was a novice producer and in over his head. The show demands paralleled a Cirque de Soleil show with over 27 aerial cues and a fly system far more sophisticated than any Broadway theatre could bear. Taymor was given full creative direction, and with that she initiated the complete renovation of the Foxwoods Theatre to the tune of US$8 million. Instead of revisiting the book to make the story work for the venue, Taymor was given the go-ahead to rebuild the theatre. The technical demands were uncharted territory, and extremely dangerous, but despite all the warning signs, the producer signed off and postponed the opening for the construction of the theatre. The show was now moving towards spectacle and was way over budget.

Communication and generosity

A lack of communication persisted as the members of the team created in their bubbles, rather than cohesively in the same room. Taymor wielded the power and treated co-book writer Berger more like a "yes-man" rather than an equal. In an effort to dodge her wrath, he remained agreeable – up to a point, as Berger recounts. The advice he upheld from the beginning echoes throughout the process, to a fault. "Stick with Julie," Seth Goldbum, Taymor's attorney, told him. "Whatever you do, whatever happens, *stick with Julie*."[3]

Unfamiliar with the process of collaborating in theatre, Bono and Edge wrote songs independently. They found the process frustrating and lacking mutual respect.

The technical aspects of calling the show demanded more of the stage management team than any previous Broadway production. There were injuries. Daniel Curry's foot got caught between the mechanical stage lift and the stage during a performance, while during a preview, the Spiderman stunt double, Chris Tierney, fell 30 feet from a hydraulic platform. Both survived, but sadly, after many surgeries, Curry's dancing career was altered. There were others. Finally, "plan x" was put in place to secretly remove Julie Taymor and replace her with Phil McKinley to direct and Roberto Aguirre-Sacasa to co-write the book with Berger.

After six years of contentious collaboration, six delayed openings, a new creative team and cast replacements, *Spiderman: Turn Off the Dark* opened, a year later than the original opening date. The project began with Adams' sudden passing and never recovered from that loss of vision. The unchecked power of the director, overly ambitious technical demands, a lack of leadership, and millions over budget, "plan x" seemed inevitable and ultimately enabled the opening, which did not include Taymor.

Many people invested years of their lives in the project, and some even sacrificed their careers. The enterprise sparked many conversations on the internet before and after opening, and during the production's existence on Broadway. The show is recognized as the most expensive failure on Broadway.

Despite horrible reviews and numerous challenges, *Spiderman: Turn Off the Dark* ran on Broadway for three years. So was *Spiderman: Turn Off the Dark* a complete failure? The average length of an original musical is less than a year[4] and a quarter of Broadway musicals never recoup their costs. A Broadway show isn't considered a "hit" until it has recovered its investment. While it never recouped, it ran to full houses until the producers were unable to renew their insurance. This was their sign to cut their losses.

Sometimes you get there however you get there, and *Spiderman: Turn Off the Dark* cannot be blamed for a lack of tenacity. Berger jokes that he thought Adams might have intervened cosmically to see it through. In hindsight, the flaws are clear to anyone who has worked on a production and experienced similar challenges, but the stakes on Broadway are too high to allow for this kind of experiment to ever happen again. Why would you risk so much for a play? Perhaps this is where learning from others' mistakes becomes a central point.

Berger was told from the beginning, "Stick with Julie." This reverberated over the years and forced a loyalty beyond the call of any collaborator. Alliances in collaboration do not work when the power is wielded by one. Berger had small children and during one of the pauses in the process he went home to see his family and go back to his day job at PBS. "I had no idea how depleted of common sense and mutual respect my days had become until an amicable and lucid discussion of a plot point in a conference room sent me to the floor of a men's room to bawl my eyes out," he said.[5] The collaborators with whom he had worked at PBS reminded him of what Bono had shared about musicians' collaboration. "When something is good, there is no arguing."[6]

In 2012, *Spiderman: Turn Off the Dark* won the Tony Awards for Outstanding Set Design (George Tsypin) and Outstanding Costume Design (Eiko Ishioka). Ishioka sadly passed away before nominations were announced and died never knowing she had won a Tony Award.

Restaurateur Joe Allen was asked whether *Spiderman* would live on the infamous Flop Wall in his frequently patronized restaurant by the theatre community, and he said, "Any show that plays for three years on Broadway, providing steady employment to members of the theatre community and pumping money into the local economy, is no failure in my book."[7]

Case Study 2: *Ragtime* (1995–2000)

The takeover of Canadian producer Garth Drabinsky's stake in The Odeon Cineplex Theatres in Canada motivated him to purchase the small live entertainment division of the company and renamed it Live Entertainment Corporation, later becoming Livent. In the early 1990s, Livent produced *Phantom of the Opera, Kiss of the Spider Woman* and *Showboat* in Toronto. *Phantom of the Opera* ran for ten years in Toronto and *Kiss of the Spider Woman* and *Showboat* transferred to Broadway.

Driven by his cautious immigrant upbringing and his childhood trauma of living with the repercussions of polio, Drabinsky's motto was, "Never give up. Never yield."[8]

Drabinsky wanted to change the way musicals were being created. The process of making a musical at the time was the writers would create the work and then seek producers to back it. Instead, Drabinsky came up with the ideas, secured funding, and hired the creative team of his choice to write *Ragtime*.

The writing team of Stephen Flaherty and Lynn Ahrens (*A Man of No Importance, Anastasia, My Favorite Year, Once on this Island, Seussical* and *Ragtime*) was one of eight teams that submitted audition material to the producer to create the musical of E.L. Doctorow's best-selling historical novel about America at the turn of the century.

Ragtime opened at the Ford Center for the Performing Arts (now the Lyric Theater) on Broadway on January 18, 1998. It ran for two years on Broadway and took home the Tony Awards for Best Book (Terrance McNally), Best Score (Lynn Ahrens and Stephen Flaherty), Best Actress (Audra McDonald), and Best Orchestrator (William David Brohn).

Stephen Flaherty shared that, "Many of the songs we wrote for that demo ended up in the show: the opening number, 'Till We Reach That Day,' and the end of Act I, for example. The material clicked for us very early on."[9]

Clear vision

Drabinsky assimilated the team that aligned with his vision. He remained true to the source material, E.L. Doctorow's novel. To ensure this, he hired artists who aligned with this central goal. Going into the process, this was the constant that drove the creative thread in all areas in order to create a cohesive and powerful story.

Drabinsky gave himself an insurance plan by choosing a creative team that not only shared the vision of his project but with which he already had a working relationship. He first hired Terrence McNally to write the book. After a 60-page treatment, Drabinsky met with E.L. Doctorow and, over caviar, Doctorow expressed how true the treatment remained to his work. Although he attempted to pass on the caviar, Drabinsky insisted, as a sign that he would spare no expense to achieve the success of the musical adaptation.

Frank Galati was chosen to direct and Graciela Daniele to choreograph, and Stephen Flaherty and Lynn Ahrens to write the score. The composer/lyricist team had achieved success with *Once On This Island* (eight Tony Award nominations in 1990 and Best Musical in the revival in 2017). Their earlier shows, *Lucky Stiff* and *My Favorite Year*, though well crafted, never gained wide recognition. *Ragtime* secured the team's longevity as one of the most celebrated writing teams in modern musical theatre history.

Stephen Flaherty shared that:

> On *Ragtime* everyone on the team was over-qualified. Virtually everyone on the team could do and had done more than one discipline in the past. Frank Galati, our director, had also acted in and written other theatre projects. Graciela Daniele, our choreographer, had also directed. Santo Loquasto, our costume designer, had also designed sets in the past. Lynn, whose job description was "lyrics by" had also written many books for other musicals as well:

> Frank also encouraged the actors to bring their own ideas to their characters. For example, the Ellis Island scene was developed during the rehearsal process in Toronto when Frank asked our Ensemble to "improve" the immigrant experience. He asked them to create their own individual back stories and asked them to use specific props to illustrate these stories, and to illuminate their emotions as they walked through Ellis Island's gates for the first time. He asked me to accompany the improv at the piano, creating music on the spot. Every time Frank would yell "Gates!" the music would need to illustrate the large gates rising and falling down. We would eventually create and layer vocal counter-lines, Lynn adapting texts in different languages, creating a tapestry of chaos and urgency, finally uniting everyone on the word "America." A perfect example of collaboration between a director, a cast, a composer and lyricist. It's all about trust![10]

Communication and generosity

It is worth looking at the writing team's process to share why their collaboration has longevity and why their work is now so prolific. The two had the secret to collaboration from the beginning of their relationship:

> When I met Lynn at the BMI workshop, I knew we would complement each other. We both wrote music and lyrics and, because we have experience in both areas, we are perfect editors for one another. We are intuitive. Sometimes, we forget that we are two different people. It's just like any relationship, romantic or otherwise; it's challenging to be part of a team, to know that you're committed, that you have to communicate and grow together. In my adolescence, I used to think the creative process was about being solitary and brooding and wearing a lot of black. With Lynn, I realized that collaboration and sharing is extremely fulfilling. Lynn was more influenced by the pop world, and that perfectly complemented my more traditional Broadway sound. Lynn helped bring back my sense of play.[11]

Lynn added:

> Collaboration also improves with age. Stephen and I have been working together for more than three decades, and at this point we don't pretend to like something if we don't, nor do we try to bully our ideas through. We're honest, direct and polite, and if we shoot down the other person's idea, we try to at least make a suggestion in its place. It's like any good relationship – it continues to evolve ... When we sit down to write, our collaboration is a lot like a ping-pong match. We bounce ideas back and forth: "What if ..." "No, but how about ..." "That's good, and what if we added ..." Something musical usually bubbles out of these conversations. Stephen will put his hands on the keys, or I'll type something, and an idea grows from there. Often, our solutions end up changing or being thrown out as the show develops, but that's normal. And if we can't find a solution, it probably means the moment doesn't want to be a song. [12]

Stephen advises students who are pursuing this collaborative field:

> If you are more interested in showing the world your own unique "solo vision," then collaboration in the theatre is definitely not for you ... It's the synergy of different approaches that makes it all exciting and keeps the writing alive. The theatre is ultimately about working with others, about finding common language and about the sharing of different ideas to your colleagues, which in turn lead to new ideas.
>
> I think tension can be a good thing at certain times. I know a deadline can be an excellent motivator, at least for me. It gives me something to shoot for on a specific schedule. As such, I don't believe I've ever missed a deadline in my life. But daily/weekly/monthly tension in a creative

partnership is not a good thing. It should be a given that you are in the room with your partner and collaborators because you admire and respect them and their work. You trust that the partnership can bring out the best in your own work. But personally, you need to be focused and relaxed while creating. So outside, interpersonal tension is not a helpful thing.[13]

Lynn concurred:

As for fighting for our points of view, we don't fight. We simply keep talking. Stephen Schwartz said that nothing can go on a stage that the collaborators don't all agree with. So, in my opinion, there's no point in fighting and there's no need for tension. It's all about coming up with an idea you both like. And it doesn't hurt to keep an open mind and try what your partner is suggesting. The best idea wins, and it doesn't have to be yours.[14]

Stephen added: "I think it's very important for everyone to be able to put across their ideas and point of view. Ultimately your idea might not end up in the final piece, but oftentimes a discarded idea can lead to something else, something new and hopefully better. You owe it to the show and to the collaboration to speak up!"[15]

Stephen shared that their "best form of communication in collaborating is honesty. We owe it to one another to be honest and direct but hopefully in a kind, supportive way. At the end of the day we both have to be happy with the song and how it relates to the rest of the score."[16]

Both Lynn and Stephen believe great collaborations are both luck and a learned skill. Stephen said:

I think all successful people-pairings in life are part luck, part destiny. And a lot of hard work in between. The fact that I met Lynn in the fall of 1982 when I moved to New York City from the Midwest, was writing with her six months later, and am STILL writing with her is a testament to commitment, hard work and perseverance on both our parts. That sort of large arc teaches you to have faith, too. Faith that "there's more where that came from", that shared ideas can manifest more shared ideas if you allow that faucet to stay open. I remember Graciela Daniele quoting Martha Graham, saying that "our job as creative people is to keep the channel open." She's right. That IS the job in a nutshell.[17]

Lynn added:

You learn to put up with your partner's annoying foibles or selfishness or bad work habits. (Not that Stephen Flaherty has any!) You learn to discuss things openly. You develop a shorthand. You get over being self-conscious and shy. You appreciate each other's sense of humor. A successful collaboration is lucky, and also learned.[18]

Stephen closed with humility and honesty:

We need to strive to be generous and kind to those we love and work with, and that starts with awareness. We might not always succeed – I often get crabby if we are having a hard time wrestling a song into submission – but each day is a new start. And the days add up.[19]

Comparing the Case Studies

Both case studies reveal that trust and respect between collaborators are the life-blood that keeps creation alive, and it is those relationships that produce the best work. Under a positive and healthy framework with joy as the fuel, the "getting there" is ultimately a lot more fun. Life being short and not knowing or being able to see into the future makes this one of the most important lessons to take away.

Both shows "got there." Both shows won awards and sold tickets, but they got there differently. *Spiderman: Turn Off the Dark* ran for a year longer than *Ragtime*. The road was challenging and most of the time not enjoyable. The question becomes how do you want to get there? Was all that the *Spiderman* team went through worth it? For each person, there is a different answer.

Drabinsky did everything right when he produced *Ragtime*, but in 1999 he was arrested for fraud and sentenced to seven years in prison for adjusting the company's books and was not allowed to produce theatre in the United States again.

In 1998, *Ragtime* received 13 Tony nominations and won four Tony Awards, but lost Best Musical to *The Lion King*, directed by Julie Taymor. And there's the irony of theatre. But is it really about awards? About ticket sales? About how long the show ran?

Is there any true measure of success? Most of the commercial measures of success in theatre are fleeting: awards, money, ticket sales, gross receipts. But what are lasting are the relationships and the impact the stories make on people's lives. *Ragtime* made a powerful impact on people's lives – everyone who saw it, everyone who participated in it, everyone who will participate in productions in the future and the collaborators who developed their work together and who continued to create in the years to come.

Looking at relationships objectively, it seems that many of Taymor's collaborators were afraid of her and deferred to her to avoid her wrath. We can agree this doesn't promote the most effective creations. When confronted with her directorial vision not working, she continued to hold onto her vision, even after it was clear that it was never going to work. She assured Berger that "the only shows that really succeed are the ones that were the result of one vision".[20] *One vision* and a *clear vision* are different directing styles.

Taymor's statement reveals that "one vision" does not serve the unified purpose. It merely serves the director's purpose. In fact, it excludes contributions to the whole, whereas a clear vision (led by the director) includes contributions in support of their vision – such as Frank Galati's improvisation of the opening scene of *Ragtime*. This is a more generous approach to creating, and in some ways lifts a tremendous burden off the director, who is trying to move mountains on their own.

Sondheim's lyric, "a vision's just a vision if it's only in your head",[21] brings home the point that vision is meant to be shared so collaboration can inspire creativity and success for all.

Creating is one thing; interpreting it is another. One person attempting both can muddy the storytelling. These lines were firmly delineated in *Ragtime*, but in *Spiderman: Turn Off the Dark*, they were not. Flaherty shared that when working with director Frank Galati:

> Frank, to his great credit, was able to create an atmosphere where everyone was able to speak their mind in production meetings, whether it was about their "department" or not. It was a very "group theatre" approach. There was a lot of cross-pollination going on there! And a lot of good ideas that were freely shared.[22]

However, the boundaries are clear. Ahrens stated that, "The director is definitely the driving force for the members of the design team, but in general, it's the writers who have the creative vision for the piece. The director is the *interpreter* of that vision."[23]

Both musicals came from source material: *Spiderman: Turn Off the Dark* was from Marvel Comics and a successful motion picture; *Ragtime* ranked as one of the 100 best English-language novels of the twentieth century, but the movie was not well received. It is important to reiterate two factors that gave *Ragtime* an edge over *Spiderman: Turn Off the Dark*: First, with *Ragtime* the material came first, giving the creative interpreters solid ground from which to work. The source material for *Spiderman* was volumes of comics, of snapshots, and although Taymor seemed to embrace this aspect early on, the origin somehow got lost. Second, Flaherty and Ahrens had worked together before. It takes time to develop a team as you learn each other's vocabulary, aesthetic, and process. Trust is developed over time, not on just one project, but on multiple projects.

One final advantage enjoyed by *Ragtime* was that the material was appropriate to the venue. Just because a conglomeration believes its source material should be on Broadway, that doesn't mean it's a good idea or even feasible. *Spiderman: Turn Off the Dark* might have achieved success in a venue more adept at supporting the technical demands of such a huge spectacle.

Eventually, the producers replaced Taymor with Phil McKinley as director and Roberto Aguirre-Sacasa was hired to assist with the book; Chase Brock created additional choreography (Danny Ezralow was the original choreographer).

Berger asks himself, looking back, whether it was all about hubris? After all:

> Julie said Arachne made the noose because her artistic impulse had been thwarted … Julie said, Arachne wasn't punished for thinking she was more talented than the goddess of weaving, she was punished for actually being more talented. Julie had unwittingly reinterpreted one of the most iconic myths about hubris as not being about hubris at all. Was that a symptom of hubris? Or was it one artist sympathizing with another?[24]

Taymor sued the producers and Berger offered his support, but when he learned he was also being sued, he realized this wasn't about money. It was about communicating hurt. Revenge. Berger was reminded of an exchange he had with Bono nearly a decade earlier when Bono was asked, "What leaves you speechless?" Bono answered, "Forgiveness."[25]

Berger brings home the point. It is about a bunch of "egos run amok".[26] Why? What for? Is it for art? Is it for fame? Is it for money? It became clear to Berger that the longevity of a collaboration is about love. When he watched U2 in concert, he shared, "Their earnestness could make you cry. Bono reaches out a hand and reminds you that the same hand that clan flip the bird can also reach out in yearning toward the infinite. Toward love."[27]

Interestingly enough, where all these collaborators intersect is Icarus. Drabinsky said:

> I never take tranquilizers nor do I ever take a drink, so I had no way to come down off the terrible humiliation of losing my company. All I had to do was climb again, back to the warmth, up into the heights … In

Greek mythology, Icarus plunged into the sea when he flew too close to the sun. It's supposed to be a lesson in the sin of hubris. I think the bastard just gave up too soon. He should have gotten himself another set of wings and taken off again![28]

Drabinsky was found guilty of fraud and not allowed to enter the United States until decades later. Once again, we are reminded of the dangers of hubris.

Ahrens maintains that the single most important aspect of collaboration is

the ability to take joy in the creative process, to have fun with your partner. A shared sense of humor. Theatre is hard, there can be disappointments for sure, but no matter what the outcome of the show, if you've had a joyful time writing it, that makes it all worthwhile. That's what a writing life should be all about – spending every day doing something you love. It's "the getting there" that matters, not the outcome.

And Stephen echoed, "The joy of creating, the process, the journey of it all. The shared history, the ups and downs, the daily commitment to 'keeping the channel open.' It's not always easy but it's always worthwhile. It's about the 'getting there.'"[29]

Of course, the challenges of working on Broadway are unique, and far removed from the educational collaboration, but human nature is just that – and the values inherent in collaboration are exactly the same.

Notes

1   Glen Berger, *Song of Spiderman* (Simon & Schuster, New York, 2013).
2   Berger, *Song of Spiderman*, p. 228.
3   Zachary Stewart, Book Review *Song of Spider-Man: The Inside Story of the Most Controversial Musical on Broadway History*, November 5, 2013.
4   Ken Davenport, *Some Startling New Statistics on Broadway Musical Vs. Original Shows*. Accessed February 24, 2021 from www.theproducersperspective.com/my_weblog/ 2014/05/some-startling-new-statistics-on-broadway-musical-adaptations-vs-original-shows.html.
5   Berger, *Song of Spiderman*, p. 255.
6   Berger, *Song of Spiderman*, p. 254.
7   Berger, *Song of Spiderman*, p. 355.
8   Steven Cohen, "The Cultural Critic: The Making of Ragtime." Originally written for *Inside Magazine*, June 1998. Accessed February 24, 2021 from https:// theculturalcritic.com/the-making-of-ragtime.

9   Raven Snook, "Flaherty & Ahrens: The Smarts of Making Art," *Theatermania*, 21 November 2000. Accessed February 24, 2021 from www.theatermania.com/new-york-city-theater/news/flaherty-and-ahrens-the-smarts-of-making-art_1127.html.

10 Stephen Flaherty, interview with Maria Cominis, August 28, 2020.

11 Snook, "Flaherty & Ahrens."

12 Lynn Ahrens, interview with Maria Cominis, August 28, 2020.

13 Stephen Flaherty, interview with Maria Cominis, August 28, 2020.

14 Lynn Ahrens, interview with Maria Cominis, August 28, 2020.

15 Stephen Flaherty, interview with Maria Cominis, August 28, 2020.

16 Stephen Flaherty, interview with Maria Cominis, August 28, 2020.

17 Stephen Flaherty, interview with Maria Cominis, August 28, 2020.

18 Lynn Ahrens, interview with Maria Cominis, August 28, 2020, email correspondence.

19 Stephen Flaherty, interview with Maria Cominis, August 28, 2020, email correspondence.

20 Berger, Glen *Song of Spiderman*, Simon & Schuster, 2013 pg., p. 246.

21 Sondheim, *Stephen Sunday in the Park with George* (Putting it Together).

22 Stephen Flaherty, interview with Maria Cominis, August 28, 2020.

23 Lynn Ahrens, interview with Maria Cominis, August 28, 2020, email correspondence.

24 Berger, *Song of Spiderman*, p. 280.

25 Berger, *Song of Spiderman*, p. 348.

26 Berger, *Song of Spiderman*, p. 350.

27 Berger, *Song of Spiderman*, p. 350.

28 Cohen, "The Cultural Critic," p. 5.

29 Lynn Ahrens, interview with Maria Cominis, August 28, 2020, email correspondence.

5
Boundaries
Theatre Intimacy Education and Safe Working Environments

The Power Dynamics Problem

At the center of the collaborative enterprise is the actor, who tradition-ally is an open, demonstrative and emotional creature. Producers hold the power of the purse and the director holds the power of the part and actors hold the power to please, which can be a vulnerable position in this power dynamic. While we strive for complete equity in collaboration, there is no denying that power dynamics, whether structural, personal or political do exist within the production process. We will look at areas of power dynamics - sexual, emotional and psychological - and suggest proven methods in establishing boundaries in the theatre, which can minimize the abuse of power.

Institutional Responsibility

It is no secret the entertainment industry is tainted with sexual misconduct, harassment and assault. The #MeToo movement began as a voice of soli-darity in 2006 to expose wrongful actions, but it was not until 2017, when victims pressed charges against Harvey Weinstein, Co-Founder of Miramax Entertainment, that acts of sexual misconduct became widely acknowledged, accelerating change and accountability. Weinstein was found guilty and sentenced to 23 years of imprisonment in March 2020.

Years of abuse of power have caused enormous damage to victims within many institutions. The Actors' Unions have initiated solutions to protect victims in the work place by placing standards and policy which help to create a culture of consent and clear expectations of boundaries within the

DOI: 10.4324/9780367810252-6

professional setting. Identifying boundaries and the codification of intimate work is a first step in providing a safe environment to all collaborators that enables the work to be the focus.

SAG-AFTRA (Screen Actors Guild and American Federation of Television and Radio Artists) responded by adopting standards and protocols for highly sensitive scenes that feature nudity and simulated sex. These standards enhanced and strengthened policies already in place, including the Four Pillars of Change Initiative, which confronts harassment and advances equity. The resources include a Code of Conduct, Empowerment through Education, Expanded Intervention, Building Bridges and Safety Nets and Guideline No.1., which includes "Putting an End to High- risk Locations for Professional Meetings and Taking a Support Peer."[1] SAG-AFTRA believes the implementation of these standards and protocols will provide a safety net for performers and establish specialized support that empowers both cast and crew.[2]

SAG-AFTRA identified the necessity for intimacy coordinators in film and television productions where nudity or simulated sex is involved in the storytelling. The theatre culture has come under scrutiny, exposing the need for much-needed change. Intimacy education is gaining ground in theatre training as more plays and productions are asking for increasingly explicit intimacy on stage and as boundaries in collaborations continue to be blurred amidst a complicated power structure.

AEA's national diversity and inclusion strategist, Bliss Griffin, shared that AEA currently has no policy statement, but the following are in development:

- a new, intersectional definition of intimacy
- member education about how to convey your boundaries and consent at every phase of a show's life-cycle
- employer resources with guidance for best practices for understanding boundaries and consent in both auditions and rehearsals.

Education

Two organizations were responsible for leading the educational path in this relatively new area of training that is changing and growing rapidly: Theatre Intimacy Education (TIE) and The Intimacy Directors International (IDI), which closed its doors on March 15, 2020:

The artists and professionals who have been the heart of IDI are still working independently, and with other companies, to continue to support the growing needs of the industry and this movement to bring consensual and sustainable working practices to theatre, TV, & film making worldwide.[3]

Chelsea Pace, co-founder of Theatrical Intimacy Education (TIE), shares that intimacy training facilitates a consensual culture and "dedicated to empowering artists with the tools to ethically, efficiently and effectively stage intimacy and sexual violence in educational theatre."[4] The training desexualizes the handling of the content to keep boundaries clear and helps collaborators to discern the difference between professional and social boundaries in a working environment:

> Gender or sexuality does not matter; both victim and harasser can be anyone. Sexual harassment can be verbal (making sexual comments, innuendos, jokes or advances), non-verbal (making gestures, facial expressions, blocking paths or following a person), or physical (touching, brushing or grabbing). In the theatre, it can occur onstage as well as offstage.[5]

This inherit power dynamic and sexually charged material put working relationships at risk if tenets are not adopted to navigate these tricky waters of collaboration.

Not unlike the fight choreographer, who is hired to stage the simulated physical violence onstage, an intimacy choreographer/coach/director functions as a collaborator who creates the simulated sexual events in a play. The intimacy choreography is created by collaborating with the director and utilizing their vision of the play within the boundaries of the actor's instrument while sustaining the artistic integrity of the work.

Tonia Sina and Alicia Rodis, co-founders of Intimacy Directors International (IDI), saw a tremendous need for a solution to the confusing message intimacy created on stage. Sina recalled:

> The second our lips touched it was not rehearsing. It was just kissing. We both felt it. We both knew. It ended up spiraling. We ended up leaving our partners for a month and we had a showmance. It caused a lot of mayhem in our personal lives because we couldn't let these characters go. We didn't have a safe way to do the intimacy, and we didn't have a safe way of coming out of it.[6]

Sina published her thesis, titled "Intimate Encounters; Staging Intimacy and Sensuality," in 2006; it was based on these challenges as an actor.

Alicia Rodis witnessed and was a victim in such scenarios throughout her career. After almost chipping a tooth when a scene partner decided to intensify a kiss onstage, she was told, "That's part of the profession. Get used to it." Knowing there were hundreds of other women who would gladly take her spot in a show if she left, Rodis thought she had to accept that kind of behavior for the rest of her career. "We sort of learned that's not the case, and we don't have to just take it. We can actually be part of the process and work together," Rodis said.[7]

Sina and Rodis, along with co-founder Siobhan Richardson, created the pillars (see below) to codify the process. Until recently, the organization made them available to the public to encourage ongoing education. At present, IDI instructors have branched out and currently coach, direct, and teach independently, and their contributions serve as the foundational building blocks for theatre intimacy training.

The Pillars

Context

Before any choreography can be considered, there must first be an understanding of the story and the given circumstances surrounding the scene of intimacy. All parties must be aware of how the scene of intimacy meets the needs of the story, and must also understand the story within the intimacy itself. This not only creates a sense of safety, but also eliminates the unexpected and ensures that the intimacy is always in service of the story.

Communication

There must be open and continuous communication between the director, intimacy director, stage management, and the actors. This communication includes, but is not limited to, discussion of the scene, understanding of the choreography, continued discussion throughout the rehearsal period, frequent check-ins during the run, and an openness to dissent any actions in the process. Avenues for reporting harassment must be made available to the entire ensemble.

Consent

Before any scene of intimacy can be addressed, consent must be established between the actors. Permission must be given by a director, a script, or choreographer; however, consent can only be given from the person receiving the action. Starting choreography from a place of understanding consent ensures that all parties are clear about the actions to which they are consenting, and it provides actors with the agency to remove consent at any time.

Choreography

Each scene of intimacy must be choreographed, and that choreography will be adhered to for the entire production. Any changes to the intimacy choreography must first be approved by the intimacy choreographer. It is the job of stage management to ensure that the choreography is performed as intended. Stage Management must also address any discrepancies that may appear in the rehearsal process and all performances.

Closure

At the end of every rehearsal or scene of intimacy, actors are encouraged to develop a closing moment between them to signify the ending of the work. This small moment or simple ritual can be used between takes or runs of the scene, and/or upon the close of rehearsal. We encourage this as a moment to leave our character, relationships, and actions from the work behind, and walk back into our lives. Likewise, we suggest that all parties (including outside eyes) exercise proper self-care during and after the run or filming of intimate projects.

As of January 2021, the organization is now called Intimacy for Stage and Screen, which is a network for directors and choreographers in the United Kingdom.

Theatre Intimacy Education (TIE)

Chelsea Pace, co-founder of Theatrical Intimacy Education (TIE), shares that intimacy training facilitates a consensual culture and is "dedicated to empowering artists with the tools to ethically, efficiently and effectively stage intimacy and sexual violence in educational theatre." The training desexualizes the handling of the content to keep boundaries clear and helps collaborators to discern the difference between professional and social boundaries in a working environment. Pace notes that the definition of intimacy is expanding to include heightened material that leverages one or more of an actor's protected characteristics. That includes sex, gender (including pregnancy), and sexuality, but this definition also includes race, color, national origin, religion, disability, age, and citizenship status.

Chelsea Pace and Laura Rikard, co-founders of Theatrical Intimacy Education, share their mission: "We train the whole company, department, or ensemble in TIE best practices so that you aren't on your own when the choreographer goes home. This is about culture change, not just choreography."[8]

In *Staging Sex* by Chelsea Pace, with contributions from Laura Rikard,[9] specific language is used to give collaborators a say in the process in service to the storytelling. Primarily established for production, it has been successfully utilized in acting classes, and in students' independent rehearsals. When intimacy education language is established within a company and the demands of the production are small, the director and actors can work independently without a designated intimacy coach. If the production's demands of intimacy are pervasive, then it becomes necessary to have one. Pace and Rikard share the work through workshops in support of creating a consensual culture in all working environments.

Below are some key points related to the intimacy training:

- *"Button"* is a self-care cue word used to pause the work so the actor can briefly pause the action and ask for what they need in the moment. This tool is an efficient step in the process for actors to be in the driver's seat of their instrument and work intimately within their personal boundaries. Theatre artists can create their own word to pause the work, but "button" was chosen as a quick pause without derailing focus and concentration on the work.
- *"Fences"* is the verbal boundary that reinforces a physically established boundary, which is informed by boundary practice.
- *Boundary practice* is the exercise that defines the individual's personal boundaries. In this exercise, the actors identify and communicate what is off limits and what areas of their bodies they are okay with their partner touching. In practice, they identify these areas and the level of pressure to which is appropriate to use their instrument and communicate this to their partner and the intimacy choreographer. The choreography is informed by and held within these boundaries.
- *Gates* are places that are negotiable boundaries, which are dependent on the context of the touch. Permission may be given for these areas by the actor.

- *Ingredients* include distance, levels of touch, tempo and counts, and shapes, to name a few. These ingredients are what the choreographer uses to articulate the movements. Rikard shared that it is possible to stage an entire show with only "distance." There are a lot of ingredients and new practitioners can get overwhelmed. Their motto is that "a little bit better is better."

- *De-roling* is identifying the differences between the character and the actor. De-roling is a de-escalation process to avoid re-trauma while allowing the actor to create the character and sustain their sense of truth.

- *Stop stepping in.* One of the most challenging elements in this work is not stepping into the work as a director. It is one of their non-negotiable tenets in the training, and key to respecting the philosophy of the work. This means the director does not "show" or "demonstrate" how an intimate moment is done. This is a boundary that both Rikard and Pace feel is non-negotiable.

- *Non-negotiable tenets.* Pace shared that she and Rikard held themselves to two questions if a rule was going to become a best practice or non-negotiable tenet. When putting the work to the test, they asked themselves whether the practice could be recommended to the collaborator who might be a candidate most likely to cross a boundary, and whether the practice was appropriate to use for the most vulnerable in our profession. If it is, then they can call it a best practice.

A boundary can be broken in two ways: a mistake and/or the actors making an agreement in their boundary practice with one another and forgetting to alert whoever is in the leadership position of the production at the time. If the boundary crossing is a mistake, an acknowledgment is required to rectify the issue. Addressing this with the stage manager in the rehearsal and/or after a performance is important. When boundaries are accidentally crossed by anyone, there is a four-step process to be followed: (1) say what you did: "I crossed your boundary" (2) apologize; (3) acknowledge the power dynamic by bringing it to their attention that the mistake was received: "Thank you for letting me know"; and (4) figure out a way to move forward.

This step normalizes the truth that boundary-crossing happens and gives the team a positive way to move forward. It takes away fear and actional steps to move forward in the creative process. Pace stated that, "In a personal environment, I have the choice to walk out when a boundary is crossed but in a rehearsal the work needs to move forward."[10] If boundaries are identified from the beginning, it is part of the collaborative rules in this process and "creates acknowledgement and accountability."[11]

If the actors reestablish their boundaries, remind them that it is important to document any changes if they are needed. Pace and Rikard go into more details about the nuances necessary in intimacy education in their book, which provides a valuable resource for educating everyone in the collaborative environment.

Identifying physical, mental, and emotional boundaries assists those who may have experienced trauma and may be triggered by charged material. These boundaries can assist when choosing plays and scenes on which to work in class and gives the actor the option to opt out of the material if it does not serve their instrument and might retrigger trauma. The work is not to discourage challenging artists from going beyond their comfort zone, but rather to challenge them within their own instrument.

Pace and Rikard acknowledge that nothing in theatre is comfortable. Characters live in conflict and that is very uncomfortable, but choosing choreography that is within the artists' fences and gates, which are the parameters to work within, offers a degree of reassurance. Rikard offered the example: "If offered the role of Medea, I would need to pass because the emotional boundaries of Medea do not serve my instrument after the traumatic birth of my twins."

This work trains the actor to identify and understand their mental, emotional, and physical boundaries without shame or apology. It prepares the actor for a profession that requires them to seek the autonomy essential for a professional career.

Ideally, when a director knows that a play or concept requires nudity or contains intimacy, they can be more specific with the actors in the casting process regarding expectations. This makes them more likely to cast the actor who best fits the role and is comfortable with the requirements of the role. This gives all collaborators agency in the process. In giving agency to the actor, it also places responsibility on the actor to refuse a role if they know they cannot fulfill what the role requires. Of course, sometimes limitations can only be discovered in rehearsal, in which case Pace and Rikard acknowledge that "sometimes the most supportive way to support a boundary is to re-cast."[12]

Rikard likens the rehearsal relationship between director and actor to that between a conductor and a violinist. In an effort to achieve the desired sound, the conductor might ask the musician to put the violin on the floor and step on it while they play. The musician might say, "I can't do that. The instrument costs a lot and I've spent years caring for it. What is it you're looking for and perhaps I can use my technique to get the effect you need?"[13]

Sometimes a director might ask a question that is rhetorical. For example, "Can you recall having sex with him?" Not all actors are aware that these questions are rhetorical. This gray area needs clarifying to avoid assumptions. Actors become the character and are taught to create from "I," so language is important. However, this is where Augusto Boal's concept of de-roling can be helpful.[14] Keeping it clear that the actor is creating the character from their own instrument as this process is taking place, it is an emotional and psychological process that should be given the care it requires. While some actors are very comfortable about talking openly and freely, some prefer to work in a more private and quiet manner.

There are many styles and processes of directing, and even more in acting. The director can adjust their process to the needs of the actor. If, for example, a director's process involves personal investigation, and they have cast an actor who is uncomfortable investigating the character in front of others, the director might consider another solution. This prevents interrogation that can imply crossing a professional boundary.

When I was a young actor, I had more than one director say to me, "Be more sexy." Or maybe you have heard, "Be more manly." "Be more Black." I knew how to do what the director was asking, but shame came over me in how this directive was communicated. It made me feel objectified. But I, like many actors who've been on the receiving end of this direction, never spoke up and just did it. As a more experienced actor, I translate the result-oriented directive into action. "To be" is not acting and it implies stereotypes of what the director thinks of as sexy, manly or Black. A more productive directive might be to ask, "What do I (the character) do (action) that is sexy? What do I (the character) do to my partner (the other character) in the scene that helps me pursue my objective, which is to go to bed with them? And what is the nature of my character to the relationship to the other character?" Those actions are in the writing of the play, dictated by the playwright, within the given circumstances. The answer (as the character) might be, "I lure", "I caress, taunt, tease, push away/pull in my lover of one month." All actions of the character within the world of the play, the nature of the relationship and how long the characters have been intimate, will inform what "sexy" is.

For each director and actor, the idea of "sexy" is different, so it is important for everyone to stick to the given circumstances for clarity and respecting personal boundaries. If the result of this process is too technical for the director's aesthetic and they want something more personal, another option is to say just that: "Work on deepening and personalizing this." This directive gives the actor control of personal intimate boundaries and is more specific to the results desired. If the actor is open to discussion, they will initiate conversation, but it should be up to them since it is their instrument that is doing the playing. Using the play as the source focuses the work on the play, the character, and the world, and removes the pressure for the actor to share personal information.

The "Me Too" movement has brought into light that crossing a professional boundary – whether physical, psychological, or emotional – not only damages collaboration, but can be harmful to the individuals involved. All collaborators are responsible for setting the stage for professional and safe working environments, and it begins with establishing a process where everyone speaks the same language and is free to ask for what they need and address what is off limits.

Safe Learning Environment in the Classroom

Sometimes it is not clear whether a student is ready to be pushed and challenged in the moment. Many acting teachers side coach like athletic coaches – it is how many are trained. Jerzy Grotowski, the Polish director who taught in America in the 1970s, believed an actor must train like an athlete. This work, and others of the era, taught resilience and strength in the actor's instrument. Today, we teach differently because we live in a different world. However, there is something to learn from this style that encourages resilience.

Coaches and teachers today get on the sidelines and feed actors subtext to galvanize a more active pursuit if an actor is playing passively. The intimacy education language is a tool that can be utilized in these encounters as well.

Identifying emotional boundaries ahead of time can help to prevent breakdowns, which can take over class and derail the learning. Establishing a foundation of trust, respect, and resilience within the educational laboratory can give everyone in the room ease to know that the goal is to stay on topic with the work.

The student who may still be processing trauma can identify topics in plays that are off-limits for them at this time. This opportunity gives the student/

actor agency to acknowledge works that might not serve their instrument. In the case of individuals who have experienced trauma, some circumstances can recreate trauma that educators are not equipped to handle.

Author Sidebar (Maria)

I have often danced around whether or not to challenge a student. When I see a student who has tremendous potential who might be holding back, I often want to push them through the scene with rigor. This can be seen in actively feeding them their subtext and giving them the will to push through the moments when they have no will of their own. At times, I have pushed too far emotionally. It is and was never my intent to hurt someone's feelings, but rather to get to the other side of the challenge. I learned that when someone has no will of their own, it is risky to give them your will and it is also not my responsibility to decide whether they are ready to activate their will. It must be their choice completely.

Over the last decade, I have erred on the side of caution, and perhaps this has watered down my coaching style for some students. I realized I am not serving the student who wants and requires the push to excellence so necessary to succeed in this business. I ask myself, "Why cheat them of this?" So I had to find the way to stop guessing and give us both permission to do the hard work in order to grow and surprise ourselves.

I created a system of dual contracts with my students. I have my contract – the syllabus – which states what I expect from them. Their contract tells me what they expect from me as a teacher/coach. I then know what their emotional boundaries are. They share topics that are gates. They share topics that are fences. They can change at any time, but it must come from them. It is so much simpler this way. There is no guessing. There is trust and respect on both sides. I have returned to these contracts when I see a student holding back.

When working on *Venus and Fur*, I realized I was pushing a student and the student's will shut down. So after class I re-read their contract and realized the material might be setting off some buttons. I emailed the student and checked in to see whether the material was working for them and if they were still compelled to work through the scene or if they needed to stop. I made sure they truly knew it was entirely their choice.

The student told me that the mere fact I was aware of and sensitive to their emotional needs gave them the permission to let go, and go for it in the next rehearsal. Knowing it was safe for them to step into difficult, emotional material empowered them and gave them permission to take the risk, knowing they could stop at any time. It was a scene and not reality. Honoring their feelings allowed them to move past the roadblock and use the power of their will. The scene took off and the actor achieved their goals. Keep in mind that this is a student who has worked through these issues and had time to heal. Not every situation is this simple.

Sexual Harassment in the Academic and Professional Setting

Mariel Mulet, labor and employment lawyer and senior investigator at Public Interest Investigations, Inc., worked as a Title IX Coordinator and investigates complaints of sexual and gender-based harassment and discrimination in the workplace and the academic setting. After having investigated hundreds of complaints, she has a first-hand understanding of the importance of a safe environment for learning and working, but also acknowledges that the learning environment in theatre or the arts should not be sterile or rigid. There must be a balance between professional behavior and the freedom to respectfully express yourself. Her suggestion to students and faculty is very simple: "Know your and others' boundaries, and if you do not know them, ask." She recommends talking about this at the start of the class and encouraging students to speak out if they do not feel comfortable with any play content, choreography, or movement. She shared that the most common cases of problematic crossing of boundaries which could be interpreted as offensive occur when someone assumes others will take the person's comments, jokes, innuendo, or gesture (hugs, kisses, rubbing of the shoulder, neck, leg) as a symbol of understanding, affection, or camaraderie. If you do not ask, you may not know whether or not the person receiving those gestures is comfortable with them. If you are on the receiving end of the behavior, communicate your wishes or feelings to the person. Also, if you are the one engaging in the behavior, be aware of the power imbalance inherent in the professor–student relationship and understand that some people may not be comfortable in answering your questions honestly or even discerning their options. To avoid that, create a safe space that allows students to respond genuinely by, for example, knowing when and how to ask those questions and account for feelings of intimidation or fear of retaliation in interpreting your students' answers.

In arts education, our relationships are informal. Theatre people are affectionate by nature. Jokes can sometimes go too far and can be inappropriate, causing division instead of unity. If a joke offends someone's gender, race, religion, or sexual preference, it divides rather than unifies.

Because physical contact can be misconstrued, Mariel suggests that touching between student and faculty is altogether a bad idea. This blurs the boundaries, which are not only physical but can be emotional and psychological. In the case of acting class, the work gets very personal, which is why Mariel recommends frequent checking in to see whether the student is working within their boundaries and to ensure their instrument is okay with the work. It is not permanent. You can change your mind at any time.

Mariel also advises to practice no assumptions; rather, communicate and ask for permission. She said, "Personally, I am not sure there is ever a need for a hug in the academic environment. In some ways, I find it sad that we are not as affectionate with one another, but unfortunately some individuals have blurred these lines with bad behavior, so innocent or spontaneous affection towards colleagues is now not the norm."

This can also be applied to emotional dependence. Your professor or director is not your therapist, and in most cases they have an obligation to report what they hear from a student if it relates to a possible violation of the sexual or gender-based harassment or discrimination policy, or where a student might be in danger. This should not dissuade sharing something that impacts your learning, but ongoing meetings about personal issues can result in compromising the professional relationship, and sometimes misunderstandings or harassment.

Out of Rehearsal

Once outside the rehearsal, some individuals think boundaries change. They might change, but they might not. Some people like to hug and some people find hugging people or being hugged stressful. For some, hugging impinges on their personal space. We can see this in different cultures. Some kiss both cheeks and hug people they barely know. With respect to all people and cultures, ask, "Is it okay if I give you a hug?" The answer might be, "I am not a hugger, no offense." Or it might be, "Of course. Come here! I love working with you." Once the boundary is established, the awkward moment has passed and the relationship is established.

Identifying boundaries does not intend to dissuade intimate friendships or relationships. It merely desexualizes the working environment by providing the tools to discern the difference between professional and personal boundaries. For some people, this has been very unclear and because of that a solution was needed.

Defenses might come up and some might feel rejected when boundaries are clearly defined. But if, as Pace and Rikard promote, consensual culture in the theatre is to become the new normal, a little awkward is better than the alternative, and consent and accountability will then become the new normal.

Allies

Sometimes you may need to find allies to help you resolve a problem that cannot be solved on your own. Theatre intimacy education was created so artists do not have to suffer alone in silence. Allies are those who will hear you and support you when you need assistance in righting a wrong, so your work can shine and you can feel heard and seen. Your allies include the stage managers, union equity deputy (a peer), department chair, or college dean. Their job is to be an ally and to help find the proper channel to correct the situation, not to sweep it under the rug. Before going to an ally, you might address the issue with the source of the problem. If that is unsuccessful or you are afraid, then find an ally to help you resolve it.

Theatre intimacy education was created because of ongoing issues in the workplace. Sexual or gender-based harassment, assault, and misconduct do not just happen to binary individuals. In 2013, Human Rights Campaign began tracking violence against transgender or non-conforming people, the majority being Black and Latinx transgender women.

Some universities have affinity programs to bring people together to feel supported and to educate others. If you don't know about these resources, you can learn about them through associated student or human resources, or diversity, equity and inclusion departments in your school and in your community. Another ally is the National Center for Transgender Equality, a resource for understanding the basic definitions and better understanding non-conforming collaborators. Not one in our community should be dismissed because we don't get them.[15]

Alexandra Billings brings love and acceptance to every classroom. She is an activist, an actor, a Viewpoints teacher and a beacon of hope for change:

> Gender is learned behavior. Gender is behavioral. We can look at physiological differences because of hormones or what not. Scientifically there was a study (UCL-PaLS, November 2017, mentioned in Chapter 1), 20 people, all different genders, sizes were hooked up to a monitor and they found when the lights went off, every heart began to beat at the same rate and it remained that way until the curtain came down. Everyone was in sync. If there were differences in gender that would not be true. But there were not. We're all from the same star stuff. So that thing inside us, whether you call it a soul, the spirit, or your heart or heart space, is shared. When we are all in a sacred space and we all make an agreement – and that's the big caveat, we all have to agree that we're in a sacred space – we change the molecular structure of the room.
>
> So, I say all of that because, and you know this as a teacher when you get women in a room and men in a room and you go through an emotional exercise, men go to fists and women go to tears because that's what they are taught. I know this because I was in that world for 19 years. I remember it vividly and what I was supposed to do. There was a lot of expectation for both genders.
>
> I will never forget when I first started to transition and I was 20, it was 1980, back when it was illegal and I spent many times in jail just for walking across the street just because I was transgender because it was against the law. You couldn't walk around like that. I spent a lot of time in California and boys in California are half dressed. Shorts and that's it. I found that as my transition began, all of a sudden, I couldn't do stuff. I couldn't open up my own door, I couldn't carry my own packages and I couldn't light my own cigarette back when I smoked. I had to cover up. I had to cover up! They talk about other countries. Why do they cover? The same thing in our country. The exact same. I went through it. You gotta put on a t-shirt. Why? I haven't worn one in 19 years. Oh, I have breasts now, no one wants to see those.
>
> So, all of my power started to go away. And I had to tell people (men), I can open my own door. "Those are a lot of packages." "No, I'm fine!"
>
> So, I say that because all of that stuff is learned. So, when we bring up the subject of *gender* in ensemble, in my humble opinion, the revolutionary act of the non-binary human is the change we've been waiting for and it's disturbing as hell, it's disturbing as fuck for everyone, me included. I think it's a large, life-size reflection about how we're behaving. And none of us wants to look at that. There is a constant

reminder there is no word and there is no container. I behave the way my spirit tells me to behave. They [binary individuals] may get jealous and pissed off. *How come they get to do that? That's dumb. I'm not calling you that. That doesn't make any sense. You're not telling me what to do.* If you can call a boat a "she" and you can call an actor "the rock" you can call somebody "they."

We use terminology all the time. It's so ridiculous and it's such a waste of time for us to discuss our differences when we really could be sitting at a table, instead of monitoring each other, we could be sitting at a table mining each other's gifts. Because here's the thing: we have an artistic expression living above our heads all the time. It's constantly sending us messages and we're constantly ignoring them. That's our basic instinct and everyone shares them.

Remember all those humans in the theatrical space. Everyone shares the same heartbeat. Everyone. So, our job, I believe, is to get into the room as collaborators and try and see past what we have known and have been taught. That's our job. See past it. And that takes work. And you can say that in the room. I say it all the time. Especially as a mixed-race person. We just got to see past the *thing*. We have to acknowledge and honor it.

Theatre is a community, it is social, and it is up to all of us to look out for one another and respect one another. If theatre is truly to be inclusive and represent everyone like our history suggests, then it is up to us to honor each other by calling each other by our names, our identifying pronouns, and remove judgement from those we don't understand. Making theatre is how we can come to understand one another as we tell everyone's story.

Our racial and cultural divides are also major barriers to safe boundaries and healthy working environments, which will be addressed in the next chapter.

Do Boundaries Compromise Collaboration and Connection?

The work in the theatre is dependent upon accessing the freedom to express one's self in the moment. It requires us to speak our minds and think on our toes. Our work demands that we create with tactile expression and human contact. How do we reconcile caution in collaboration to keep ourselves and others safe with the need to connect at a deep personal and meaningful level?

One of the tenets in our guiding principles is *trust*, and *trust* is essential to both sides of this coin. Trust is essential to create the work in a meaningful way with one another and it is imperative to have faith that all collaborators will respect one another, both in the work environment and outside of it.

Is it possible to have a professional, open connection and protect one's self from potential deception without compromising the integrity of our work? Theatre intimacy education provides a language to understand how boundaries are set within the professional setting, but what about when we are just people, enjoying each other, bonding outside the work environment and socializing? For many people, the camaraderie and bond between artists are the attraction of the theatre. Many meet their spouses or form long-term relationships. How do we continue to build healthy, happy relationships without being rigid?

When guiding principles #1 and #2 are practiced, there is no guessing where boundaries are. When trust, respect, inclusivity, and communication are practiced, it sets a solid foundation for any healthy relationship, whether professional or personal. Many lifelong friendships are made in the profession, and these are valuable. If a consensual personal relationship evolves out of a working relationship, boundary work does not prohibit it. Best practices suggest that if a consensual intimate relationship occurs, then discretion needs to be used while in the professional environment. However, it is probably a good idea not to date your teacher. If both adults feel the same after graduation, then there is no conflict of interest. Due to the power dynamic, it could be a problem that neither party wants to deal with.

The "It" Factor

A long time ago it was called the "it" factor. Later, it was called sex appeal. Today, it is called … you can fill in the blanks. It is no secret that being desirable and alluring is part of the profession. Does this concept over-sexualize our business? Perhaps. But it is a fact, and we cannot ignore it. Presence is another way to put it. Confidence. Will. Great artists radiate presence and emanate vital, exciting, powerful, and sexual energy. This is often what makes an audience interested and invested, and it is necessary in the context of much of the work.

The great Russian actor and teacher Michael Chekhov teaches that, "An actor must burn inside with an outer ease." This does not just apply to actors but is relevant to all artists. Passion is what drives storytelling. It is also what bonds us and excites us to connect to each other. The theatre is built by passionate people, and its universal language is love for the human race – as well as pain, which is inevitable. The theatre is made of both because these are the ingredients of the human condition. It is what keeps the audience coming back because humans need empathy, compassion, and identification. If we look at where theatre began, we can see it has shown humans how people, society, and our world have evolved. Boundaries will not take this away.

Anyone who is called to this work and stays in it for the long haul comes to it from loving it and loving the people in it. That is not to say it is not filled with grief, disappointment and sometimes even betrayal. That is why Shakespeare coined it the "mirror" to nature. Establishing boundaries will not take the depth away, or remove joy or passion from the work. It will only allow artists to work within personal, acceptable boundaries, which are vastly different for each individual. The effect of this is actually to create a freer and safer environment for all those working within it. True freedom needs structure and boundaries provide this.

How do artists access this energy that is so essential to the theatre artist? If we look at it closely, it is a presence. A confidence. A sure-footedness that draws others in. If you look around you, it is not only actors who possess this quality, but designers, directors, producers, and musicians as well – anyone who has that light inside of them that burns with an outer ease.

> Students do not realize how important concentration is and how necessary is the feeling of a "stone" or "spear." The theatre today is poor and the audience bored. It must be won with love and not fought. A man goes to the theatre after a good dinner, he sees a badly acted love scene and is perfectly justified in asking what he is getting of value from it. But the new theatre will be something different. We will have the audience on their toes – tense.
>
> – Michael Chekhov[16]

Collaboration depends on clear professional boundaries in working relationships. During the COVID-19 pandemic, we were forced into a new relationship with each other. Touch was no longer an option. Families could not hug or kiss one another. Babies less than a year old had never met another baby. School-age children did not engage socially for a year. This experience will inform our connection in the years to come, both onstage and off, but perhaps it can remind us that theatre is a meeting of the minds and hearts, which unites us to create all our stories on stage together. If we can support one another, respect one another, and trust one another as we do this, then the process and the theatre will be better because of it.

Scenarios for Discussion

Scenario 1: Intimacy in the rehearsal room – awkward stage kiss

Cast

The Director: Me, a gay man, early in my career as a director
Actor 1: Josh, a straight man playing an experienced older gay man
Actor 2: Bruce, a young straight man playing a young, but experienced gay man

The play in question, which we'll call *Awkward Stage Kiss* (no, not Sarah Ruhl's *Stage Kiss*), tracked the journey of a transgender person that included three other gay characters. At the time this story takes place, there were actually very few plays about gay men, and those that did exist avoided any overtly physical expressions of sexual engagement. This play had, for its time, a fairly explicit make-out scene between the characters – Joshua and Bruce.

Casting the two roles had been challenging, and Josh accepted the role the day before rehearsals started – it was that hard to find a man willing to play an older gay man who makes out with a younger gay man. Josh was friends with the playwright and, at the last minute, agreed to take on the role as a favor. He lived in New York City (rehearsals were in Los Angeles) so he asked for a week to get his life together. With no other options, I agreed and began rehearsals without Josh.

This upset Bruce, who was playing Josh's lover. His major relationship in the play was with an actor who couldn't be there for a week, and he felt cheated out of necessary time to develop a believable relationship with Josh. I explained that it wasn't ideal for me or Josh either, but we had to deal with the hand we were dealt. I was unable to mollify Bruce, which made the first week of rehearsal without Josh challenging for us both.

Josh finally arrived, and the portions of the play that focused on Josh and Bruce got underway. Everything seemed to be going fine until they started staging the makeout scene. This was in the days (not so long ago) before intimacy coaches were even a concept. Actors knew the play, knew the requirements of the play, and were expected to jump in and go for it.

However, just as they got to the kiss, Bruce stopped the rehearsal and said, "We have to talk about this."

    Me:"Talk about what?"
    Bruce:"I don't know how to kiss a man."

My jaw dropped. It had never occurred to me that this actor would have an issue kissing another man. It never came up in auditions or during table work; neither I nor Bruce ever thought to bring it up as a potential problem. The older actor, Josh (who had also never kissed a man), was completely game and ready to go, but Bruce became very resistant. Just as I was about to lose it, another actor burst through the door with another problem. I was given a reprieve – for the moment – to figure out how to move forward.

Before you say this would never happen today, note that Sarah Ruhl's play, *Stage Kiss*, has a scene almost identical to the above scenario, except it is between two actors of the opposite sex who were married and have to do a love scene together. Actor discomfort with on-stage intimacy is real, and it has to be dealt with.

What would you have done if you were me? Let's add the given circumstances that the production company, like most theatres, is poor and can't afford an intimacy director. Think about the following questions:

1. I was obviously blindsided in rehearsals. What could I have done to better prepare the actors for this scene?
2. Is there something I could have done in casting that would have alerted me to potential challenges with intimacy? Should those *potential* problems be taken into account when casting?
3. Is replacing (firing) Bruce an option? Under what circumstances would you/wouldn't you take advantage of this option?
4. *Weird Stage Kiss* is a new play. Is it an option to go to the playwright – a collaborator in this production – and ask them to rewrite the scene and omit the sexual activity? Why or why not?
5. What responsibility does the actor have for alerting the director to potential problems before they get to the scene? What reasons would an actor have for not disclosing issues they may have with the scene – or other scenes of a similar nature?
6. How might this scenario inhibit or inspire collaboration? What effect – positive or negative – might this cast member's "problem" have on the other collaborators in the company?

Author Sidebar (Mark)

About 20 years later, I saw Sarah Ruhl's *Stage Kiss* with "Bruce" (the same actor in scenario 4). I didn't know the play, so when I found myself watching a scene where this actor (in character, in a play) stops a rehearsal just before a kiss was about to take place and says, "We have to talk about this" – well, it was the most surreal moment I've ever spent in the theatre. My eyes became glued to the "director." In some weird way, I was watching my younger self deal with the problem – and anxious to see how he would solve the problem.

Scenario 2: Exercises to make the actor feel safe in a sexually driven play

Let's take a look at *Lysistrata*, a play centered on women withholding sex from their husbands to end a war. The play requires the actors to physically experience their sexual desires in front of the audience. Imagine the language one must consider to create a brave space where everyone feels safe, open, and willing to play.

1. Without formal intimacy training, what language would you develop for everyone in the room to feel safe?
2. How would you approach a show with sexual content requiring sexual actions by the actors?
3. How would you make the actors feel safe?
4. How would you aid in releasing their inhibitions?

Notes

1 SAG-AFTRA, "SAG-AFTRA Unveils Landmark Industry Standards and Protocols for the Use of Intimacy Coordinator." Media release, Los Angeles, January 29, 2020. Accessed March 1, 2020 from www.sagaftra.org/contracts-industry-resources/workplace-harassment/intimacy-coordinator-standards-protocols.
2 SAG-AFTRA, "SAG-AFTRA Unveils Landmark Industry Standards".
3 Accessed March 1, 2020 from www.facebook.com/IntimacyDirectors International.
4 Chelsea Pace and Laura Rikard, "Theatre Intimacy Education (TIE): Mission". Accessed March 1, 2020 from www.theatricalintimacyed.com/mission.

5 Stefanie Maiya Lehmann and Celeste Morris, "Facing and (Fixing) the Problem of Sexual Harassment in the Theatre." *Southern Theater Conference Journal*, 59(4) (2018), 9–23.

6 Carey Purcell, "Intimate Exchanges." *American Theatre Magazine*, October 23, 2018. Accessed March 1, 2020 from www.americantheatre.org/2018/10/23/intimate-exchanges.

7 Purcell, "Intimate Exchanges."

8 Pace and Rikard, "Theatre Intimacy Education (TIE)."

9 Chelsea Pace and Laura Rikard, *Staging Sex* (Routledge, New York, 2020).

10 Chelsea Pace and Laura Rikard, interview with Maria Cominis, June 10, 2020.

11 Chelsea Pace and Laura Rikard, interview with Maria Cominis, June 10, 2020.

12 Chelsea Pace and Laura Rikard, interview with Maria Cominis, June 10, 2020.

13 Laura Rikard, "American Theatre Artists Online." Stefan Sittig interviewer. May 3, 2020. Podbean. Accessed August 31, 2021 from www.podbean.com/media/share/pb-etyhg-db4785.

14 Augusto Boal, *Games for Actors and Non-Actors*, trans. Adrian Jackson (Routledge, New York, 1992).

15 https://transequality.org/issues/resources/understanding-transgender-people-the-basics

16 Chekhov, Michael, *Lessons for Teachers*, Expanded edition, MICHA pg. 6–7.

6
Culture and Collaboration

We have spent a great deal of time in this book so far identifying and exploring the principles that are essential to successful collaboration. Essentially, we have been articulating ways to create a "culture of collaboration" and we have used terms such as "theatre culture" and "culture of consent," as well as focusing on professional and academic cultures.

In this chapter, we will take a closer look at culture, focusing on the cultures of the stories we tell and the culture of the artists who tell them, particularly the cultures of people of color. Much of the experiences in this chapter will be the stories of Black artists, in part because this is the culture that has been most aggrieved by the culture of the American theatre. Ultimately, we hope to share ideas and practices that will help to honor and embrace all cultures in the collaborative process.

Culture

If the theatre studies, analyzes, dissects, and embodies the human experience, how do we begin to embrace that fact? When do we seek to understand the beauty of all cultures? When we start to understand people from all walks of life honestly, we increase the human volume of stories, begin to see each other, hear each other, understand each other, and create.

Culture is what families from all walks of life do behind closed doors. Culture is how, why, when, and where people worship or not. Culture is the passing on of customs. Culture is placing the preposition at the end of the sentence at home, but not in public. Culture is passing on traditions, recreating traditions, and sometimes restructuring traditions. Culture is food and Friday night fish fries, matzo ball soup, or maybe fufu. Culture is music, country, hip-hop, jazz, Benga, Ubango, Hindustani, calypso, Mambo, acapella, Celtic

DOI: 10.4324/9780367810252-7

chant, bossa nova, bluegrass, gospel, and blues. Culture is rich and diverse. Cultures can create a melting pot of untapped masterpieces.

Culture is:

- learned through active teaching, and passive habits
- shared, meaning that it defines a group and meets common needs
- patterned, meaning that there is a reoccurrence of similar ideas – related cultural beliefs and practices show up repeatedly in different areas of social life
- adaptive, which helps individuals meet needs across variable environments
- symbolic, which means that there are simple and arbitrary signs that represent something else, something more.[1]

Culture and basic human needs

Collaborations present amazing opportunities to bring the insights, creativity, and experiences of multiple individuals together in ways that enhance the quality, authenticity, scope, depth, and ultimately the dynamism of collective work beyond what any single participant could have envisioned or executed on their own. However, there are also instances where power dynamics prevent the mutuality through which collaboration takes flight. Multiple parties dig in their heels, such that the battle and clash of ideas and personalities prevent the merging and meshing that are integral to synergistic endeavors, or differences in individual understandings of the nature of collaboration lead to miscommunication, judgements, and tensions that hamper cooperation. Embedded within these challenges are divergent approaches to the fulfilment of basic human needs, many of which are culturally patterned. For example, the focus of one's work on self-actualization (follow your passion) versus community actualization (serve the people you love), the positioning of emotional involvement as essential for or detrimental to professional relationships, and the broader pursuit of extrinsic or intrinsic rewards as central to wellbeing, happiness, and ultimately satisfaction with collaborative endeavors. Thus, an essential ingredient for effective collaboration is an understanding and willingness to allow for multiplicity not only in ideas, but also in behaviors, communicative styles, and broader worldviews. This is not a technical skill to master, but a reflexive positioning to embody and embrace in order to unleash the true potential in a collaboration, and to actively bring to light and build from those aspects of collaboration that are often hidden, silenced, or bridged over in ways that can dissuade individuals from collaborating again in the future.

– Arianna Hun, anthropologist

Before going further, it is important to consider our shared humanity, which is also at the heart of the theatre. We tell stories in large part to share our experiences and deepen our understanding of one another, leading us to continually rediscover that there is, in fact, more that unites us than divides us, and that at our deepest core, we all share the same basic wants, needs, and desires.

These desires are shared by those who collaborate with each other, so before we can successfully collaborate and embrace cultures that are different from our own, we must first acknowledge the basic needs of *all* people, regardless of race, gender, or ethnicity. There are three on which we will focus here that are especially significant to collaborative culture: attachment, control, and self-actualization.

Attachment

The human desire to attach to another person is one of the most potent psychological needs.

The ability to achieve successful relationships on a team is contingent on how artists connect to each other and attach to the vision. Attachment occurs when a person feels safe and respected, and has a sense of autonomy. The goal should be to set timelines, ensure clarity of goals, and not to micromanage. We must create a space where the artist feels free to develop and contribute.

Control

Control requires checking in, testing the vision's ideas with exceptional clarity, and verifying the experiment. To have clarity about a situation is to have a sense of control, and options become more apparent. When we don't know what is going on in our environment, there can be high levels of stress and anxiety. Checking in with your creative team promotes conversations and shared ideas while remaining open to various options. Testing ideas for the concept keeps all voices in the conversation. The discussion allows agreed-upon changes while working towards the vision. These exchanges provide clarity and understanding, which establishes orientation. The conversations solidify the artists' work and support their artistic integrity as they preserve control of their ideas around the concept. Although the final product – the show – is not verified until tech, it is here that the experiment's collaborative success is tested.

Self-actualization

Self-actualization needs refer to the realization of a person's potential and self-fulfillment, seeking personal growth and peak experiences. In a theatrical collaboration, it means encouraging all to create from their life experiences to their full capacity.

Meeting basic human needs in a collaboration

The following are three examples of how basic human needs impact the collaborative process from the experience of Rufus Bonds.

Example 1: Basic needs fulfilled

I was directing the play *Lysistrata* at a university. The set designer was a student under the tutelage of one of the professors. Through many conversations, we were able to refine the idea for the set into a vibrant playground. Arriving at the final ground plan was the result of a long process: presenting proposals, rethinking ideas, and dismissing ideas until the vision, budget, and artistic agreements matched. The exploration process was guided by asking questions and enjoying discoveries while providing constant respect, support, and appreciation.

The many shared conversations prompting questions and solutions created a relationship of mutual trust that satisfied the first human need: attachment. The student not only believed in the concept for the show, but also in my direction. Knowing precisely the vision's needs gave the student clarity, understanding, and control of her ideas, satisfying the second human need: control/orientation. The third human need, self-actualization, is accomplished by continually supporting, respecting, and expressing appreciation for the student's craft. The support allowed her to achieve her goals and beyond.

Example 2: Basic needs unfulfilled

When the inability to articulate honest conversation occurs, the three human needs go unmet and collaboration disintegrates. In the same production of *Lysistrata*, talks with the costume designer projected the illusion of mutual understanding. However, during the developmental period, there was a lack of meeting timelines, completing designs, and providing articles for rehearsals. The lack of communication between the designer and the director strained the human need for attachment. Although her thoughts appeared to attach to the vision, it was challenging for me to support her ideas without being able to view her materials. The artist stated that she does not show her designs or costumes to prevent her work from being rejected. Making a choice not to share information was a way of her controlling her vision. The action taken by the designer to determine who saw her work and when operated against the team being able to collaboratively control, check, and test. Although the designer was encouraged and supported, her need for self-actualization proved unsuccessful. Tech tested the designs, and a number of the costumes required changing. This did not stop many of the costumes from ultimately being successfully realized, but the opportunity to experience the joy of collaboration was never achieved.

Example 3: Basic needs challenged, yet resolved

Another encounter involved the struggle for power over a set piece built by the technical designer. On the set, the actors needed a way to exit an upstage platform. In agreement with the set designer, the technical designer created steps for the actors to exit the stage to solve the problem. The stairs posed a safety problem for the actors. The distance from one step to the other was too deep and it was challenging for the actors to step down. The costume lengths presented an issue for mobility on the stairs and maintaining a pace for all to exit the stage promptly. The idea of the steps was tested and found unsuccessful. I continued to ask the technical designer questions to keep the conversation moving toward a solution for the problem. The technical designer tried to place the issue on the actors, implying they could make it work. I requested that we meet in the theatre and try to understand the logistics of the issue. His attachment to the set piece created a disconnect in the communication, which presented a challenge to resolving the problem. We met and he continued to defend his position until I finally asked, "What is it about these steps? What is it you're holding on to?" I could see the technical designer taking in the question, taking a breath, and then he replied, "Nothing." The technical designer finally stated he felt that the steps represented himself, and if the piece was ineffective, it might reflect on how his abilities were viewed. In his mind, the prop expressed his inability to achieve self-actualization, his desire to work at a level using his full capacity. Because I continued to seek and understand the technical designer's attachment to the set piece, we discovered a solution. Understanding how he viewed himself at that moment and choosing to support him through it allowed us to address the issue and solve the problem.

> You know I've worked with quite a few directors. George [C. Wolfe] has a way of making sure that everybody feels like their voice is heard. That's the whole trick to collaboration. Everybody needs to listen to everybody else. And you know George will stop, he'll say what he has to say, then he'll say, what do you all think, and sometimes will go around the room, sometimes somebody will raise their hand not so timidly because he wants people to speak out. It might not be the right idea, but at least you feel comfortable and safe in voicing it, and you know it's up to him after that to see whether we try it or not, and most of the time he'll say, you know, let's try it. That's the other part of collaboration; you just don't shut people down. I mean, let's talk about the first few days of the table talk. George is the person who not only wants to know who you think your character is, he wants to know who *you* are, and he wants you to feel safe being able to express whatever doubts you have because if he can help you with those problems, he's making a better show for himself.
>
> – Daryl Waters, composer, arranger, orchestrator,
> conductor, musician, *The Cher Show, Shuffle Along,*
> or *The Making of the Musical Sensation of 1921*

Beyond Collaborative Culture

The word "culture" has many definitions that are helpful for our discussion:

- a particular form or stage of civilization, as that of a certain nation or period
- the behaviors and beliefs characteristic of a particular group of people, as a social, ethnic, professional, or age group

- the shared beliefs, behaviors, or social environment connected with a particular aspect of society
- the values, typical practices, and goals of a business or other organization.

This last definition applies most specifically to the culture of collaboration that is the primary focus of this book. It is, however, the other definitions that are most in need of attention by the American theatre community.

We are a very diverse country, consisting of people from a remarkable variety of cultures, each with their stories to tell – and each with their own storytellers who bring a richness of understanding of those cultures to the table. As we will see, if we ignore these cultures, we are actually denying ourselves the richness and truth of experiences that are essential to a vital and dynamic theatre.

Let's look how culture is expressed through the stories we tell and the artists who tell them, and discuss ways in which these cultures can be explored and presented with authenticity, even when the artists aren't of that particular culture.

Culture of the story

All plays and musicals tell stories that are rooted in a specific culture. In America, that has been dominated by White European and American culture. There are also many plays and musicals that represent other cultures, including Black, Asian, Latinx, Native American, African, feminist, LGBTQ+ and many others. The list is as diverse as the population served by a theatre. Working on a play or musical of culture requires the same investigative process as any other piece. The script is analyzed and scrutinized to understand every aspect of it: underneath, around, inside and out, and in-between. Looking through the words and the color of the voices helps us to discover truths, secrets, and hidden nuances.

Research about the culture should be a given. If you omit the work to understand people's customs and circumstances while clumping them into one category, the result can only live on the surface. Seeking to uncover the grit, danger, pain, buoyancy, and scope of the people will take you toward a path of verity. One must understand the language and the reasons why the words connect in a particular pattern. What are the physical movements of the community and the gait of its people? Inquire about their land and the connection their souls might have to the soil. Seek to understand their spirits and who they are behind the eyes. Journeying into the depths of the souls reveals answers. Here is where the work begins.

Researching will not provide all the answers. Sometimes in works of culture, questions may persist, and the answers can only be learned by going to the source - the people who can offer their experience. One can investigate, study, and analyze a culture academically, but situations will arise where you must engage in conversations with people of that culture to bring truth to the stage. The most significant expression of the research's impact on the production resides in the bodies of the artist. Communicating honestly, acknowledging they are the experts on their experiences while seeking truth, opens the door to priceless collaboration. Answers can be found by listening, asking questions, and collaboratively investigating the world of the play.

Once on This Island is a musical set on an island in the French Antilles in a society whose social divisions are based on the lightness or darkness of a person's skin. It is based on a novel by Rosa Guy, who was born in Trinidad and raised in New York City. The book and lyrics were written by Lynn Ahrens and the music was by Stephen Flaherty, both White and born in New York City and Pennsylvania, respectively. The production was directed by Graciela Daniele, an Argentinian born in Buenos Aires and the set was by Loy Arcenas, who was born in the Philippines. The cast consisted primarily of American-born Black performers. How does a team of artists this diverse authentically create a story set in the Caribbean?

Kecia Lewis, who originated the role of "Asaka," describes a rehearsal experience that gives us a number of clues to the answer:

> When we were doing *Once on This Island*, we were preparing a dance that was supposed to be kind of a ritualistic Haitian scene dance, asking for safety and forgiveness to the gods of this mythical Island. Graciela [Daniele], our director choreographer, was very clear from the very beginning that she had no idea how to authentically duplicate what we should be doing on stage. And what I loved about it was that Graciela had done her research already concerning Haitian culture. She was very well read and prepared when she walked in the room, which has been, unfortunately, not the norm in my career experience. But when it came to this particular area, she felt she did not have a clear vision on how to execute the dance. She came to the cast, and she asked if any of us had any African dance training. A few of us did. We talked a little bit about that as a group. We talked about what those movements might be in relation to African dance. Could we use specifically African dance? So, there was a lot of back and forth, discussion, collaboration, physical movement that we all watched and said, I don't know if that feels

right. I don't know if this feels right. And that's how we came up with this dance that, um, winds up being a highlight of the show for many people.[2]

This is a perfect example of investigating a culture that may be foreign to the artists involved. The director/choreographer brought research to the table, then opened the creation to the group, first ascertaining the experience of the company before inviting the artists to give expression to that experience, then engaging the entire company in developing the ideas before solidifying them into a dynamic dance number that contributed to the success of the production. Investigating culture brings truth to the story.

When Graciela requested assistance from the cast, her approach was to engage with the cast with great care and honesty. She led with trust and respect while including the cast in the process. Collaborating with the cast created a profound moment on stage and in the actors' lives that continues to endure decades after the show closed. Note that a director doesn't relinquish their power by using the full breadth of experience and talent of their company to bring truth to the stage. Instead, the power of collaboration establishes rich relationships built on mutual trust and respect. Bringing care, sincerity, honesty, and generosity into the room creates a space where all feel welcome to contribute.

In August of 2014, I had the pleasure of portraying the title role of Porgy at the Regents Park Open Air Theatre in London. I was delighted to observe how the creative team led by Timothy Sheader worked as one force. In the room, their sharing of ideas occurred throughout the rehearsal process. After working on a scene, the team gathered – David Shrubsole, musical director; Liam Steel (choreographer); Diane Alison-Mitchell (assistant choreographer); and Ola Ince (assistant director) – to determine whether the moment was successful and how to make the adjustments. It was clear they collectively chose to make sure the story was straightforward. Although Timothy was the director, his process of listening to his team and cast was honorable. Everyone was allowed to voice their opinions about a specific moment. The action was very time-consuming. As I was sitting and listening, I was thinking, "Can we just do it?" I learned the time allotted for shared opinions allowed everyone to be on the same page and created a unifying bond between the cast and the creative team. Everyone felt a part of the collaborative creation. Everyone felt safe, seen, and acknowledged, while playing in an environment to achieve their best work.

Timothy was adamant about making sure cultural actions were honest. There was a scene where the women were cleaning fish. They created a setting where each character was specifically identifiable. The women's hierarchy was clear, even with the women singing the same chorus and performing the same physical actions. Timothy and Liam successfully developed the bond among the women by listening, sharing, and understanding the community. The scene was so powerful that the audience suspended their belief and imagined the ladies were cleaning fish, even though the prop for the fish was a rag. The truth of the moment was achieved by Timothy asking questions, not assuming, and staying open to the information shared.

Working in London as an American with a culturally diverse cast of Black British men and women was fantastic. Going to work every day was a joy beyond belief. Creating with artists with the sole focus on telling the story fostered a magical atmosphere. Being American and depicting an American account, my input was not only welcomed but requested.

Although the director, choreographer, and musical director were not people of color, it was clear that the goal was to bring to life a culturally authentic, dynamic story. The production is a real example of when the guiding principles are the process, collaboration thrives.

Ignoring the story's culture

Unfortunately, not all productions invite this kind of collaborative investigation of culture. The result is often failure. Take, for example, the case of the off-Broadway musical *Dessa Rose,* another musical by Ahrens and Flaherty directed and choreographed by Graciela Daniele.

Dessa Rose, based on both fact and fiction, weaves together the stories of two real women who struggled for different kinds of freedom in an era defined by men. Ruth Sutton is a white woman abandoned by her husband and living on an isolated farm. Dessa Rose is an escaped slave on the run from a bloody slave rebellion with a newborn infant to protect; she seeks refuge on Ruth's farm. Ultimately, the two women's uneasy alliance transcends racial barriers as they find the strength to confront the world on their own terms.

Whitewashing is when the language or action of a story of culture is changed to make it more palatable for a White audience. It is when factual truths are changed, either because the producers, directors, or adapting authors – often White men – cannot believe the historical fact or choose not to present themselves in a particular way on the stage. Whitewashing is the watering down of a culture's story for someone else's benefit. The procedure of Whitewashing works completely against cultural collaboration and destroys all the guiding principles. There is no respect, trust, or communication, and the voices of the people of color are silenced; there is no act of generosity. In the case of *Dessa Rose*, the concept imagined by the director moved forward without a unified vision.

Kecia Lewis, a member of the original cast, remembers:

> So, there was a different way culture was handled in a production that I did at Lincoln Center. The [original] version of the show was not favorable to Whites. When it was presented to the producers in a run-through, there were immediate changes made against the director's wishes by the producers, because it wasn't palatable to them. It was Whitewashed. And there was a White actor in the show who, you know, as we sit in the green room and chat and, you know, get to know each other, he was adamant that he had never seen anything like it in his career. And it couldn't be anything but racism. He said we have a beautiful story here. Why are they doing this? Why are they making these changes that are important to the story? They are necessary to understand these characters and their motivation, but the producers wanted things changed because it was not favorable to the White folks in the show or the characters we [the Black cast] were playing. And we were dealing with slavery. So it was just an aspect of slavery that wasn't well known, but it happened. Their argument: this wasn't feasible; this didn't happen. It's like, excuse me. Yes, it did. You're just uncomfortable with it.

In this instance, the producers refused to accept the historical fact that Dessa Rose, the slave, would hold an emotionally dominant position where a White male would beg for and be driven insane by her insolence and refusal to love him. The producers demanded that the story be changed. Because of their disbelief, there was the washing away of the truth to tell the story they wanted.

Culture of the artists

When a Black cast enters a space to create a theatrical experience, the room receives them. The entire room welcomes the unspoken history between everyone in the room. Collaboration begins the first day of the rehearsal, the moment they step into the space. It becomes a space where they can just be themselves. Trust and respect are present in the room. Generosity exists, and if a problem arises, it is resolved through constant and open communication. Is this always successful? No, but the attempt is made, and everyone works to remain on the same page.

However, many times people of color enter the space and are immediately challenged regarding how they react to events in their culture. This action does not invite collaboration but creates the opposite. Trust and respect must be earned. One earns this by listening and seeking truth to create an authentic world. When you think you understand a culture better than those in the room, the shutting-down process begins, and sometimes trust and respect are destroyed.

> It is essential for the director to create a welcoming space from day one. During my time in *The Lion King*, never did I hear Africa mentioned by the director. The action became very perplexing to me. Julie spoke much of Bali: conversations involving her trip there and the inspiration she had garnered.
>
> I was putting in the work to understand the complexities of the show, yet at times I felt the puppet on my head was more important to her than the actor. At times I felt the scope of my culture and race ignored.
>
> In my first week of rehearsal, I witnessed an issue between Lebohand M. Morake, who was responsible for much of the additional music in the theatrical production, and Julie Taymor, the director. They were at odds over how Mufasa's song, "He Lives in You," which Lebohand wrote, should be sung. Julie wanted the song to be more spoken and staccato, while Lebohand intended the vocal to be lyrical with more musicality. There was no way to win in this situation. We all made it through this moment until tech many weeks later. We completed the song, and Ms. Taymor on the bullhorn, in the dark from the audience, bellows, "Rufus, I've heard you sing this right before." When a person of color – when any person – does not feel safe, heard, or honored, collaboration is not possible.

Being in a Black production directed by someone who is not a person of color presents its own set of challenges. Issues arise when the director has not researched the culture, when the director pretends they can teach you the Black experience, or when we are told our authentic emotional impulses from a cultural reaction are undesirable or too emotional.

It is essential for a director of a different race or culture to acknowledge that they are not the authority in the room on the Black experience – or any experience not their own. If you find yourself directing a group of actors who are different from you, it is okay for you to ask questions – *once you've done your research*. When you honestly seek to uncover the truth by being open with the people who might have the answers, you will establish trust. It is about respect and communication.

Kecia Lewis recounts her experience during the mounting of the Broadway production *Leap of Faith*, which powerfully illustrates this point:

> A large focal point of the show was the Black gospel choir. I should say gospel choir because there were White members of the choir, but it was 95 per cent black. Initially, the creators, who were White and had no experience in the gospel world at all, first called on some well-known innovators in the gospel music field to help with creating the choir, giving them some schooling on how things should be sung, the culture of it. I played the choir director, and so there's a very specific way that a soloist/choir director sings and performs with a choir.
>
> So, they [the creators] initially listened to these experts. And then, once things didn't work out for the experts to remain a part of the collaborative process, they took it upon themselves to consider themselves experts. And so, as the process went on and we got closer to Broadway, there was a lot of clashing. This was our life experience. We were being told the proper way to execute gospel music in a church, which I found absolutely appalling. And it got to a point where I had a big clash with the music supervisor, who made a comment to me about how I should behave as the choir director and how I should even sing the soprano ad lib.
>
> I've learned over the years to just not play tit for tat, not swallow it, but speak up. I just went to the writer of the musical, sent him an email and said, we need to have a meeting. And I need to know how you feel about what I'm doing, what your plan is for what we are doing, so I can be clear, and whose direction do I need to take. This is not Kecia the actress playing a part [about which] I am needing to do research. I have lived it and have been in church since I was a small child. You and your creatives, on the other hand, have not for one second been involved in this culture at all. So it got a little heated, but we got to the bottom line, and they thankfully kind of acquiesced and said, you know you're right. You let us know what you think should be done here.
>
> When we don't speak up as actors of these various cultures that are being depicted by others who are not of the culture, if we don't open our mouths, we are going to get caricatures, and the stereotypes will just keep going on and on and on. Whenever people create something that they know nothing about and consider themselves experts, you always have some kind of inauthentic mess.[3]

This situation could have been avoided with a little openness and generosity. Everyone in the room wants to achieve the same goal: to create extraordinary, authentic, bold, thought-provoking work. As a friend once said, an actor will jump off a mountain for a director if you make them feel safe.

Of course, not every experience ignores the specific experiences and understanding of culture that their cast brings to the table, but when a company truly sees who you are and *wants* what you have to offer, you remember it and seek it in all of your collaborations. Celise Hicks, assistant choreographer of Disney's *The Lion King* Worldwide, remembers a truly collaborative experience that, for her, was unforgettable:

> My best experience was when I danced with Ron K. Brown's company, Evidence. I was a dancer, but I found that to be, honestly to this day, one of the best creative experiences of my life. We were all People of Color.
>
> I think there's an understanding that you don't have to explain certain things. So, I feel like there's an underlining comfort and trust that you don't have in other spaces just because it's a comfortable environment. *I feel collaboration becomes a success when there's no fear involved.* [Italics added.]
>
> Collaborative things I've done when I was just an artist, was me and everyone around me truly believing in the vision, but also not threatened by anybody. You were able to show up as yourself in the space every day, and you felt there was no other motive. There was nothing but the art and the people. It was the energy and there was no fear involved, no insecurities, no egos. Even with the artistic director, speaking of Ron K. Brown, there was nothing attached to it. If people are fearful, you can't collaborate.
>
> I think true collaboration is beyond culture. I think it has everything to do with an individual, and if they show up to whatever space, as their whole self, as their whole vulnerable self.
>
> Ron led with the work. It was definitely just about the creative process and not him. I felt complete after every rehearsal or show; I felt connected. It was spiritual for sure.
>
> As I keep going in this business and now being on the other side for so long, my first objective is to make sure everyone in the room feels better, or I want to try. I'm not going to say I'm always going to succeed at that because I'm a human being too. I'm flawed like everybody, but they should feel better leaving than they felt coming in. It's art, and art should heal you. They [the artists] as well, they are the facilitators of the art. To get the best out of someone, you have to really be supportive and understanding and allow them to show up as themselves.

Black hair and makeup

The sensation of being ignored and unseen is a system established to control and ignore one's culture. Being seen and embraced for your racial and cultural identity extends to every aspect of your being, especially for the performer. Black hair and makeup emerged as a *major* concern during the recent demands the Black community made on the theatre community, because hair in the Black community is more than hair: it is spiritual and cultural.

Unfortunately, it is the norm for many hairstylist in the theatre to be ill-informed about how to address the natural hair of Black people. The lack of skills and education can lead the hairstylist to disrespect the actors, especially children. Some children are told their hair is difficult, bad, and not easy to manage. These words placed in the child's mind will stay with them for the rest of their lives. The lack of sensitivity for a person's being is why we are where we are today. You cannot assist the actor if you do not seek to understand what the actor needs. Implying that straight hair is good hair is the same as saying the closer your hair is to the texture of white hair, the better.

Broadway hair and makeup supervisor Cheryl Veronica Thomas points out that:

> There has been an avoidance of dealing with natural hair in the theatre in my opinion. An example from the extreme is the request for an actor to cut or shave their dreadlocks. African hair and hairstyles have been a means of pride in social ranking and tribal connection. Slaves were broken down from their tribal distinction by shaving their hair for the slave journey crossing the Atlantic.

Understanding this can improve the collaborative culture by avoiding design choices, maintenance care, or the lack of care for wig-wearing that will make the actor feel invisible.

Similarly, issues with undergarments, and stockings exist. Black actors will be given undergarments and stockings that will not match their skin tone. You will never hear of a white actor given brown undergarments or stockings. How is this not taken into consideration when the costume plot for the actor is designed? It says to the actor that they are not seen in their totality: their culture and their essence are invisible. Research must be undertaken to purchase the makeup required for the beautiful range of skin tones of Black actors. The makeup exists. Once again, the problem of invisibility is in the room. To be better, we must do better. See the actor, see their culture, and find the solutions. The response will be one of great gratitude and generosity.

Hair and makeup artists have a unique position seated between management and the actors. By being in such close proximity with the artist on a day-to-day basis, a shared trust evolves. The actors express their concerns, achievements, and gratitude. The hair and makeup artist's aim is to keep both sides of the spectrum happy:

> Understanding how to work with Black hair in American society has been avoided as much as people saying the N-word, which is taboo. Not being taught Black hair in cosmetology schools and working with it in theatre, it is understood that you don't know what to do. Natural hair courses are considered specialty courses in most cosmetology schools and not a part of the core curriculum. Comments are made it [Black hair] is difficult and hard to work with, whereas Black hair is one of the most delicate and fragile hair structures of the human hair.
>
> Some actors have been told that their natural hair is difficult or ugly. African hair was peculiar and distasteful to White Americans. The pride of African hair began to be chipped away, being described as woolly, kinky, nappy, unattractive, and unruly, to name a few.
>
> There has been a lack of training to understand Black hair because it is not considered important, in my opinion. Being told that you don't have good hair is disrespectful. Hair is neither good nor bad; it is healthy or unhealthy.
>
> – Cheryl Thomas, hair and makeup supervisor
> of *Aladdin*, Broadway and Worldwide

When Culture is Ignored

Invisibility and the harm it does to collaborative culture

Visibility and sensitivity to the race and culture of the artists of a production must begin with the very first conceptual steps of a production, and must permeate every aspect of the production. *Everyone* involved – including the management side of the production team – must be aware that insensitive choices can damage the collaborative culture of any production. Stanley Wayne Mathis, who was cast as Schroeder in the 1999 Broadway revival of *You're a Good Man, Charlie Brown*, presents us with an extraordinarily sad, completely avoidable cautionary account:

> There are people who will hire Black people in their shows and then commence to Whitewash you. Example: *You're a Good Man, Charlie Brown*.
>
> You go through all this trouble to be diverse with the cast. All we are, are assimilated Negroes, assimilated Brown people, you know. BD Wong was basically an assimilated Asian, and I was an assimilated Black person.

I had gone to my director at the time for *Charlie Brown*, and I brought pictures and everything, 'cause you know, you have to be really careful. It's like you're going to court with them. You have to really state your case and be prepared, well prepared, and present your arguments and everything because they just aren't trying to hear it. I brought the director pictures and photos of children and people from the ages of babies all the way to 100-year-old adults, people from all different professions and also Jamaica. They were all wearing locks, wearing dreads. And I had a lot of pictures of children in particular because I wanted them to see the dynamic of how playful that looks. When they see locks, they see homeless people. They see threats.

He [the director] loved it. He just thought, Oh, this is fantastic. Cause I told him, "I can't very well match Schroeder's blonde bouffant. What if I did that? What if I match that dynamic with locks?" and he loved the idea, so we were in the process of getting that done. When the producers found out that that's what I was doing, they were like, "Oh no, no, no, no, no, no, no. We're not. No, absolutely not!" And I just thought, "I don't understand why you would bring people of color into your productions, if you don't want them to bring themselves to the table. And if you wanted everything to be White across the board, then you should have just hired an all-White cast." If you're going to diversify a cast, they're going to bring elements of who they are, as far as identity, and culture, and language and nuance to the table. It's not like, take off your galoshes and your legal glasses and your coat at the door when you come into the room. And that's what they ask us to do.

And it's infuriating because you're not allowed to exist in the space. They don't even realize, but they're preserving their White spaces. I've done eight Broadway shows, and there have been instances in it for most of the shows that I've done. You just go, "Boy, is it ever going to change, is it difficult to ever fricking change?"

And they've been living with this construct for so long that's put into motion, and generations have grown up on it. There's a cognitive dissonance there that they are not even aware of. If ever you attempt to show them that, put a mirror in front of them, they become disturbed, shaken almost to the core. Some of them [get] angry and violent because of it. Others are hurt and defensive about it. We live inside of it. They construct it, but they live outside of the inside boundaries, and we live with thousands of microaggressions a day. To the point, you become numb to keep from experiencing it.

Things like *Charlie Brown*. When we shot the commercial, we got into the little bus that they made for us. It didn't occur to them that perhaps you shouldn't put Schroeder (Stanley's character) in the back of the bus. When I saw the commercial and you know, how they do cutaways and edits and stuff like that, you know? So, they went down the line, they started at the front of the bus, and just before they got to Schroeder at the back, they cut to another scene.

Theater Magazine did a whole cover story on us, and the cast ain't that big, Rufus. You know, it's just a handful of us. Every character was on the front page, except Schroeder. Even if it's not your intention, do you not know how those things appear?

[In] *Kiss Me Kate* [another Broadway Revival that featured Mathis] I have the big number, "Too Darn Hot", and it's the opening of the second act. It became a big thing. The critics talked about it. There were publicity posters that went up all over town with the headline *Too Darn Hot*. I wasn't even paying attention. I had people come up to me and say, you know, I saw the posters around town for *Too Darn Hot*, and you weren't in any of them. I started walking around town, and I look, and I'm looking at the posters, and I'm seeing all different types of variations of people in the cast. And I am not in any of the posters. And it says *Too Darn Hot*, and they eliminated the person who led the number. I was not called to the photo shoot. The publicity people started Whitewashing the show. And how is this supposed to make you feel going to work every day?

To eradicate Stanley Wayne Mathis from the *Theater Magazine*, to eradicate Stanley Wayne Mathis from the promotions around New York City of *Kiss Me Kate*'s "Too Darn Hot" is Whitewashing and racist. How does a producer choose this action and believe it is justified? How is his work honored on the stage, but his very image cannot represent your musical in the world? He was erased, while the historical pictorial documents will forever present in history Anthony Rapp, Ilana Levine, B.D. Wong, Kristin Chenoweth, and Roger Bart – but not Stanley Wayne Mathis. As for Stanley Wayne Mathis, whoever decided to photoshop him out of the photo or not invite him to be a part of the photoshoot also decided to erase his image, his person, and his essence from history. How can we speak of collaboration if the approval of erasing a Black man's image on the highest stage of our industry, Broadway, is allowed to occur? Stanley is a darker-skinned man. If the tone of his skin was lighter, would that have made a difference?

Through his voice, you can experience the lack of respect, visibility, and significance afforded him. In this situation, communication occurred without the act of listening, understanding, or caring. Generosity was non-existent. Someone had a clear vision – not for the show, but for how Mathis's image would exist or not, globally. When this happens to a Black actor, how do you think it makes that person feel? What happens when you awaken in the morning, knowing you will go to work for an organization whose only desire is for you to sing, act, dance, and leave. What arises in you when seven o'clock arrives and it's time to head to the theatre? What stirs in you when you walk through the stage door, cast members are moving in the space, happy go-lucky, and you carry the weight of being disrespected? You put on the face. You collect the check. You make sure your agent fights for you as the establishment tries to discard your essence. How can you trust? What do you do? You do your job 100 per cent from the totality of who you are. You lead with generosity and stay true to the director's vision and the vision for your life.

Negating Black experience

The following stories address situations from plays and musicals involving the Black Church. There are some institutions in the Black community that exist as the cornerstone for survival and the Black Church is arguably the most important of these. Historically, the Black Church was the one place where Black people could worship freely and fully exist. This space represents a sacred place of healing and gratitude. Hopefully, there was no cost against your life in this space.

Unfortunately, crimes against Black lives walked into this institution in Charleston, South Carolina, taking nine members' lives. This hateful crime did not destroy the faith of the congregation nor the cornerstone of the institution. The Black Church still stands and is the seat of survival, education, protection, honor, love, and praise. When the Black Church setting is present in a play, it must be understood and respected. To disrespect it will alienate your cast. This alienation occurs when a director of a different culture behaves as if they are the authority in the room. This action does not practice trust, respect, or communication.

Kimberly Harris, the "Church Lady" in the original Broadway production of *The Color Purple*, shared these experiences with us:

> There was this incident where – I believe I blocked it out, but a fellow castmate brought it up not too long ago. She reminded me of when we were rehearsing a church scene, and the director (a White man) said something like, "Stop, Stop! Does this White man have to come teach you all how to be Black in the church?" or something like that.
>
> The room went silent. Everybody looked at him and at each other, thinking, wow, here we go. Not knowing or caring that his words were offensive. He was making an assumption of what Black people would do

in the church, maybe something he saw in a movie, I don't know, but there were quite a few instances like that.

I remember being in [the musical] *Abyssinia*, and the director was showing us how to dance in church. He was doing the shaking jazz hands up in the air kind of thing like "Oh Lordy, oh Lordy" and I just, I told him, I said, "Listen, what you just did, it is what a White person would think a Black person does in church, dancing. I've never seen a Black person do anything like that, except for on those minstrel shows, old movies or a White person in blackface." He didn't use that step. He knew he didn't know what he was doing on some level. He knew that.

It is hard to imagine, but the above experience is not all that unusual, as Stanley Wayne Mathis describes his experience in a production:

The play was called *Greensboro* by Emily Mann. And we were out there in Princeton, New Jersey, and a British director was directing. It was about the Greensboro massacre, and in short that's what the play was about. There were three Black cast members, and the director proceeded to sit us down and tell us the history of the Black Church in the 1960s. What the Southern Black Churches were about, and so forth and so on. So, at first, when he started off, we were listening attentively and then all of a sudden, we start, you know, side-eyeing each other. I was like, "Wait a minute. Is he trying to tell us about being Black in the 1960s and the Southern Black Churches?" We were all looking at each other, and I know out of the three of us, I don't think any one of us was Catholic. I'm looking at Carol, Carol's looking at me, and then we're looking at the other guy, and we're looking at each other. So, after a while, as he's just going through giving us this grand lecture or history lesson, it was like, "Are you serious?" First of all, none of us was under 40 at the time. You know? It's like, we were old enough, we were Black, and most of us came from the South. I really don't need a lecture on the Black Church in the South, in the 1960s. You need to tell me where to stand. It was weird that this white director from the United Kingdom thought he needed to tell us this information. I'm just looking at him like, is he serious? How long is this going to go on? And I thought to myself, I can't take it anymore. I finally looked at him, and went, "We know, we were there."

He sort of stared blankly at us, the lecture ended, and he proceeded to direct. The production came off very cold and austere. I don't know if that's a thing with them over there, but I think they think Americans are too emotional. Maybe y'all are not emotional over there, but over here, we are. It was like he didn't want you to feel. It was a massacre. People were being shot and killed. What is it you didn't understand? It's interesting: here's somebody who's outside of the experience, even outside of the Southern White experience, outside of the American experience altogether. He was projecting that whole British sensibility to it.

Which I felt like, first of all, that really don't apply here. You're telling an American story. I mean, there are certain things you could do style-wise or whatever, but it was very confusing. It seemed like he was so hell-bent on trying to tell us how to express ourselves.

By this point, you're probably making a vow to yourself never to participate in a production of a show that doesn't reflect your own culture, but if you are, you're missing the point. Theatre from beginning to end is an exercise of the imagination. We are inhabiting a story, not real life. We *all* are playing make believe, and our participation in stories of cultures different than our own are just as important as audiences being exposed to shows that are outside their experience. The theatre gives artists a chance to imagine living different lives in different times and in different places, and to walk away from that – or be intimidated away from that – is to miss out on one of the great gifts the theatre has to offer all of us. Yes, we have an absolute responsibility to authenticity; after all, if an audience doesn't embrace the world of the play, then the story will have no impact. It is *vital* that the audience see what's on stage as believable. So, we *must* make choices in casting, personnel, designs, every aspect of a production, that aid in the story's authenticity.

The point is that the individual artist in the collaborative team – every part of them – must be seen and embraced *from the very first encounter*. And these individuals must see, research and investigate the *author's* creation, including the culture of the world in which the story is situated. It *is* possible to do all of this and create fulfilling, rewarding, and even joyful experiences in telling stories from all corners of the Earth, and with people of all races, ethnicities, and cultures. To illustrate this, we are going to conclude this chapter with a series of experiences by Black artists in which they felt seen and heard, and their contributions were *valued*.

When Culture is Embraced

The experience of creating the role of Jim Conley in Hal Prince's production of Jason Robert Brown and Alfred Uhry's *Parade* was extraordinary. The care given to crafting the story by Prince, Uhry, Brown, and choreographer Patricia Birch proved remarkable. The creative team operated as one unit. The music propelled the story, the choreography represented the same story, and the book guided them both.

Early in the process, I discovered that the team's objective was to honor and free Leo Frank. In order to do that, Jim Conley would need to take the blame. As an actor and as a Black man, I could not convict a man who had not been convicted. I was asked by Prince to make an exit following the murdered little girl, Mary Fagan. That action would condemn my character. As an actor, I always try to honor the request of the director. After that moment, in the dark from the stage of tech rehearsal, I bellowed to Hal, requesting to speak with him. As I exited the stage, I went through the audience, and arrived in front of Mr. Prince. I learned before I arrived that someone had informed Mr. Prince about why I needed to speak with him. I stood before him. Mr. Prince stated, "Don't take the exit. You don't need to follow her off." I thanked Mr. Prince and returned to the stage.

I made a choice that could have gone another way. Mr. Prince had every right to hold to his direction. He had every right if I chose not to take the note to release me. Mr. Prince decided to listen, hear me, and respect my choice.

I also discovered the team had not researched the Black culture involved in the story. I continued to gather information on Jim Conley, learning valuable tools for my character. I would ask Alfred Uhry about the information, and he was unaware. Later in the revival, an additional character, Mini, Frank's maid, was added. I came across this lady while researching the Black community and mentioned her to Alfred. There was a moment in "Rumblin' and Rollin'," a song shared by the show's Black community. Some lyrics were not authentic, something we, as Black people, would not say in the moment. I discussed the issue with Jason; Hal stopped to listen. He said, "He's right," and Jason changed the lyric. Here we have another example of listening, hearing, understanding, and making an adjustment.

Music supervisor and orchestrator Daryl Waters reminds us that when people are willing and open to learning from others, energy erupts in the room that can be infectious. He believes collaboration in the theatre is the only way:

Again, it depends on who the person in charge is. Hopefully, it's a person that's very sensitive to the fact that it's a culture that they might know on the surface, but they have to count on other people, like myself, and like the actors to be able to flesh it out. So, I've worked in situations where it was disappointing, and I've worked in other situations where you know it was absolutely just thrilling to be in the room as you watch somebody learn at the same time as much as you can throw at them.

Kimberly Harris is an original cast member who experienced the journey of *The Color Purple* from reading to Broadway. As we have already seen, being a person of color in a production from one's own culture directed by a person of non-color and *not* of that culture can present challenges, and those challenges were not absent from *The Color Purple*. However, there were successful collaborative efforts, which Ms. Harris speaks to in this memory of her experience:

> What I saw and experienced, *The Color Purple* was very collaborative.
>
> The creative team (composers and lyricists) Allie Willis, Brenda Russell, and Stephen Bray were all engaged. They were all appreciative of each other's talent and their contribution. My impression was they all contributed. Brenda might come up with an idea, and Allie and Steven kind of would jump in and then maybe write the lyrics and vice versa. I saw that happen a couple of times. I never witnessed any like, ego kind of thing. It felt like they were really open to each other's suggestions and ideas. For Mister's song, Oprah didn't feel like it was enough of a redemption or a turn-around for Mister. So they worked overnight or all through many nights trying to figure things out, and then they came up with what's in the show.
>
> I definitely felt like we were listened to. There were a couple of times when, because we had such a knowledge of our characters, we could ask, "Wouldn't we be in this scene? Wouldn't I do this? Or wear that?" And they were able to see what we did, and sometimes write whatever it was into the show … I felt like in that rehearsal process, and the reading process, we came up with a lot of things that ended up being kept in the show.

Finally, Stanley Wayne Mathis describes his experience with the Broadway production of *Jelly's Last Jam*:

> *Jelly's Last Jam* was a great collaborative experience. Here's the difference. The writer was Black. The director (George Wolfe) was Black. The composer and musical arranger (Luther Henderson) was Black. The costume designer (Toni-Leslie James) was Black. The choreographer (Hope Clarke) was Black. Gregory Hines and Savion Glover did tap choreographer, and they were Black. You see where I'm going? So we were very well taken care of. The story was Black. It wasn't a Black cast doing a White show. That's been a problem too. It's one of the things that I can't stand. I do not want to do Black versions of White stories. It says to people that we don't have stories of our own to tell that are interesting and compelling. We were telling a Black story surrounded by Black people, not just on the stage, but behind the stage creatively. Susan Birkenhead is White and Jewish, but she works closely with George, and she was the lyricist. So, it was Black up into there. And I felt that I could live inside the culture without apologies. George insisted that you brought that to the table. He absolutely insisted upon it, and that was refreshing.

How Do we Move Forward?

We conclude this chapter by asking our readers to look inside at the root of what we need as human beings. Attachment, control/orientation, and self-actualization are part of those needs. Everything we do takes us onto the path to satisfy these three human needs. In all situations, people from all walks of life want to be seen, heard, respected, and allowed to succeed.

Theatre is a sacred space with the pursuit of these human needs on and off the stage. On the stage, plays are vehicles for expressing society's ills, the misunderstood, the abused, the elevated, the educated, systems, pains, glories, and so on. The human voice rings on the stage in search of some deep desire, a need to take hold of something, the hope of shaking out a better life, the bitter quest to destroy the unhuman suffocating pain of assault, the undeniable sensation of finding love. This place is a mirror of the conditions in our society as well as those in the world. The act of diving into the text to uncover the character's need to attach, grasping onto gaining or losing control, and making sense of their state of being while discovering their place in their world is a given. The work proceeds to search and tear through layers to find the character's core. One builds upon their essence using unlimited imagination. Incredible magic on the stage springs forth from this investigative work.

This same magic extends off stage. The magic of a vision that inspires the creative team to feel safe in offering their gifts. Building a work area where all ideas are welcomed and honestly considered. Space where all are allowed to imagine.

Imagine a rehearsal room where everyone's presence is acknowledged – even yours. Imagine a space where all voices are welcomed, where the tension of fear is removed and replaced with the energy encouraging fun, play, and truth while seeking to dispel insecurities. A room where the result does not outweigh the process. A room where it's okay not to know the answer about a culture, but it is celebrated that you knew to ask. A space where people of color feel honored, wanted, and seen for who they are as their full selves – an atmosphere where shared experiences of various ethnicities combine to create a dedicated American theatre, dedicated to telling everyone's stories.

Imagine an America where everyone is seen – even you. An America where students learn everyone's human experience. Where students interact and view each other as whole beings in an acting scene. To establish a new generation of students whose intellectual curiosity is triggered by plays, musicals, or literature by people of color. This action teaches us all how to see beyond, yet embrace, the physical; to seek understanding. This action is at the seat of collaboration, checking in with one another, listening and testing ideas to see how the experiment unfolds at the end of the process.

When collaboration succeeds at being of service for all, those like Stanley Wayne Mathis will never be erased. Dessa Rose's true story will be represented in theatre history. There will be more shared experiences like Kecia and Graciela's, and there will be more voices invited into the shaping of a scene as the experience with Timothy Sheader in London. More extraordinary work emerges using George C. Wolfe's guiding path as he makes sure everyone feels their voice is heard.

At the root of all of this is love.

> On the American Theatre Wing Webinar, Not Going Back to Normal, Moving Forward on August 6, 2020, Binta Niambi Brown (moderator) asked the panel: playwright, Dominique Morisseau, advocate, Marilyn McCormick and artist and cultural dramaturg, Amara Brady: "How do we take the idea of love, true love, the self-examination and use it to make our theatre and our society more equitable?" Dominique answered. "That's the theatre I want to be a part of." She continued: To love is to learn, to listen, to understand I am not the expert. I am not the authority on that experience, and therefore I have to serve you, not the other way around.

Love is the most significant power in the universe. It is this power that creates a shift in our lives, our work, and our students. When we teach our students to learn the full scope of everyone's human experiences, their minds will expand. The expansion will reach beyond the classroom and move into the world with kindness, generosity, love, and respect. The culture of collaboration will become the norm.

Scenarios for Discussion

Scenario 1: A harmful demand by the producer

You are the director of a show involving animals. The team has carefully thought about the design and style of the show. The goal was to ensure the production would not be culturally insensitive. For this reason, the creative team was in agreement not to design a literal world. The costumes would incorporate strips of fabric to simulate the movement of the animal. Gorilla costumes were not a part of the design; instead, tribal markings on the actors' faces represented the makeup concept. The lead actress is Black, playing the role of a female gorilla.

A problem arose when the producer became insensitive and requested that a literal prop, a gorilla doll, be carried by the Black leading actress. The director, who was also Black, felt that the prop was culturally insulting and refused to put it into the production. The producer became very angry, insisted that the prop be used – and then stormed out of the rehearsal room.

1. What should the director do? Do you stand your ground? Do you quit? Do you concede?
2. How does this affect the relationship between the director and the producer?
3. Which guiding principles of collaboration would you use to resolve the problem.?

Scenario 2: Perpetuating stereotypes

It is the week before technical rehearsals for *Sonnets for an Old Century*, I asked John how he sees Character "X" – what he might wear, his outer appearance. The character talks about killing people and says he would do it again. I said, I see him in a hoodie and chains. I immediately went to a gangster stereotype, but John said, "I don't feel comfortable wearing something that perpetuates the stereotype." I back-pedaled and said, "Of course not. What do you want to wear?" But the damage was done. This micro aggression and obliviousness to rushing to a stereotype had clearly severed trust. X's last line is, "Don't none of you think I'm gonna change."

It was not the first time John had been cast and a director's choice had gone towards a cliché. For him, this was years of being limited and the character he was cast as being seen as one-dimensional.

Questions

1. If you were John, what would you do?
2. If you were the director, what would you do?

Notes

1   Lumen Cultural Anthropology. "What is Culture?" Accessed January 10, 2020 from   https://courses.lumenlearning.com/culturalanthropology/chapter/what-is-culture/#:~:text=Culture%20is%20the%20patterns%20of,a%20nation%20or%20time%20period.
2   Kecia Lewis, interview with Rufus Bonds Jr, December 10, 2020.
3   Kecia Lewis, interview with Rufus Bonds Jr, December 10, 2020.

7
Including Students in the Collaborative Process

By this point, we hope it is clear that the principles of collaboration apply to any field or situation where people must work together towards a common goal – which is pretty much everywhere, including, of course, the academic environment. However, the academic environment presents challenges that have no equivalent in the professional theatre. These focus on the students and the educator's educational obligation to train them to become successful collaborators. In professional collaboration, there already exists an understanding that everyone is an equally valued and necessary collaborator. For the student entering a university program, however, the confidence from believing you are necessary and valued is not something that comes naturally, and must be encouraged, nurtured, and reinforced before they can truly participate as collaborative equals.

In this chapter, we will look at the educational institution's responsibility to its students, as well as ways to empower students to engage fully and collaboratively in their theatre training and education.

Understanding an Institution's Vision and Mission

Vision: "the act or power of anticipating that which will or may come to be."

– Dictionary.com

Where there is no vision, the people perish.

– Proverbs 29

Vision is everything. It guides us. It helps us set priorities and make choices. It is an essential component of leadership. It is vitally important in professional fields such as politics, religion and, of course, the arts.

DOI: 10.4324/9780367810252-8

The professional not-for-profit theatre is structured around vision, or mission, in relation to the theatre's place in its community as conceived by its artists. Every professional theatre has a unique mission statement, and has at its helm an artistic director, producing artistic director, or an equivalent, charged by a board of directors with fulfilling that mission. Every piece of work produced in a theatre *should* be measured against its ability to fulfill the institutional mission.

Good mission and vision statements make it clear to those both inside and outside of the institution why the institution exists, what its goals are, and what values it pursues. These become guiding principles by which the institution determines its priorities, specific actions and decisions, and assesses its failures and successes. It says to the world, "This is who we are and what we strive to achieve through our programs."

Academic institutions are also mission driven, as are the departments that populate the academic community. At the heart of most department and academic missions is the student. Frankly, we wouldn't exist without them, and for many of us who teach at these institutions, they provide the primary sense of joy and satisfaction that keeps us returning year after year. Every course we offer, every curriculum we develop, must therefore focus on the student: their education, their development as people and artists, and their preparation to become productive contributors to the "real world."

Understanding and adhering to the program's mission and vision are fundamental to faculty and students' successful collaboration within that environment. If you have found a home where you feel you can thrive, the chances of your collaborations thriving are great. If, however, your vision of theatre doesn't align with a department's mission – if, for example, you're looking for a great professional training program, but the department's mission is to produce scholars – you will probably be better off looking for a program whose mission is more closely aligned with yours. Once you've found a "home," you will still have to navigate other challenges in order to get the most out of your education. For the student, the most daunting of these can be the dynamics of power.

Academic Theatre Power Dynamics

The most challenging obstacle to successful collaboration for students is the inherent imbalance of power that exists between them and the faculty who teach, guide, and mentor them. A student director is not going to feel comfortable exercising power in a production meeting populated by faculty and staff. A student cast in a rehearsal room with a faculty director may find it hard to express themselves freely, both from a desire to please and a determination not to rock the boat. It thus becomes essential for those with power to develop collaborative skills that empower those with whom they work with to do their best work. Before we look at ways to accomplish this, let's first look at power and think about how it works.

We've all been told that "power corrupts, and absolute power corrupts absolutely," but what we must understand is that power is *essential* if we're ever going to accomplish anything. Rather than approaching power with a sense of mistrust, we need to understand it as an essential tool that, when exercised by ourselves *and* others, can lead to the best collaboratively created productions.

Power is the ability to do or act, the capability to do or accomplish something. In the collaborative milieu of the theatre, we all need the "ability to act" and we all must exercise authority or influence over others. In the academic environment, educators and directors must possess some level of control or command over students. Without the *necessary* exercise of power, a collaborative enterprise will lack cohesion, focus, and a singularity of purpose. Without these, it is impossible for collaboration to succeed.

To understand why, we must remind ourselves that with great power comes great responsibility. The converse is also true: responsibility *needs* power in order to meet the responsibility. Look at the response to COVID-19: if the CDC has the responsibility to protect us from disease, but doesn't have the funding or support of the executive to research and prepare, it will fail in its response to a new biological threat. The response of the United States to the pandemic was initially a huge failure, in part because those with the most ability and resources to deal with COVID-19 were not given the power to do so. In the academic environment, teachers have a responsibility to educate their students. To do this, they are given great freedom in determining how and what they teach. They are also in control of the discipline within their classroom and are allowed to establish rules for classroom conduct and the power to enforce those rules. In a university setting, the rehearsal room is a classroom, with the director afforded the same responsibilities and powers as in any other classroom.

Effective educators – and this includes those in the rehearsal room – understand that the power they wield can be used to nurture the talents and abilities of their students by *sharing* their power with the students. We call this "empowerment" – the giving of power by a person of authority to another so that they are most able to succeed in fulfilling their responsibilities. Empowerment can mean resources, time, or simply, in the case of actors, permission to take control of their character or role.

Sometimes, responsibility and its subsequent power cannot be shared. Directors, however much they may want to, cannot ultimately share the responsibilities inherent in the execution of their role as director. Professors cannot share the responsibilities of their job with students. At the end of the day, directors and educators are held responsible for their performance in ways that students cannot be, and are accountable in ways from which those with whom they work are exempt.

Students can understandably see themselves as powerless within the academic structure, but the student must overcome these attendant insecurities if they are to participate fully in the theatrical collaboration – *and the educators must empower them to do so*. It must be noted, however, that students are *not* without power. Their significant power comes from holding faculty and staff accountable for fulfilling their responsibilities to educate and support. Taking possession of this power can become very challenging for the student who is concerned about grades or standing within the program, and who doesn't yet have the skills, knowledge, or expertise to execute their responsibilities to the standards set by the department and/or director. However, the student can work with their faculty to overcome this by focusing on what the student needs to successfully fulfil their role(s) and communicating it to their faculty.

In the academic theatre environment, you will find a certain rigidity in the power dynamics that doesn't exist in the professional world – or at least not to this degree. Within such a rigid power structure, then, how is it even possible to create a collaborative experience for all those involved? Not surprisingly, the best strategies can be derived from the principles of collaboration, so let's look at them in relationship to power. We're going to take them in a somewhat different order, in part because of the nature of the academic environment.

Let's begin with "pursue a clear, unified vision". We start here because it places the focus on the work, and keeping the focus on the work is one of the best ways to develop and practice the other principles of collaboration. A clear, exciting vision – whether put forth by the director or created by the team – can keep everyone motivated to give their best and to avoid the smaller, often petty, tensions that can derail a collaborative effort.

Next, "encourage generosity in yourself and others" – and make sure that you extend that generosity to *everyone*, regardless of status. Generosity will ultimately make it easier for all collaborators to "practice trust, respect and inclusivity." When power is shared by faculty, it inherently says to the student, "I trust you and I respect your abilities." If trust fails, the failure can become an essential teaching moment – as well as giving faculty the chance to practice what we always preach: you learn more from your failures than you do your successes.

In an ideal world, trust is given from the beginning – and that makes it easier on *everyone*. When trust is initially withheld, for whatever reason, it will have to be earned – and there is no easy way to do this, other than to focus on the work and do the best work you possibly can. You develop trust by coming prepared, listening, respecting others and fully engaging in the ideas of others by trying them. Eventually, if you keep at it and don't give up, you will develop mutual trust.

Gaining trust is one thing; losing it is a whole other problem. When trust is lost, it is important to acknowledge the loss of trust and articulate a path back to trust so that the offender has a clear path to restoring trust. Everyone must work through it *together*. The times when trust should irrevocably be withdrawn should be very, very rare, and be set aside for only the most grievous of sins. The key thought is that *you must always allow for a path for trust to be attained and/or restored. Collaboration cannot happen without it.*

Author Sidebar (Mark)

I learned my rehearsal process from two great directors: Lifetime Tony Award recipient Marshall W. Mason and the legendary Anne Bogart. Marshall – and the company of artists with whom he collaborated at Circle Rep – taught me the value of process over product. Anne, for whom I was the associate director on the original production of Paula Vogel's *The Baltimore Waltz*, taught me a specific process that encourages collaboration in the rehearsal room. I've used what I learned from these two my entire professional and educational career, and what has surprised me is that it has worked just as well with students as it has with seasoned professionals at the top of their game. So I can honestly say that my process at CSU Fullerton is no different than my process at Circle Rep or any other professional theatre where I have worked. This process demands collaborative participation from all of the actors in the room – including those with only a line or two – and the results have always been gratifying.

There are, of course, as many different processes as there are directors, but the main point here is to encourage faculty directors to develop a process that treats students as active participants and collaborators. With time at a premium, too often we focus on the product – the end result – but after working for many years in summer theatre with its *greatly* abbreviated rehearsal periods, I can attest to the fact that a good process provides a stronger foundation for a more rewarding product than rushing to get something on its feet before the actors are ready.

We have left the hardest part for last: "maintain constant and open communication." This is hard because everyone is so busy and their focus is so divided that it is very easy for even *huge* elements to fall through the cracks. *Maintaining* good communication begins with *developing* systems of communication that work. If they already exist within your department or program, then you are 90 per cent of the way there; if not, then it is important to establish a clear system of communication as early as possible. It is not enough to have the system in place. *Everyone* on the collaborative team – students, faculty, staff, and guest artists – must understand how to use the system and, just as importantly, understand their responsibility to engage in the system on a regular basis. You can have the best rehearsal notes in the world, but if no one reads them, they will be useless. Failures of communication will inevitably occur; when they do, it is important to first find out why the failure happened and then take steps to fix it. Generosity comes into play here by treating the person responsible for the failure with respect. Hold them responsible, yes, but do so with the respect that everyone on the team deserves.

Some Thoughts for Students on Navigating Power Dynamics in the Academic Environment

- Remember that you are in college to learn from people whose experience exceeds yours. You may have a better grasp on the latest cultural innovations – what's new and hot and exciting – but you do not have as much experience as they do. That experience can guide you to quicker, better ways to solve problems, so practice generosity and keep an open mind, even when your instincts tell you otherwise.
- Many students arrive at university theatre programs with a healthy sense of accomplishment, but don't let that fool you into believing that

you've "arrived." You may believe that you're already a "great" actor, designer or director, but one of life's great lessons is that learning never stops and without a sense of curiosity about how the world works, you cannot grow. Curiosity is one of the best ways to cultivate a true collaborative relationship with your professors. We all love to work with students who are curious because, to be quite honest, we learn the most from them.

- *You* have power – and, like everyone with power, you can use it wisely *and* you can abuse it. Strive to use it wisely by honoring truth, listening, and refusing to jump to assumptions that are unproven.
- Throughout your professional career, you will *always* be intimidated by someone in the room who you perceive as having more power than you do. Use your time when you are working with faculty to learn how to navigate that dynamic in a way that empowers you. Never be shy about asking for what you need. Listen carefully to what is being said. Earn trust through meeting your responsibilities to the best of your abilities.
- Put the principles of collaboration to work for you. With them, you will earn the trust of your artistic team, including faculty. The more faculty trusts you, the more power, responsibility, and opportunities they will give you, and the better prepared you will be to enter the professional world.

Practicing with a net

Students have three tendencies that can hamper their ability to effectively participate in true collaboration: a desire to please the director, a view of rehearsal as a place to "get it right," and an absolute fear of failure. All are actually counterproductive to full participation by the student in the collaborative process, and all three are closely related. Your director/educator can go a long way towards helping you mitigate these tendencies, but the hard work of taming these tendencies is yours.

The tendency to please the director is rooted in the basic actor-to-director question, "What do you want me to do?" What is absolutely true is that you will never get the best performance from an actor – professional or student – if that question is at the forefront of their mind. The director therefore needs to shift the student's focus from "What do you, the director, want?" to "What do I, the character, need?" The director can do that by asking questions *and* not providing answers. During rehearsals for the original production of *The*

Baltimore Waltz, whenever an actor would ask Paula Vogel, the author, a question, she would invariably answer, "I don't know – what do you think?" This said to the actors, "I recognize you as a collaborator in this process, and you need to stop looking to me for answers and step up to the participatory plate." Students can become full collaborators when they learn how to ask themselves questions that prompt them to possible choices that they can bring into the rehearsal. A basic question for the actor is always, "What do I want?" The next step is to ask, "What are the options?" The answers to this second question can be brought into rehearsals, where the next step is to try them. This process keeps you from waiting for someone to tell you what to do and frees you to participate fully in the collaborative process.

Which leads us to our second problematic tendency: the tendency to want to get it "right." This tendency is particularly dangerous to collaboration because it shuts the student off from the others who share the stage with them. In trying to get it "right," the student focuses on their own role and not on the collaboration with the other actors on the creation of an event. Remember that theatre is an art, and in art there is no "right or wrong" – there are only effective choices and ineffective choices, and it takes trial and error – experimentation – to *discover* the most effective choice. There is no such thing as a mistake, which allows us to take the damaging impact of "that was wrong" and turn it into "that was a choice that didn't work; let's look for a better one."

We should stress that there is a difference between a technical mistake – a mispronunciation of a word, an unmotivated cross, a wrong note – and trying a new choice. In a professional environment, the actors have the skill and confidence to execute a choice that students do not yet possess. There is absolutely a period of time where the fundamental skills need to be stressed and enforced. As we are fond of saying, "Learn the rules – and then you can break them." However, there is always a balance that we are striving to achieve as educators – the balance between support and freedom. Support without freedom leads to a breakdown in collaboration, where the actor looks to the director for all the answers and brings nothing to the table; freedom without support leads to a lot of wasted time that can demoralize the student actor and sap their desire to collaborate.

Finally, there is the fear of failure. This is a fear we all know well because we never fully conquer it. Every actor will tell you that they live in constant fear of someone discovering they have no idea what they are doing – even when they really *do* know what they are doing. The insecurities never completely go away. The same is true with directors and educators, and just about everyone whose success and personal identity are tied up in each other.

Ironically, we stress the value of failure without ever really providing a safe space for it. "We learn more from our failures than our successes" is a meaningless and trite maxim if we don't truly allow room for it.

And what better arena to provide a safe space for artistic failure than the academic theatre program? In fact, it may be the *only* place outside of a professional lab situation where an artist *can* freely fail. Make no mistake: failure is not a goal, and for *all* of us who have experienced it, it's not fun, but without the *freedom* to fail, true collaboration is not possible. The fear will always keep someone from sharing or trying an idea, to the detriment of the entire company.

The only way we can address the fear of failure in the academic environment is to place a premium on experimentation and to eliminate judgment. We can learn to couch our judgments in terms that are not personal, but rather focused on the choice, encouraging growth and building on what is learned from a failed choice.

Author Sidebar (Mark)

I was once brought in to take over the direction of a play at the beginning of technical rehearsals because the director had a family emergency that took him out for the remainder of the tech/preview period. The cast contained some of the finest actors I've ever had the privilege of working with: Academy Award-winner William Hurt, theatre and film veteran Lois Smith, and then-unknowns Calista Flockhart and Melissa Joan Hart. At the first rehearsal I attended, William (Bill) immediately pulled me aside and asked me to give the cast the opportunity to try different choices. The director had tried to lock in choices at the very beginning of the rehearsal period. Bill said to me, "We are good actors and our initial instincts are almost always right, but we need the chance to try the wrong choices so that we have confidence in the choices we instinctually made." This was an eye-opener for me, and from that point on I instituted a rule: we try *every* idea. In the theatre, you don't really know if an idea works until you try it.

At the end of the day, even with their differences, academic theatre departments and professional theatres want the same result: the most exciting, engaging, fully realized production that resources allow. In both cases, this is made much easier when there is a clear vision – *and* when the focus is always on the work.

Scenarios for Discussion

Scenario 1: A question of generosity – *The Play About the Cat*

Generosity is the willingness to listen to and consider all ideas and, when the time comes, to embrace the consensus decision as fully as you would if it were your own idea and choice. As you read this scenario and discover the challenges it contains, think about root causes, power dynamics, opportunities for problem-solving, and possible outcomes.

Cast

The director (Cheryl): A second year graduate student directing her first mainstage production with full design and technical support.

The mentor (me, Mark): An associate professor at the university on my way to tenure.

The production manager (James): A full, tenured professor who has been head of production for several years; also teaches scenic design. He also sits on the department's Play Selection Committee.

The chorus: We'll call the rest of the production team the chorus. It consists of a team of student designers and student heads of technical areas, along with their mentors.

Not in attendance: the department chair, Saundra, who is also the department's producer.

The play, which we'll call *The Play About the Cat*, or "P-Cat" for short, was chosen in the middle of the previous academic year. By the first full production meeting, the set has been designed, the play has been cast, and the director is about ready to go into rehearsals. What is important for you to know is that the ending of the play involves the appearance of a live cat on stage, which comes into the room of its own accord and engages with the lone actor on stage. Since it is the end of the play, it is one of the most important moments, essential to the story. Essentially, the playwright has created a challenge – a problem, if you will – that the team must solve. Why a playwright would make such a choice – an essential cameo appearance by a cat (not known for their willingness to cooperate under the best of circumstances) – is a topic for an entirely separate chapter, but the point is that the producing organization, by deciding to program the play, has embraced the challenge as something that *should* be able to be accomplished within the resources of the department. The director, aware of this challenge, has located the cat and secured its services. (Note that in a professional situation, this would *not* be the responsibility of the director, but would be delegated by the production manager.)

At this first production meeting, which I am attending as the mentor for the director, the conversation turns to the cat – which seems to throw James (the production manager) for a loop. He seems to be unaware of the need for a cat, and it quickly becomes apparent that James has never read the play – even though he sat on the Play Selection Committee. It also becomes clear that he hates the idea of the cat and begins to throw roadblocks at the director: university policy won't allow it, it will take too much time to get permissions, have you thought about who is going to take care of it and where it will live between shows?

From that point on, every production meeting (held weekly) devolved into a discussion about the cat. Each week, James (occasionally with the support of other staff members) would throw a new challenge at the director. Each week, I would advise the director to investigate the challenge (which sometimes proved factually incorrect – the university had no policy that would prohibit us from having a cat on stage, for example) and bring back the information. Each week, she would answer the challenge with a solution and a new challenge would be thrown back at her by James.

Finally, about a week before the production was to go into tech rehearsals, I walked into the production meeting and there, sitting on the table, was a toy cat that, when activated, meowed and wagged its tail. "What's this?" I asked. James replied, "It's our solution to the cat situation." "Are you kidding me?" I asked back. I looked at the director: "Did you know about this? Did you approve?" "No," she said. This, for me, was the last straw.

I will stop here, except to say that we wound up with a live cat on stage for the production. The cat survived the four weeks of performances, no one got rabies, and the show got its ending.

In thinking about the above scenario – and how to work towards a more collaborative process in the future – it can be very helpful to think about and discuss these questions:

1. Do you see any of the principles of good collaboration at work in this scenario?
2. Which of the principles of good collaboration were violated – and at which point(s) along the way?
3. Where did the collaboration get off track?
4. What reasons could the director have had for insisting on the cat? What reasons could the production manager have had for not wanting the cat in the show? What role should I, the mentor, have played? Is there a point where I should have intervened? Was it my place to intervene? Was there anyone else who should have been involved in the decision-making process?
5. How do you think we arrived at the final consensus – to allow the cat to appear on stage? Do you think we were able to reach consensus?
6. What actions could have been taken to resolve the conflict earlier in the process?
7. What would you have done differently to resolve the conflict in your favor had you been the director? The production manager? The mentor?
8. How and when could generosity have come into play in this scenario?

Scenario 2: Communication is a two-way street, not a dead end –*Lysistrata*

Cast

The director (Chris): A full time professor with tenure.
The production manager (Amanda): A graduate student in stage management
Assistant technical director (Aaron): a new hire to the program.
Amy: A student designer

The rest of the individuals are student designers, their mentors and production staff.

It is the first official production meeting in the Fall semester for *Lysistrata*, the musical. Chris, the director, is handing out Greek cookies to the team as he shares his vision for the story. Chris is very passionate about the project. In the corner of his eye, he sees one of the staff members, Aaron, roll his eyes and, in agreement, one of the student designers starts to giggle. Although annoyed, Chris ignores this and finishes his concept speech. Aaron is not fully attentive, but the student is still distracted from his previous commentary.

"So, if you have more questions you can reach out and I can elaborate more. I can see some of you are not following, but the goal is to bring in old Greek traditions, dance music, and folklore into the piece." One of the student designers, Amy, raises her hand and asks whether there will be consumables on stage since he brought cookies today. Chris laughs and says the cookies were to bring everyone together – to break bread together in a way. To connect. He also tells Amy he supports the idea if there is money in the budget should he decide to add food. After all, it is an important ritual and that is part of the culture. Amy is in agreement.

Meanwhile, Aaron, the new guy who rolled his eyes, is texting. Chris does not know this staff member, so he says, "Excuse me, I apologize that we didn't go around and introduce ourselves. I don't even know your name. That was my fault. Let's do that now and include preferred pronouns. I got right into sharing my vision and forgot." The team does so and we learn that Aaron was recently hired in the second week of school. He is the assistant technical director and will be taking over on this production to relieve the load of the technical director, who is overworked.

After learning everyone's name, Aaron says, "I don't see half of what you're talking about on the ground plans. Is this the updated ground plans?" Chris replies, "This is still only the first production meeting; we are still developing the set design and our guest designer is still out of the country and will be back next week."

Aaron replies, "I can't do my work unless it's on paper. When did you plan on telling me? What this is? I mean, we need facts. On paper." Chris asks whether we can table this until after the meeting, as we have a few more people to hear from, where we do have information to share. Aaron huffs and pushes his chair away from the table. The rest of the designers share their progress, there is laughter and collaboration. As the meeting ends, Aaron storms out of the room. Chris, calls out, "Aaron, we will get that ground plan to you as soon as we can." Aaron returns and says, "If you're meeting, I suggest you include me on that meeting. I need to know what you're thinking to even let you know if it's possible."

Chris decided to let it go and not address Aaron's wish to attend design meetings. He is a year from retiring and hoped he wouldn't have to work with this new staff member ever again.

However, the following year a similar event happens. Chris has to fill in on a production whose director has taken ill, and finds himself in the same predicament. Aaron, now more confident since he has been there a year, is emboldened to continue to cross the line on expectations and demands. As Chris begins talking about how he is going to approach the change, again Aaron throws shade and starts texting and not listening.

Questions

1. What should Chris do?
2. Do you see any of the principles of good collaboration at work in this scenario?
3. Which of the principles of good collaboration were violated – and at which point(s) along the way?
4. Where did the collaboration get off track?
5. Was the director sensitive to the room or did he give up his power?
6. How do you think this communication breakdown could have been prevented?
7. What actions could have been taken to resolve the conflict earlier in the process?
8. What would you have done differently to resolve the conflict in your favor had you been the director? The new staff member?
9. What are some ways in which communication and professionalism could have improved?

Scenario 3: Exploring culture in context

The demographics in the acting scene study class consist of four White males, two White females, three Latina females and one Black female. Scenes are being chosen and the teacher asks the students to choose scenes and partners from a contemporary American realism scene list. Trying to be sensitive, the teacher asks the Black student, "Do you want to work on August Wilson or maybe Lynn Nottage?" The student answers, "But there are no other Black people in this class." One of the White students chimes in and says, "I would love to work with you if we can find a scene we both like."

Questions

1. How do you think this scenario might make you feel if you were the Black student?
2. How do you think this scenario might make you feel if you were the White student?

3. Should the teacher have singled out the Black student?
4. How might the teacher and the students handle inclusivity in scene selection?
5. What if a White student wanted to play a role written for a Black individual because they wanted to learn what it felt like to step into someone else's shoes?

8
Past, Present, and Future of the Theatre

On March 9 here in Southern California, we closed our doors [Cirque de Soleil]. Now, I have 20 artists in Los Angeles who lost their visas and lost their salaries. They are in hiding because they can't get home to their countries, and now they're hiding out from ICE. They can't work out, they can't train, and Cirque de Soleil is bankrupt. I have seen how team-work manifests really great things. I've seen other artists take these poor artists into their homes to keep them safe, and keep them fed. It's nine months, and they still haven't received a paycheck, and they still can't get home. I'm encouraged, and I have a lot of hope, and the reason why I have hope is because I have seen community.
– Ron Kellum, artistic director, Cirque de Soleil

The need for collaboration exists everywhere in human societies. There is very little that can be accomplished without collaboration. This book is a collaborative effort between three theatre professionals and educators. We each have very different backgrounds and we each come from different places when we think and talk about collaboration. We didn't always agree. In fact, we had a lot of very difficult conversations about much of the content in this book, but we held to a very basic agreement that as authors, we all had to be comfortable with every word in this book. We had to be honest with each other, communicate our concerns, listen to each other, talk with each other, debate with each other – and decide together. There were times where the whole thing could have fallen apart, but we persevered together because we were writing about a topic about which each of us cares deeply and with which we continue to grapple in our professional lives.

We thought we would end this book with a chapter that lets you see how different we are and how our very disparate professional pasts have shaped who we are today, as well as how we see the future of collaboration – and the theatre. These essays are our own voices, without the influence of each other's views or opinions. They are very personal and reflect our individual

DOI: 10.4324/9780367810252-9

passions, struggles, disappointments, and hopes. What is the same is our passion for the theatre, our belief in the principles of collaboration, and our respect for the women and men of all races, ethnicities, sexual orientations, abilities, and genders who devote their lives to making theatre.

Past, Present, and Future: Mark

The past

I began my professional career in New York City in the mid-1980s. I arrived in the city in 1983 as a closeted gay white man with directing degrees from CSU Fullerton (BA) and the University of Texas at Austin (MFA), as well as a one-year apprenticeship at the Asolo Theatre in Sarasota Florida under my belt and an Equity card as a stage manager, which I received working at the Philadelphia Drama Guild.

One of my first experiences as a New York City audience member was Lanford Wilson's *Angels Fall*, directed by Marshall W. Mason at Circle Rep. What I saw was the physical manifestation of what I aspired to: a seamless production in which every element worked together to tell the story. There was magic in this tiny little theatre that seated 160, which transported me from a noisy, busy area of the Village to a quiet church in New Mexico. I had already been exposed to the work of Lanford Wilson, first through a production of *The Gingham Dog* directed by my grad school colleague (who had written Lanford for advice – and received an impressive, and very lengthy reply), and later through my first professional (well, first paid) directing assignment, a production of Lanford's Pulitzer Prize-winning *Talley's Folly*. I had read about the legendary collaboration between Marshall and Lanford – still, I believe, the longest such collaboration in the American theatre – but this was my first time seeing its results in action, and I was mesmerized. I recognized this as the kind of theatre to which I aspired. We all need examples early in our career that help us define what we want to achieve, and Marshall was mine.

A couple of years later, through a wild fluke of coincidences, serendipity, and just plain luck, I wound up at Circle Rep as Marshall's administrative assistant. It was his last year as artistic director of the company, and in the interview I was told there was no room for advancement and that I would have the job for two years maximum. Within the first months – again, through a string of flukes – I was placed in charge of casting(!) and eventually became the company's associate artistic director, the second highest artistic position in the company after artistic director, as well as becoming a member of the company in my own right as a director. I was there for seven years.

Circle Rep was where I cut my theatrical teeth. It was where I learned everything I know about process and collaboration – and I learned it from directors like Marshall, Anne Bogart, and Norman Rene; designers like Kenneth Posner (lighting), Toni-Leslie James (costumes), John Lee Beatty (sets) and John Gromada (sound and music composition); actors like William Hurt, Tony nominee John Dossett, Joe Mantello and Cotter Smith; and playwrights like Craig Lucas, Paula Vogel, and Keith Curran. Most of all, I learned from Tanya Berezin, who became the acting then permanent artistic director of Circle Rep during Marshall's final year. Without her support, my time at Circle would have been very brief and my career path very different. Through everyone at Circle Rep and the Circle Rep Lab, I received the best professional theatre education imaginable. I made a lot of mistakes (many of which horrify me to this day) and cried a lot of tears (literally), but I wouldn't trade it for anything. It made everything else in my life and career possible.

During these seven years (1986–93), I rarely heard or used the word "collaboration"; instead, we practiced it. The structure of the collaboration was fairly typical of the time and what we would call very hierarchical today. What made us unique was our process – a process that Marshall introduced and made a way of life in the company from its inception in the late 1970s. It was an extraordinarily collaborative process, one that treated all four designers as equals, including paying each the same fee – something that was unheard of at the time. It was also one of the first, if not *the* first, theatre companies to designate a company sound designer and make the hiring of a sound designer standard for every production (also unheard of).

At the center of the process were the playwright (we produced primarily world premieres – five a season) and the actors. In a very real sense, they held the power in the company, and everyone, including the director, worked in service to the play/playwright and actors. Directors who didn't embrace this found themselves directing at Circle once – and never again. And on more than one occasion, a director was released in techs with a "thank you, we'll take it from here" by the artistic director when the director became a barrier to collaborative growth (in the eyes of the artistic director).

The collaboration extended past the rehearsal room. We were a *company* of theatre artists (around 40), and part of our mission was to develop plays and develop talent, a responsibility taken very seriously by the company "elders."

During previews (which lasted about three weeks), the artistic director would convene the director, playwright, and company elders at the Lion's Head (a local bar a block away) and discuss how to fix the play and production. (It always needed fixing; there were always notes.) It didn't matter who the director and playwright were, this collaborative approach was a part of the process. I remember one time we were producing *The Destiny of Me*, Larry Kramer's prequel/sequel to *The Normal Heart*, and after an early preview, Marshall, Larry, and Lanford took off to Marshall's apartment, just down Christopher Street, and spent the rest of the night "fixing" the play.) At times, this process could be very intrusive into the collaboration between the director and playwright – and on occasion, it damaged the play (in my opinion) – but on the whole, it made Circle a very exciting, artist-centric place to work.

Play development was at the core of everything we did. Every Friday afternoon, we would read a new play, often with an amazing cast (the first Fall I was there, actors who read included Holly Hunter, Kathy Bates, Richard Thomas, and Dustin Hoffman – it was quite heady); we would follow each reading with a formal discussion of the play that would be followed by a more informal discussion over wine and cheese. We also did eight workshops a year of the most promising new plays – rehearsed readings that were then performed in front of an audience of subscribers, followed by a discussion. (Even our audience participated in the collaborative development of new work!) Lanford held retreats for playwrights twice each year at his home in Sag Harbor, where playwrights and actors would gather to read and discuss work in progress from tiny snippets to full drafts.

We also had a "junior" company called the Lab Company that, during the season, would produce workshop productions (fully rehearsed and mounted) of new plays. This is where I cut my directorial teeth. We were given nothing but encouragement (and a $50 budget), but to a young director in New York with no place to practice his craft, this was heaven – a kind of exciting playground of young playwrights, directors, actors, and designers, many who would go on to become major figures in the theatre and beyond. The workshop of Paula Vogel's *The Baltimore Waltz* was produced in the Lab (directed by Anne Bogart), and eventually led to a full production on our mainstage. Other artists who were part of the lab included director Joe Mantello, author, screenwriter, and film director Peter Hedges, television start Bill Fichtner, and many, many others.

I'm taking all of this time to describe my Circle Rep experience because it is foundational to my understanding of what collaboration is and how it worked. I experienced collaboration as being extremely vital and necessary, creating an energy that resulted in a lot of activity involving hundreds of artists. We fought like crazy and pissed each other off constantly, but we did it in the spirit of pushing ourselves – and everyone else – to reach the highest standards of the profession. It was a remarkable home – one that, sadly, was forced to close a couple of years after I left it. The reasons for its demise are many and very complicated, but at the heart of it – as with many failed enterprises in American life – the cause was overwhelming debt. Those of us who were a part of this extraordinary organization in this extraordinary time still lament its loss. Efforts to start it anew are ongoing and have been implemented in both New York and Los Angeles, but so far nothing has even really begun to replicate the life of this remarkable institution.

The present

Almost 30 years have passed since I left Circle Rep. I've led two theatres as artistic director and served at another as its associate. I've worked as a freelance director, and have taught and directed at universities. And until recently – within the last five years – the collaborative process I learned at Circle Rep has served me well. Today, the present, I find collaboration to be very challenging, and not so much fun as it once was.

What happened? What's different? Writing this book was, for me, a way of exploring these questions – and I'm still working my way through it and probably will continue to do so for the rest of my life. It's a "process." But I do have some thoughts that are informed by my experiences as a director, an artistic leader, and an educator who primarily teaches young directors, and it's part of my obligation in writing this book to share these thoughts with you. Before I do, I want to stress that these are my very personal perspectives, and will not be shared by those of my generation. One of the things I *do* know about the theatre is that everyone's journey is unique, and our successes and failures impact each of us differently. My story – my understanding of my experience – is no different.

I think it's important here to reiterate an observation that was stated early in the book: theatre reflects society. This extends not just to the plays we produce, but the way we produce them. If the society is cohesive, collaboration will be easier; if society is fractured, working together will become harder. This leads me to my first thought about "what's changed": the hierarchical structures that I grew up with have been challenged and are being dismantled. This is not inherently a good or bad thing, but what has resulted – in both the theatre and American society in general – is a lack of faith in leadership and the institutions that are the foundation of our society and art. This is reflected in a crisis of leadership, one that makes it hard to address the problems that face us and produce work that moves us forward. I would go so far as to say that it's almost impossible to lead in America in the current milieu because in our culture, leadership must have the consent of the governed. Successful enterprises of any kind need leadership as much as they need collaboration. Without leadership, you have an unproductive Congress, anemic responses to crises, and a general inability to solve problems.

Without leadership, the focus shifts from the work of the whole to the complaints of the individual. This is my second thought about what's changed: we've migrated from working on something that was greater than us – the theatre company, the production – to a focus on the needs of the individual. We are more protective of ourselves, more vocal about problems without offering solutions, and simply more afraid. We have developed a very dangerous way of thinking: "I can't do my job because *you* have created a bar-rier." For example, I received an email from a student saying, "I'm intimidated by you, so I can't do my best work." This is language that prepares the way for failure, and allows the student – or collaborator – to place *their* failure at the feet of someone else. This further inhibits openness and real communi-cation, which have become harder as we shut out or shut down people who disagree with us. We find ourselves trapped in our own echo chambers. All of this fights against good collaboration practices.

There are, of course, changes that have increased our ability to collaborate at a higher level. These include:

- *More opportunities*. There are so many more opportunities to create theatre in this country than when I first started. More opportunities for work mean more opportunities to collaborate. It is possible, I believe, for a theatre artist to find or create a theatrical home in every city of size in this country. The downside: the pay in most of these venues isn't enough to live on, and financial struggle is a part of everyday life for these companies.
- *Better training*. Actor training in this country is producing actors, dir-ectors, and designers of extraordinary skill. The theatre's greatest resource will always be its artists, so the better trained the artist, the more likely it is that the result of the collaboration will be of high quality.
- *Social awakening*. The Trump era pushed playwrights and theatre com-panies to focus on work that spoke to the current crisis. The American

theatre seems to have made a shift from the personal to the political, and I personally feel this is a positive trend. Political and social causes ignite passions; passionate work is exciting work; and exciting work galvanizes the energies of everyone involved in the collaboration – and beyond.

In balance, I think that immediately prior to the COVID-19 pandemic shutting everything down, theatre was the healthiest I'd ever seen it, and I was very optimistic about the future of the theatre. Broadway was vibrant and producing truly challenging work including *Slave Play*, *Hamilton*, *Hades Town*, *Indecent*, *Sweat* – diverse, cutting-edge work that we are forever lamenting the absence of.

But the pandemic, along with social and political events exacerbated by the pandemic, revealed tremendous divides – not just in our country, but in our theatre and in our academic institutions. I found that we were a deeply unhappy society at a time when there was – and is – so much to celebrate. Now we are our own worst enemies, tearing everything down without regard to what we have that is of true value – and with little or no real vision of what we will replace it with.

The future

This brings me to thinking about the future. Before I head there, I want to spend a bit of time talking about what I believe will never change in the theatre, because this is the bridge from the past and present to the future.

The theatre has been around for 2500 years. It will always be with us, and at its heart it will always be people telling stories about people. It will always be a communal experience. It will always be ephemeral, existing in the *now*.

The need for a live experience – to sit in a space with other people and be moved, inspired, awed by something that illuminates the human condition – will never go away. And people will always have the need to act out these stories in front of other people. To those worried about the theatre (in the broad sense) surviving the pandemic, this is why I have no doubt it will. Yes, specific theatre companies will not survive, but the profession as a whole will always be with us.

The profession will always be difficult, not matter who you are, or how talented you are. Make no mistake, making a living in the theatre is next to impossible *for everyone*. I have known Tony Award winners who haven't been able to get a job *after* winning the award, and very successful artists not having enough money to pay their rent. It is a brutal, hard profession that has broken more hearts than it can heal. There will always be more people who want to participate professionally in it than there will be opportunities.

So, those are the things I believe will never change. What, then, will change? What will the collaborative experience grow into?

I have no idea.

As I head into the last chapter(s) of my life, the future beyond me is both bleak and hopeful. Bleak because we, as a nation and a world, aren't addressing climate change, which threatens our very existence. Bleak because we seem to be becoming more divided, not less – and as such, we can't seem to be able to solve the problems that confront us. Bleak because more and more we are talking to each other less and less. Social media is robbing us of our ability to think for ourselves, to deeply connect with each other, to compromise and work together, to really listen to one another.

Hopeful because we are capable of change. Hopeful because we still believe in the healing power of art and storytelling. Hopeful because we're still curious about the human condition and still have deep-seeded desires to understand. Hopeful because eventually we will realize that we need each other – deeply and profoundly. I was drawn to the theatre because it is one of the few places where we openly acknowledge that we can't accomplish what we need without working together – without collaboration.

So, even though I don't know where we will wind up, I do know that we will get there through working together – through collaboration. And I truly believe that collaboration is always better and more joyful when we practice trust, respect, and inclusivity; communicate freely, openly and honestly; approach our work and colleagues with generosity instead of judgment; and pursue a vision that is larger than any single individual.

Past, Present, and Future: Rufus

The past

Theatre was not accessible to me as a child. Being shy, timid, and overweight, the church was my moral guide and a place where I could communicate by singing what I could not speak. The music and singing became my voice. To sing was to give myself over completely, disappear and become this source of power erupting from inside to fall upon anyone in the reach of the voice. The voice could pull pain from broken spirits and allow them to cry out, release, and breathe. For those moments, I too was free. Free to express all the pain living inside of me that I could not articulate. Free to follow the voice into this parallel world of uncontrolled emotional explosions, and for a few moments I was whole, I was enough, I was. The moral journey, the gift – and I say "gift" because it was nothing I had earned, but my voice – was given to me by God. This space, the church that shaped my life, unknowingly was my training ground for my future in the theatre. My voice would be the key to unlocking doors in places of the world I knew nothing about.

Many teachers in high school tried to convince me to be a music major. My choral instructor, Mr. Robert Thomas, somehow applied to a university for me and I was accepted. I did not pursue a career in music because I felt my voice was meant only to praise God, so I majored in chemistry. Once, while home on spring break, I attended the Ohio State Theatre in Cleveland, Ohio to see *The Wiz*. At the end of the show, I sat in the theatre, unable to move as emotions stirred within my entire being, and I began to cry. It was in that moment I said to myself, "I think I can do that." I would attend the national tour of *Ain't MisBehavin'* at the same theatre a month later. Debra Byrd, a former vocal coach for *American Idol*, was in the show. Ms. Byrd had a gospel choir that would visit my church when I was a little boy. After the show, I went backstage, which was entirely out of character, and asked to see Ms. Byrd. She came out to see me, and I asked her, "How do you do this?" Her reply, "You have to want it more than anything. You must go to New York, and you must be willing to sleep on floors and sometimes not eat." I replied, "Okay."

I graduated from the University of Cincinnati as a chemist and worked for Sherwin Williams, a Cincinnati chemical company. My roommate at the time knew I was miserable as a chemist. He was Donald Lawrence, a renowned composer and artist. He was a musical theatre major at the Cincinnati College Conservatory of Music (CCM). Donald said, "You know you hate chemistry. I am going to teach you two songs, you will audition for the conservatory, and you will get in." I auditioned, and the department head, Worth Gardner, asked me, "Why don't you go to New York?" I told him, "I don't know anything." True to Donald's word, I was accepted, quit my job at Sherwin Williams, and began my theatrical journey.

When I arrived in New York, it was life-changing. My barber in Cleveland gave me his brother's phone number and encouraged me to connect with him. Little did I know it was Chapman Roberts, the four-time Grammy winner and vocal arranger for *Smokey Joe's Café*. Chapman would introduce me to Tony award winner Anne DuQuesnay, Luther Henderson, and George Abbot. The summer before I moved to New York, my dance professor at CCM, James Truitt, of Alvin Ailey, suggested I study at Nate Horne Musical Theatre. Mr. Horne had also danced with the Ailey company. I needed housing, so I reached out to a director I worked with in Cleveland, Mike Malone, at Karamu House Theatre, who allowed me to stay in his brownstone for free while he was away directing for the summer. Relationships are everything! Because of the relationship I fostered with Mike, I was able to move to New York.

Walking in the Village, I happened upon the famous Negro Ensemble Company. I cannot express the sensation that ran through my body. The Negro Ensemble Company, founded by Douglas Turner Ward, Robert Hooks, and Gerald Krone, created a space to promote great plays based on the full human experiences of people of color. It was here that Black actors found a home where they felt supported and free to collaborate and create. Seeing the building let me know my life was moving in the right direction.

I auditioned for William Finn's production of *Romance in Hard Times*. At the callback, the musical director, Ted Sperling, approached me and said, "Let's look over this song. Mr. Finn really likes you – he wrote this for you." Being so green, in my mind, I thought, wrote this for me to do what? After being cast in the show, I understood the gravity of the moment. As a gift, Mr. Finn gave me the handwritten sheet music of that song. In the show, Lillias White taught me the importance of every musical note; Vondie Curtis-Hall showed me the skill of stillness; Cleavant Derricks schooled me on how to make sure no one would take advantage of me; and Ted Sperling and Mr. Finn always treated me with the utmost respect.

The journey continued, presenting unique opportunities from *Joseph and the Amazing Technicolor Dreamcoat* with Donny Osmond, *Once on This Island* with Graciela Daniel, *Rent* with Michael Greif, *Parade* with Hal Prince, *Lion King* with Julie Taymour, *The Color Purple* with Gary Griffin, Carnegie Hall, and *Porgy and Bess*, as Porgy, in London. All these experiences taught me how to become a better artist, leader, and person.

When my son was eight years old, I took him to school one morning before I was leaving to return to a national tour. I realized he was sad. I asked if he wanted to go back to the car, and he said yes. Once we got in the car, he broke down and told me he didn't want me to go. I promised him that after I finished the tour, I would stay home, and I did. For the next nine years, I stayed home to honor my promise to my son and I began to reinvent myself. Lula Elzy and Doug Merk called and asked me to direct for the Muse Machine. I had never directed before, but they assured me I knew the craft and that they were there to support me. Ironically, directing was more a part of my eye and skill set than I realized. I continued to investigate the art of directing. I began to direct at various regional theatres. I decided to pursue a Master of Fine Arts in directing. After I was accepted into a program, Mark Ramont, the head of the directing program, became my guide into the world of imagination, specificity, the art of crafting the story, and always being aware of the audience's eye. This moment would shift me into the next chapter of my life.

The present

Today I have added my voice to a team of professors at Syracuse University. As an assistant professor, it is my mission to usher into our business, exceptional artists committed to honoring humanity. As I stand before class, we agree upon the beauty of our differences and how it is essential to bring them, and their culture, to the work.

This new academic path allows me to support young Black men and women from a place of familiarity. I know the impact of being the only Black student in the class. The students share their challenges, and together we discuss a way forward that is healthy, honorable, and empowering. We acknowledge the academic world, for the Black student is a good reflection of the industry. To support this fact, here is a study by the Asian American Performer Action Coalition 2017/18 data on racial representation on New York City stages.

> The Artistic Directors of twelve Broadway and non-profit theaters are 100% white.
>
> Whose stories are being told? 79.1% of the shows are written by white writers and only 20.8% of all NYC productions were written by BIPOC writers. Who gets to shape the stories? 85.5% of the shows are directed by white directors and 14.4% of all NYC theater productions were directed by BIPOC directors. White directors get to shape New York City's stages the majority of the time. Who gets to direct stories written by BIPOC? On Broadway, 100% of stories written by BIPOC were directed by White directors, and White directors directed 100% of Broadway musicals. White directors also directed stories that took place

in a BIPOC culture but were not necessarily written by a BIPOC writer - such as *Once on This Island*.

BIPOC directors, being given the same opportunities to direct shows written by a White person, did not happen in equal measure. In fact, it happened only 7% of the time and often when the playwright was dead. BIPOC directors were primarily paired only with BIPOC writers, a clear indication that race is primary when directors are first considered for projects.[1]

How is today's theatre different from that of yesterday? Watching an interview with Alvin Ailey, the issues he faced connected to Broadway in the 1960s are the same issues we face today. Yes, there has been movement, but until People of Color are allowed to be gatekeepers – producers, artistic directors, and theatre owners – progress will be slow.

Despite the obstacles, our history teaches us that nothing is impossible with determination, perseverance, knowledge, and the unshakable power from our ancestors.

The future

Theatre tomorrow will not look like theatre of yesterday or today. Today we are in the middle of a shift and a fight for humanity. With the "Me Too" movement, an election year that appears to be a fight between morality and villainy, the world witnessing a man, George Floyd, murdered on TV right before their eyes, and a virus creating a pandemic worldwide, nothing can proceed in the same way. Stories will erupt from men, women, and children's souls, expressing their pain of isolation and the pain living in their bodies from loved ones lost to the virus. Stories of how we made it through as a family, as a people, a nation, as human beings will burst forth. All these stories will find a place to live, and some will find their way to the stage. The question is, who will guide the narrative of the stories? Who will be the gatekeepers? Will spaces emerge for people of all ethnicities? I believe spaces will appear much as they did in the 1960s. Groups will find and build a place to tell their stories. Will Broadway remain the same? Only time will tell.

Many people are encouraged about the future of theatre. The youth's voices are strong, demanding, and determined to join together and create provocative content. Are we in a moment where the current gatekeepers are willing to relinquish power and allow others to be a part of the decision-making?

Or are we in a moment of response, where the producers, artistic directors, theatre owners, and academic institutions react to the moment because they don't want to be called out. Is this a passing moment in time, or will the industry seek to make a systemic change for business and humanity?

Past, Present, and Future: Maria

The past

When I was seven years old, my parents took me to Greece for the summer to visit the homeland of my father, who had not returned to Greece for over ten years. He was more than excited to teach me about the history of my Greek culture and the origins of democracy.

I imagine my seven-year-old self, looking up at the Parthenon at the foot of the Acropolis, and realize this family trip planted the seed of my passion for the theatre, ritual, and storytelling. I vividly remember trying to see The Epidaurus stage, sitting up on my knees on the ancient stone bench seat, in awe, seeking to connect to something bigger. It's in my DNA to belong to the theatre.

One rave review in a semi-professional production while I was still in high school was all it took to solidify my childhood fantasy of someday playing Maria in *The Sound of Music*. Except for one minor thing: I didn't look Austrian.

I worked my way through college performing in melodramas at The Bird Cage Theater (Knott's Berry Farm), the Young Americans Dinner Theatres and a few small national tours. After numerous rejections from Disney, I landed my first Actors' Equity contract with the Bilingual Foundation of the Arts in Los Angeles (thanks to my high school Spanish teacher, Mrs. Lopez-Garcia, who insisted on perfect pronunciation), where I toured and performed in a Theatre for Young Audiences (TYA) tour for about a year.

I caught the interest of agents in Los Angeles but I confused them. "You're ethnic. I'm not sure what to do with you"; "Can you lose 20 pounds and straighten your hair? You need a bikini body for television"; "Can you wasp it up?" I was 5 foot 3 and 125 pounds, curvy with big (1980s) dark, frizzy, curly hair (pre-hair products) – any Greek Yiayia would have called me a healthy young woman with child bearing hips, but I was not quite the Hollywood type.

Los Angeles agents would take me on and send me out on Spanish-speaking auditions, and I would consistently remind them I was not fluent in Spanish and there were plenty of actresses who were. I went through many agents during these days, who just didn't get me.

After two degrees in theatre, and a few prominent regional leads playing Maria in *West Side Story*, I moved to New York City in my late twenties following graduate school. I established a creative home at HB Studios after studying with Uta Hagen during my time at the University of California, Irvine in their New York City satellite training program. My husband was invited to participate in the Lehman Engle BMI Composers Workshop in New York, so start spreading the news: we moved to New York City at 29. I visualized myself with a spring in my step, walking down Broadway in my Broadway show jacket. We were on our way to living the dream.

Before long, I became Ms. Hagen's key student at HB Studios, where I eventually was given my own class and began my teaching career. As I continued to audition in New York City, I could see that the mindset about my ethnicity was not as much of a barrier in New York, but my singing voice didn't quite match my look. I was a soprano in a belter's body, so to speak. Unbeknownst to me, sopranos in musicals were blue-eyed, tall and blonde, all of which I am not. (This was before Audra McDonald opened their minds.)

New York agents freelanced with me. They took me on and put me out there to see how I did. I auditioned, I got called back for Broadway shows for ten years. I worked on soap operas, I got another TYA tour, this time on the east coast, and taught acting and acting for musical theatre at HB Studios and later at Weist Baron Television School and AMDA in New York.

Ms. Hagen told me more than once, "You're not a cookie cutter of what they want. You're unique. Create your own work." So I began writing because I always wrote, but I was a closet writer. My first venture out of the playwright's closet was with *Mommy Monologues*, tales of motherhood and identity crisis. Let's just say I went back into the playwright's closet for about another decade.

At 36, I had a few television credits, still no show jacket, and a toddler running wild in a two-bedroom apartment in New York City. My husband was working on Broadway in music preparation with big names and playing in the pits, in and out of town. As I got closer to turning 40, I came to the conclusion that the reality of my Broadway dream was not happening but the dream of being a mother, a teaching artist, and a storyteller was. I looked inward.

I realized I came alive collaborating with students in the classroom when I was teaching. I was passionate, articulate, and more myself there than anywhere. I found solutions to actors' problems in rehearsals, which led to developing guidelines for students on how to rehearse independently. I delighted in the students' progress and their successes.

Sam Groom, a well-known New York actor, taught his class at HB Studios after my class, and one of the guidelines was left behind. He stopped me after my class and asked, "Where did you get this?" I told him I created it. He asked if he could steal it and I said, "Of course!" Weeks later, he encouraged me to continue to develop this process as it was an area in training that had not been addressed.

Then 9/11 happened. Disasters have a way of taking the blinders off and making you really see what is important. I realized I didn't know who I was post Broadway dream or what I had to contribute to the theatre, which was still very important to me.

Collaborating with students and acting in readings of original works at HB Playwrights filled my artistic spirit. I loved the acting process, and my valid-ation came from the meaningful work, not who signed my paycheck.

On one my first trips back to New York City after doing a well-known tele-vision show, one of the wives of my husband's collaborators congratulated me and said, "Wow. *Desperate Housewives*. That's got to validate you." I took pause. Then the bells went off. Wait. What? Is she saying that my validation comes from the shows I've done? No. No, it doesn't. Does it? Show business doesn't define me. It's one of the things I do. One of the many things I do and care about, but it doesn't define who I am. My validation doesn't depend on Broadway. If it did, I would be nothing. My life defines me. My good work defines me. My bad-ass creative work-ethic defines me. I realized I had put my self-worth in the hands of others – and others who I had no reason to trust – and not my own. This was huge.

Sometimes we love people who don't love us back and we stay in that rela-tionship for whatever reason we justify in our heads. I was in a co-dependent love affair with Broadway, which was making me pick up the tab at every audition. It cost me every time I put myself out there because I stopped loving it. For what? To be part of a cool club (the show jacket club), a paycheck or to do meaningful work? I was already doing meaningful work. It was time to start caring for myself and get into a healthier relationship with Broadway and with showbusiness in general.

As we've said in this book, sometimes you learn more from your failures than your successes. I don't look at my New York experience as a failure because those particular stars didn't align. Broadway just wasn't my mate. We weren't a match. I am a better teacher because of those challenging successful ten years in New York. The tenacity, the grit it taught me enable me to fight every day to get up and do something I love no matter how hard it is; that is worth every disappointment because I am who I am today because of it. And once I stopped loving it, I stopped. We broke up, amenably, and today I flirt with her every now and then – sing a few show tunes, maybe do a show – for the joy of it and not for the show jacket.

Ms. Hagen recommended me to teach acting to the UCI, NY satellite program, the very program that got me to New York. At the end of the last session, I went into labor and headed straight to St. Luke's Roosevelt to deliver my baby boy. Don't let anyone tell you that you can't have everything. You can certainly try, and most of the time it turns out better than you ever imagined.

For this California girl, our 900 square foot apartment with the reverberating C train under our feet, a toddler who was bouncing off the walls and pigeon crap on the air conditioner outside our baby's window was just as much of the New York dream as we needed. My husband could work anywhere because he was traveling everywhere, opening original Broadway shows with the current Broadway Show Company's music departments. After a decade in New York City, we sold our beautiful apartment on Central Park West, and with dog, kid, and husband, I left in search of sunshine and space. We were on our way back to California.

Before we left New York City, I booked an adjunct teaching job and one job led to another. Before long, I was living on the California freeways teaching from Pasadena to Azusa to Long Beach out of my purple PT Cruiser.

One night, I had dinner with a friend in Hollywood who was working on our friend's new pilot for ABC and he said, "You must audition for this. You're perfect for it." I hadn't come to Los Angeles to try television *again* but you never say *no* when you're offered an audition for a new pilot. I hadn't even snagged an agent yet. In short, I went to audition for the producers for a role in *Desperate Housewives* that was written for someone else. Marc Cherry, the show's creator, called me to say they went with the actor he had written the role for, but the director and the producers loved my work and that if the show got picked up, he would have me on as a recurring character. He kept his promise. I was on almost every season as the recurring nosy neighbor, Mona Clark, with a pivotal role in Season 7. I found an agent who finally got me, and with whom I am still working today.

I heeded Sam Groom's advice from my HB days and finally put those rehearsal guidelines on paper after finessing them with students for many years. When I received my first sabbatical, I completed my first book, *Rehearsing in the Zone: A Practical Guide for Rehearsing Without a Director*,[2] which is currently adopted by a few prominent universities.

I am inspired by my students every day to grow and learn with them. There is never a dull moment. I heard my mentor's voice and continued to write. In 2020, my first full length play, *Women of Zalongo*, received semi-finalist placement at the Bay Area Playwrights Festival and is currently in a development workshop with professional actors. I guess I finally came out of the closet as a playwright.

My collaborations have allowed me to wear many hats. You may have heard the quote "Jack of all trades, master of none", but the full quote is actually, "A jack of all trades is a master of none, but oftentimes better than a master of one." Not getting what I initially wanted meant I had to dig deep to find my authentic path as an artist, and I'm still chipping away. Beside me is my seven-year-old self, sitting up on her knees on the ancient stone seat on the Acropolis, in awe, always seeking to connect to something bigger.

Our world now

It has been a year since the Ides of March of 2020, when every theatre closed across the country due to the pandemic. Broadway was shut down for the first time since the September 11 terrorist attacks of 2001. All forms of live entertainment came to a screeching halt.

Education went virtual and stay-at-home orders sent students packing up their dorms and apartments, hugging their friends goodbye and moving back in with their families, to wait the virus out. Scattered across the country, family members suffered the loss of jobs, and extended family moving in. Desperate times caused some students to rethink their future in the theatre.

For students, faculty, and staff who carried on, we did so with insufficient bandwidth. Students struggled those first few months as they squinted into small laptops, trying to find their light, this time not on stage but in closets and far corners of their family's garage, anywhere to get some quiet and privacy so they could concentrate and attempt to learn, albeit virtually.

We found one another in our private spaces rather than in public. We dealt with intervening family members, guest star appearances by pets strolling by computers for a scratch on the back. For the introverted extrovert, *learning from home* was not the end of the world, but it made collaboration in the theatre impossible. Performances and readings all went online, but art was still made and growth still happened. A new tenacity presented itself. We fought through the distractions but the emotional toll on families who lost loved ones and learning new ways of life wore thin. Somehow fighting for a parking spot no longer weighed on students' minds, but one more hour on Zoom seemed an eternity. Social distancing (6 feet apart) and masks in public became the new normal as non-essential businesses and institutions remained closed. To say it changed our way of life is an understatement. This is part one.

Then, the country was hit by a double pandemic. The second pandemic was racism. The racial uprising over the killing of George Floyd, Breonna Taylor, and Ahmaud Arbury paralleled the Civil Rights Movement of the 1960s. George Floyd died before the public's eyes, under the knee of a Minneapolis police officer who later was found guilty on all charges. Images of his killing were displayed on social media for everyone to witness. All over the country, people watched him die in a choke hold, begging for his life. Breonna Taylor was killed in the crossfire by plain-clothed police officers who entered her home in Kentucky on a suspected drug bust. Ahmaud Arbury was hunted down and shot by armed white men while he was jogging in South Georgia. And there are more. Unbeknownst to some people, racism was still very much alive and contaminating our society with a new fervor.

Despite the risk of getting COVID-19, people took to the streets in their masks and marched, 6 feet apart for their Black brothers and sisters. Black Lives Matter led the public outcry for justice and the institutional education on anti-racism began.

If that wasn't enough, events worthy of a Shakespeare tragedy unfolded on January 6, 2021, the day Congress was to certify the votes for the new President Elect Joe Biden and Vice President Elect Kamala Harris. This normally would be a day to celebrate with hope for the future, but instead a riotous mob outnumbered police and desecrated the Capitol in an attempt to overturn the election results. Congress members' lives were threatened and six people died, including an officer trying to protect the Capitol; two others took their own lives shortly after. Days later, Congress voted to impeach President Donald Trump for the second time for inciting violence and encouraging an insurrection. He was acquitted in the Senate on February 13, 2021 by a vote of 57 to 43, just ten votes shy of the required two-thirds majority to convict.

History seems to keep repeating itself in new ways. Meanwhile, only 49 percent of Americans are fully vaccinated even though vaccinations are readily available. Organizations continue to practice social distancing and vaccinated individuals are still required to wear a mask in public. Theatre is resuming slowly with regular mandated testing. It is a new way to connect. To be continued.

So, when do theatres open? You might say that it is irrelevant, given the state of our union as livelihoods diminish and burgeoning careers look uncertain, but someday soon. It is hard to see what their future will hold, but in no way is theatre going anywhere. In some ways, 2020 showed us our north star and how important this pause was in order to make the necessary changes. Now, more than ever, unheard voices have been given the microphone. It is time to turn up the mic and listen to the many untold stories.

There is reassurance in that this is not the first time in our history that plagues and wars have closed our theatre doors. Time will tell how this period of history will impact the life and soul of the theatre. It has asked us to look at who we are and what we stand for, and what theatre can do and what theatre we want to be a part of.

That seed that began growing inside me as a child still grows and longs for a theatre that is collaborative, kind, and generous – one that opens a door, one that may falter but gets up and tries again. A theatre more inclusive of everyone's story because when we listen to each other's stories, we learn about one another and we realize we are cut from the very same cloth, the human one. We practice empathy and compassion, and only then can we truly collaborate.

The future

Theatre has the capacity to give a nation a soul by externalizing what can't be explained. Theatre is and always has been social and, like society, it will perpetually change because humans change. We have learned: artists are resourceful. More content than ever has been created in the last year and multimedia in storytelling is no longer just an extra but part of the experience. Technology has opened up Pandora's box and there is no going back. My hope is that we don't lose who we are in this change and that the story and the humanity of theatre remain central to its focus.

Nearly two months into the pandemic of 2020, I was coaching one of my students to prepare her for her final assessment into the BFA in Acting, an audition that is the culmination of two years of training in order to get to a higher level of professional training in our program. She was preparing a monologue from Tony Kushner's *Angels in America*. Her delicate words somehow felt more resonant because of the bad wi-fi connection we were both trying to overcome. We got kicked off numerous times. We kept reconnecting. "Can you hear me?" she said. "Yes! I can. Keep going," I answered. We knew nothing about our future, let alone the future of the theatre. All we knew was that if we caught this virus, we could die. Morgues were filled to capacity in Italy and the virus was on its way to us. So the best way to deal with the unknown future was just to continue to do the work. It seemed to help.

As she pulled me into her monologue, I remember not being able to form words to give her feedback because Kushner's words said everything that captured the moment and the giant lump in my throat left me speechless:

> But I saw something that only I could see because of my astonishing ability to see such things: Souls were rising, from the earth far below, souls of the dead, of people who had perished, from famine, from war, from the plague ...

And we both froze with one another, deeply connected to something bigger – or maybe it was just the bad wi-fi connection? No, it wasn't. It was us. All of us. We both held one another's focus for a moment in time, connected beyond the bandwidth, where the words of a playwright captured the reality of our nation at that moment in time.

Historical events offer a reset button. Much is still to be learned in moving forward. When we finally reconvene in the theatre someday, let's hope we create from a place of generosity, trust, and equity, and embrace our differences where everyone's story is worth telling and representation matters. If theatre reflects our identity and reveals who we are, as it has from the beginning, we can change the conversation and keep the tragedy on stage not off, so the stories we pass down are of significance to the generations to come.

Collaborating with a host of different people will influence the art you create and in part serve the function of theatre, which is to hold a mirror up to nature – something that is inclusive of everyone. Let us be forever challenged by each other, by holding the bar higher with each production, listening to our collaborators with attention and sensitivity, because before long another house will be filled with hearts that will synchronize to your work and your work will take their breath away. That is the power and the beauty of what we get to do, and we do it together with one unified vision under collaboration with creativity and success for all.

You are the theatre's future, and your collaborations will inform the next generation. Retrospection can provide insight into the soul of the theatre to ensure it remains and progresses with your hopes and dreams. What does your theatre look like, how do you wish to collaborate and what will be your story?

Notes

1 Pun Gandhu and Julieene Hanzelka Kim, The Visibility Report: Racial Representation on NYC Stages 2017–2018. Accessed January 2, 2021 from www.aapacnyc.org/uploads/1/1/9/4/11949532/aapac_report_2017-2018_single.pdf.
2 Maria Cominis Glaudini, *Rehearsing in the Zone: A Practical Guide for Rehearsing Without a Director,* 3rd ed. (Kendall Hunt, Dubuque, IO, 2020).

Appendix 1
To the Educator

The impulse to write this book came, in part, from the frustrations the authors and many of our colleagues were experiencing with collaboration in the academic environment. The three authors came to education from the professional world and we were baffled – and frustrated – by an atmosphere that was too often combative, hostile, uncooperative – in short, anything *but* truly collaborative. We decided to create this appendix to specifically address these concerns in the hope that we might offer you constructive ways to address these challenges so you are able to continue to experience the tremendous joy that *can* come from collaborating with your students, staff, and faculty.

This appendix is geared towards faculty directors, designers and/or mentors who find themselves in positions of leadership that define and/or impact – positively or negatively – the collaborative culture that exists in your department *and* in each production. Much of this book has already addressed collaborating with students, so we will focus here on collaborating with colleagues. The three authors have performed and/or directed professionally and have extensive experience directing in the academic environment. This unquestionably informs our perspective on the issues discussed in this chapter.

Vision and Mission

We want to begin our discussion by expanding on the idea of mission and vision introduced previously, and by asking *Why do people choose to teach and/or work in an academic environment? Why do YOU choose to teach and/or practice your art and craft in an academic environment?* We know from our own experiences that this is a complicated, difficult question, but if you don't have the "education of students" at the top of your list, you will find it very hard – impossible, even – to find happiness in your work or successfully collaborate with anyone. This is not a judgment, and it is not a question with an unchanging answer; however, it *is* a question that must be asked by all of us every now and then – especially when we begin to lose our sense of fulfillment and joy.

The vision of a theatre department is much more complicated than that of a theatre company, for two very good reasons: first, the department's vision encompasses not only the theatre, but the teaching or pedagogy of theatre and its many elements. Second, every faculty member, by virtue of academic freedom, is free to pursue their own particular vision of both theatre and teaching theatre. There is no incentive – other than goodwill and occasionally dynamic leadership – for every faculty member to pursue someone else's vision. In fact, many professors come to academia with an agenda in mind – a determination to instill in their students an understanding of theatre that reflects their own vision, taught in such a way that it reflects their values, including their values of collaboration. If this agenda doesn't align with the department's and/or university's mission, it is time to adjust that agenda, adjust the department's mission, or find a new home where your vision will be appreciated and encouraged.

A faculty member's vision of both theatre and theatre education is greatly influenced by their personal background. Those who have spent their life in academia will often bring a theoretical vision of the theatre grounded in intellectual investigation and discovery. Those who bring professional experience to the program will be greatly influenced by their encounters with the professional world. Those with very successful careers will bring one understanding; those with disappointed careers will bring a very different perspective. One end of the scale is not more valuable than the other; what is important is that you *fit* in whatever end of the spectrum is supported by your department's vision and that it meets your personal needs. If not, the consequences for our students can be very adverse, as explained in this quote by Amara J. Brady, a recent recipient of a BFA:

> Because of the way schools are structured and the way that theatre programs popped up, there are a lot of people teaching there who never wanted to be teachers and then they don't know how to do it. They damage a lot of people and then a lot of people go around as damaged humans, damaged artists who create other damaged artists because their teachers had an ounce of power that they never had in the real world that they now use to manipulate people in their presence.

While this is a very dark and not particularly generous view, it contains some truth and occurs in any program where there are faculty members who have retreated to academia, rather than embraced it. These faculty can teach students in a way that "over-corrects" to compensate for the damage done to them, in turn making their students' chances of success less likely. It also can make them less willing to trust and/or collaborate with those who have had more successful careers.

As anyone who has ever worked professionally in the theatre knows, almost no one walks away unscarred, and you will encounter damaged artists – even hugely successful ones – at every level of the profession. What everyone needs is compassion towards each other. Every faculty member has something of value to teach, and very few of us truly don't want to be here. It is imperative, however, that when the negativities and insecurities begin to emerge, you personally deal with them immediately and swiftly; the longer the wounds are allowed to fester, the more damaging they become to everyone.

Author Sidebar (Mark)

The tension between the academic and professional worlds has been a constant in my life, beginning with my graduate work at the University of Texas. I understand what it is to be a "damaged" theatre practitioner who went into theatre education too soon. In 2000, the board of directors at the Hangar Theatre decided not to renew my contract as artistic director. Essentially, they had determined that they couldn't support my vision of the theatre, and unless you're a founding artistic director, the board wins – rightfully so. Luckily, I was able to pick up a teaching position as director of theatre at Rice University. However, I began the position very disappointed, believing that my professional career was over, and deeply hurt. The dismissal from the Hangar was ugly and not handled well, which left me very angry and more than just a little bitter. Without meaning to, I took it out on my students. It's not that I was a bad teacher or that they didn't learn from me, but for the first year or so I saw myself as a failure with nothing to teach – and *I didn't want to be there*. I worked through it, but my professional failures nagged at me. Towards the end of my fourth year at Rice, Paul Tetreault, a great friend who I had met at Circle Rep and had known for 15 years at that point, gave me the opportunity to return to the professional theatre. He had just been hired as the executive director at Ford's Theatre in Washington, DC and he wanted me – as his first staff hire – to help him manage the artistic side of the theatre. I jumped at the chance, finished the year at Rice and moved to DC where I was at Ford's for seven years. Those seven years allowed me to come to terms with the professional world and helped me realize that teaching is what I really love. This time, when I got hired to head the directing program at CSU Fullerton, I was ready – and *wanting* – to teach, and it has been the best experience of my life. I still am an associate artist at Ford's Theatre and work with them on occasion. And I still keep in touch with a number of students from Rice, who are wonderful – and very forgiving – people; a few even work in the professional and educational theatre 20 years later. This experience, along with others, has taught me that unhappy people tend to make other people unhappy, which is not fair to those around them. However, I also have tremendous compassion for those who, for whatever reasons (usually financial), wind up in academic theatre before they are able to deal with their professional aspirations. Many of them do have much to offer their academic programs, and as long as they are happy, more power to them. But if their wounds and disappointments ever reach the point where they realize they are damaging their students, they really should look for something else. Everyone will be better off.

Let's now assume – for argument's sake – that everyone on your faculty staff put the students first and is happy with where they're at. Let's look at some other considerations that can impact collaboration.

Power Dynamics in Academic Theatre vs Professional Theatre

Power dynamics, as discussed earlier, exist in every situation in life. In the professional theatre, there is a hierarchy based primarily on job titles (producer, director, designers, actors, technicians, etc.). In the academic world, the divisions of power are based more on institutional status and fall into three tiers of authority: on the top tier are faculty (including chair and guest artists); the middle-tier consists of technical staff; and the lowest tier belongs to the students. (For the sake of keeping things simple, we're going to leave administration and the power dynamics between departments and schools out of this discussion – that's a whole other level of power structures that goes beyond the scope of this book.) Each level also has its own power structures: tenured faculty have more power than nontenured, adjunct and guest artists. Staff with longevity will have more power than those who are new. Seniors will have priority over Juniors, Sophomores and Freshmen – and grad students will have more power than the undergraduates.

Faculty have the most power in this structure by virtue of their responsibility to educate their students. Since this is at the core of every academic institution's mission, the responsibility has a real impact on when and how faculty wield their power. Where it can become really tricky is in the power dynamics between faculty members, especially between those who serve an artistic function on a production (director, designer, actor) and those who mentor students. Struggles can erupt over the split goal of putting up a strong product and the education of the students. When the struggle is between a faculty director and a faculty mentor, the traditional power of a director in a professional setting might not hold sway; the faculty mentor with tenure and longevity may very well prevail. A student director becomes very vulnerable when working with a faculty designer or actor, and may need a mentor to step in to compensate for the lack of the student's power. Even a faculty director working with a faculty actor can find directing that actor extremely difficult because of faculty imbalances of power that have nothing to do with the dynamics that would exist in a professional rehearsal room. As you can see, it becomes very, very complicated.

The technical staff derive their power from their responsibility to ensure that productions are mounted on time, within budget, and with the highest quality possible. They also gain power through their hegemony over their specific area of expertise. While faculty will generally work on one show per semester at most, the technical staff will work on every show, which gives them a tremendous amount of power in their area. In this way, they are very much like the technical staff of a professional resident theatre. Artists come and go, but the department heads are forever. This can obviously be tricky for students who rely on staff to help them realize their goals. They may be pushed into decisions that are convenient for the staff, but aren't necessarily going to give the designer the best result. Faculty mentors may need to run interference. Faculty directors and designers may also find that the power they have isn't enough to compensate for a resistant staff member.

Faculty and staff in a university department can often be like a family that has lived together for too long. In the professional environment, artists come together for relatively short periods of time, which often allows them to hold tensions at bay. Once a project is completed, the artists really don't have to work with each other again, and move onto the next team. In an academic department, however, professional relationships can exist – sometimes for decades. Even the healthiest relationships will eventually come under stress, and built-up resentments and old arguments inevitably will surface and make their impact felt in the collaborative process. It is at this point that the focus needs to be returned to the project, and any and all personal disagreements taken outside and directly dealt with by those involved. Left ignored, these tensions will eventually negatively impact the collaborative process for the production – and beyond.

Unfortunately, the longer faculty and staff work with each other, the more chances there are to betray trust. Rebuilding trust is extraordinarily difficult and, depending on those involved, sometimes even impossible. Generosity helps, as does approaching every new project with a fresh eye and a clean slate. This, like so many aspects of collaboration, begins with the individual (i.e. with *you*), although those with the most power (chair, director, senior faculty) have the greatest responsibility to establish and maintain trust as a necessary part of the team's culture.

When Power Dynamics Break Down

Power dynamics are tricky under the best of circumstances, but they can be an absolute minefield in the academic setting. Good collaborations are a mini-version of a society, and societies function best under rules and processes that are maintained and enforced with equanimity and adhered to by all within that society. What happens, then, when someone refuses to play by the rules? The power of the U.S. President power derives from the Constitution and laws of this country, but as we learned with the Trump administration, when one party refuses to play by those rules, chaos can ensue, and trust in the laws and very institutions of the country can become damaged beyond repair. When this happens in a theatrical setting, any hope of a successful collaboration can come crashing down. In the professional world, it is relatively easy to root out those who won't play by the rules: you can simply fire the offending artist, removing them from the "society." Or, if that's considered too drastic, the producer can simply decide not to hire that person again. In the academic world, it is much, much harder. Tenure, longevity, position, and status all make it extremely difficult to remove – or even discipline – anyone who decides they no longer want to play by the rules. As a result, their power can become outsized and extremely damaging to the power structure of the department.

Imbalances such as these can't really be solved at the production level. At best, the production team can try to insulate itself from any toxicity that exists in the department at large, but ultimately it is the department itself that must take the lead in changing an unhealthy culture. Establishing goals and guiding principles by which rules and decisions are made, creating rules to support those principles and then enforcing them are a good start, but ultimately a theatre department is a collaborative body *without*, unfortunately, the same incentives that exist for a production. If negative actions poison the collective well of the collaborative community, they need to be dealt with immediately and with support from departmental and university leadership. Failure to do so may ultimately weaken the resolve of the department to deal with the corrosive environment, at which point it becomes a game of waiting for the negative influence to graduate, leave, or retire.

Hopefully, you will never experience these challenges to the degree that your department becomes a toxic and unpleasant place to work. Be vigilant and keep your eyes open, because it can happen very quickly and take even longer to heal. Keep in mind, though, that the hard work to bring a department back to a collaborative, respectful place ultimately will pay off, most importantly for the students. Toward this end, we have a few thoughts/principles/guidelines to help you avoid the deterioration of an environment before it progresses too far.

For faculty artists (directors, designers, etc.)

- Remember that those who have power don't need to prove it to anyone. This will help you exercise your power wisely and generously.
- Treat everyone with respect and learn forgiveness. Power exercised with mercy and generosity can change lives.
- Don't feel as if you need to know everything or do everything. Leading means learning how to delegate your responsibilities (when possible) and empowering others to do their best. It is *not* "telling everyone what to do."
- Remember that mistakes can provide the best lessons, so use those teaching opportunities to lift students and colleagues to a new level of performance.
- Never be afraid to admit your mistakes. It will increase others' respect for you without diminishing your power in the least.
- Listen to others, not just with your ears, but with your eyes. You can catch a lot of small problems this way and keep them from becoming larger issues.

- Don't let wounds fester, but deal with them quickly. If possible, communicate in person first, over the phone second, and lastly over email. *Never* make the concern public and certainly don't air it on social media. The damage you do will be irreparable.
- Establish expectations and rules of engagement for everyone in the collaborative team; do it as early in the process as possible. It's not a bad idea to review or modify these at each stage of the production (e.g. pre-production, production meetings, rehearsals, tech rehearsals, etc.).
- Take your responsibility to be a good role model seriously. You don't have to be perfect, but you do need to adhere to the rules and principles that you establish or are required by department or university policy.

For the faculty mentor

- Communicate as closely with the director – faculty, guest, or student – as you do your mentee. Don't assume the student will be good at communication; this is part of what they have to learn.
- Remember that you are working in an advisory capacity and treat the artists with primary responsibility, as you would want to them to treat you if you were in their shoes.
- Watch and listen to your mentee carefully when they are in meetings or rehearsals. If possible, wait until afterwards to provide insight, suggestions, etc. Avoid stepping into the fray unless absolutely necessary. There will be times when your mentee may need you to step in and flex *your* power, but that should be a last resort. Jumping in too early may undermine your mentee's authority and damage their ability to function on their own.
- On some level, you need to think of yourself as a parent and the mentee as your child: at a certain point, you can only guide them. They need to make their own mistakes. It may be hard to watch, but they will learn the most from it.
- Remember: it's *never* about you.

For staff

- Provide the same respect to faculty that you want from them. If you feel they don't respect you, take the time to sit down with them (over coffee?) and express how you feel. Don't vent to someone else before first engaging with them.

- Communicate often and never leave faculty out of the loop. If you do, you're sowing the seeds of distrust, which may result in their trying to reassert their power.
- A lot of your power lies in your expertise and knowledge. Rather than using that power to assert your dominance, learn how to share your knowledge and, as a result, your power. This may require a lot of patience, but it will help build trust and respect.
- Never forget that you're all on the same team; there are no enemies, no "us vs. them."
- Your attitude shows, so be aware of that – especially when students are present. You have a tremendous amount of power and influence over students, and they will look to you to learn professional behavior. If you teach them how to subvert the power of those with greater responsibility, you will most likely cost them a job in the future.

Division of Focus

Let's be honest: everyone who works on a production in an academic environment works far beyond what is expected from other faculty *and it is exhausting*. Professional directors and actors in the theatre tend to focus on one project at a time once rehearsals begin. It is the same with designers, but their focus becomes absolute at the beginning of load-in and tech. This singularity of purpose and focus doesn't exist for members of the academic community. In addition to rehearsals and performances, students and faculty have classes. Faculty will have committee responsibilities, as well as the pursuit of their own creative and academic projects that are often necessary to achieve and maintain tenure. For 30-plus weeks a year, schedules are full and demanding, and the ability to give one's full attention to a single project just isn't possible.

This division of focus can make collaboration very difficult. Collaboration in the professional world is successful in part because everyone understands that during this finite period of time, the production is everyone's top priority. You can feel everyone in the room focusing their energies on giving their best work in order to deliver the best product. If someone is "slacking," it is never for long because the collaborative group will not allow the focus to slip.

How do you maintain your focus on the project when it is 7.00 pm and your first class was at 8.30 am? Or you are entering their fourth straight week of tech? Or you are trying to mount a professional production at a nearby theatre while you are guiding your mentee through the tech process? It can seem completely impossible. Your energy flags and, rather than entering the rehearsal excited and full of possibilities, you just want to get through it.

We all go through periods when we are stretched to the limits. Three things can help us get through – perhaps not unphased, but nonetheless enough to make it work: prioritizing, planning, and preparation.

When everything seems important, we are forced to prioritize our tasks and obligations. Classes in an academic situation will always be a priority, but there are times – however briefly – when they can take the back seat to the priority of production. Very rarely will all the important things in your life need to be accomplished at the same time, so choices can – and must – be made.

Planning can help with this. Before beginning rehearsals, step back and take a look at everything that needs to be accomplished during that period of time – and slightly beyond. Planning needs to be more than just planning a rehearsal schedule. It is taking *all* of your obligations and mapping them out as best as you can so you build in times to accomplish all you must accomplish. You will begin to see that there are pockets of air that will make prioritizing easier and more apparent.

When planning, don't forget preparation time, which you should try to build into your daily plan. You can make the most of a rehearsal if you come prepared for that specific rehearsal *even if* you're exhausted or have a million other distractions in your head. You'll be more able to participate fully in the collaborative process, which in turn will motivate others to give their best. Preparation can mean more than just knowing what you're going to work on and how you want to approach it. A good preparation also includes mental focus, physical alertness, and emotional availability. It may require a nap, a good meal, or a cup of coffee – whatever it takes so you're able to be fully present at the beginning of rehearsal.

A successful collaboration, which continues all the way through closing night, requires that at key moments, everyone is focused on giving their best. Realistically, it is impossible in an academic environment to have everyone's 100 per cent focus 100 per cent of the time. Setting priorities, careful planning, and thorough preparation can help ensure that the focus of the team is 100 per cent present at those times that matter the most.

Most of all, be as patient as you can with each other. What we do is *not* easy. It's not rocket science – it's human communication, which is *much* harder.

Finally, it all comes back to practicing the principles of collaboration whenever and wherever you can:

- practice trust, respect and inclusivity
- maintain constant and open communication
- encourage generosity in yourself and others
- pursue a clear, unified vision.

We wish you much success and joy!

Like so many, I came to the theatre seeking an outlet to express myself and a place where I felt accepted. These two ideas have been the siren song calling misfits, triple-threats, nerds, and superstars to the performing arts. As artists we are constantly searching for the story we want to tell on stage and off, and the audience and creative team willing to hear that story. I have been shaped by the directors, choreographers, and educators that I have worked with over the years, just like everyone else. For the most part, those people showed me compassion, empathy, support, and patience. Whether they were being tough on me or maintaining their own high expectations, their criticisms were productive and built on trust. They managed to offer me everything that brought me to the theatre in the first place – a home.

I have also been shaped by other types of creatives and educators. I have been shamed for my weight, excluded because of my skin, teased for my lack of skill in one area or another, and shunned for not achieving some pre-conceived ideal of what an actor who looks like me should or should not sound like when they speak or sing. I have been devastated by the words of a producer after a very first run-through of the show. I have been denied leadership positions because of nepotism and fear that contacts would not accept me as an authority because of my race. I have been reprimanded when requesting hair and makeup supplies or undergarments appropriate for my skin tone and hair type when my White counterparts were provided whatever they needed.

As my opportunities to direct and teach grow, there are things I am no longer willing to accept. I will no longer accept shame as a motivator for a cast or crew. My collaborators will always know that our relationships and the work we do are mutually beneficial. I will no longer accept that in "the real world" toxic behavior is normal and something that my students must get used to or accept. Screaming at a group of artists is stifling to the entire creative process and has no business in showbusiness. I will no longer accept traditional beauty standards as the deciding factor for casting. Equity, body positivity, and disability visibility are the principles that will carry us into the next generation

of theatre. As an educator and director, my students will learn when to advocate for themselves and that it is safe for them to advocate for themselves.
As I look at the good work so many of my colleagues are doing in the area of
equity and inclusion, I know we are on the verge of a positive revolution in
the theatre. The theatre can be what we always dreamed it should be: a place
for self-expression and acceptance.

– Brooke Ashton Harper, actor and educator

Appendix 2
Casting in the Academic Environment

When creating the collaborative team, casting takes center stage, so we felt it was important to address issues of casting as they pertain to representation, diversity, and inclusion, especially in the academic environment. Changes in the professional environment are more likely to be implemented if we prepare and train our students to become sensitive to issues of representation, diversity and inclusion.

Representation matters. Race- and culture-conscious casting matters. Anti-racist policies matter. Gender identities matter. If we are going to encourage collaboration by practicing trust, respect and inclusivity (Guiding Principle #1), then collectively, interrogating the casting process is important. For the first time in Actors' Equity's 104-year history, the organization completed a diversity study. The 2017 study revealed biases and identified quantifiable ways to track hiring biases, including age, gender and gender identity, race/ethnicity, disability, religion, national origin, sexual orientation, and veteran status. In 2020, the actors' theatre union reported its second diversity and inclusion report. The 2020 diversity report shows some improvement, but there is room for more equity (pun intended). Theatre as a whole enterprise has a long way to go: "It is our duty to be part of the solution, to work to tear down barriers and rebuild a structure that is truly inclusive."[1]

What are some of the issues surrounding casting in an academic environment? Below are some thoughts. Collectively, we are seeking a new path forward. We will offer more questions than solutions. Frankly, we don't have the answers. As with everything in this book, however, we find the guiding principles to be extremely useful in helping us address the challenges, and we will conclude this appendix with some thoughts on that.

But first, the challenges.

The Casting Pool

The casting pool is always limited to who is available, which means the casting pool in the academic environment is very, very small. In the case of professional training programs (BFA or MFA), our choices are often limited to the actors in the program. Casting for representation moves from being an abstract concept to a very practical consideration.

If your program is committed to reflecting the diversity of the larger community, then selecting a diverse group of students becomes a major priority. If your acting pool is typically homogenous, how can you change your recruitment and admission practices to attract a more diverse cohort? Are there financial aid programs and recruitment practices that can be altered to make attending more feasible to underrepresented communities?

Programming

Casting and programming (play selection) go hand-in-hand. Play selection is about determining whose stories get told, but it is also about the training opportunities you provide your actors. Shakespeare has become controversial because of his identity as a writer in the White male Western European canon, but he is still the most produced playwright in America and his work remains extraordinarily challenging. Casting practices when it comes to Shakespeare have been extremely flexible. There are numerous examples of professional productions with incredibly diverse casts, as well as productions that embrace gender-bending. All-female casts are a popular solution. In other words, all actors can find a place in Shakespeare's canon. Can you truly provide strong training and neglect the Bard?

On the other hand, can you adequately train people of color or who identify as LGBTQ+ or are disabled if you don't provide them with performance opportunities that reflect their identities? If you have a diverse acting pool, then you're probably not serving them well by choosing plays with all White characters.

Finding material that provides roles for diverse populations can be challenging. However, the material available to us is growing exponentially on a yearly basis. It can be hard to keep up with it all – and it can mean a lot of extra work to find these plays – but it is imperative that we do so if we are going to provide opportunities for our actors. What practices can you install in your faculty, students, and play selection committees to encourage the discovery of new and diverse voices?

Casting vs Whose Stories get Told

It goes without saying that if you don't have African American actors, you can't produce a play by August Wilson. But what happens if you want to tell the story of a transgender man and you don't have a transgender male actor? Do you not tell the story? There are so few stories about trans people; isn't it valuable to your student population – your audience – to hear these stories? Or a play that calls for a disabled character? Do you not tell that story because you have only able-bodied actors?

Playwrights have a lot to say about this. The author of a wonderful play called *Teenage Dick* states in the published version of the scripts that you will not get the rights to his play unless you can cast two of the roles with disabled actors. Period. A lot of colleges and universities won't get to produce this play because their acting pool doesn't include disabled actors.

Other playwrights are more flexible, but still provide guidance. It is helpful when playwrights are specific on how representative the characters must be and whether there are alternative choices if necessary. One example is Lauren Gunderson's play, *I and You*, which she wrote for an African American boy of 17 and a white girl of 17. However, in her production notes she allows for flexibility: "The race of each character can be altered. The only essentiality is that both characters are not the same race". Guidance like this can be extremely helpful.

Student Identities

Identities – racial, cultural, sexual – are important to students, but can also prove tricky when incorporating them into the casting process. A student is not obliged to share their racial, sexual, or gender identity, so how can their identities be honored if we don't know what those identities are? Ultimately, it is a student's choice to share information; without it, directors can only guess and that leaves a greater margin of error. While this replicates professional practice (directors/casting directors can't legally ask questions about identity when it comes to race, age, sexual orientation, etc.), it makes it very challenging if a department's goal is to honor student identities and take them into account when choosing and casting productions.

One possible solution is, in the spirit of collaboration, to ask the students, "What stories do you want to tell and how can we support you?" Until recently, students did not have a say in the decisions being made, but the twenty-first century is proving their voice to be significant, so it might be wise for universities to begin to look at this cultural shift with a wider lens. One way to look at it is to see students as the consumers who are choosing to come to your school. Will your department be more appealing to prospective students if you develop a track record of embracing student input? After all, they don't have to come to your program. There are many other programs to choose from.

Colorblind vs Color-Conscious Casting

Back in the 1980s, Actors' Equity Association (AEA) made a concerted effort to increase casting opportunities for people of color through its "Nontraditional Casting Project." The goal of this program was to identify in every production those roles in which race was not a defining characteristic. New plays were submitted to a committee of actors at AEA, who determined which roles fit this definition. Casting directors were then required to see a diverse range of actors when casting these roles. It became known as "colorblind casting."

Today, colorblind casting is no longer a professional practice. Actors of color don't want to be racially invisible, but rather seen for who they are. They want their race and culture to be incorporated into the conception and performance of the role. A Black actor playing Astrov in *Uncle Vanya*, for example, doesn't want to pretend to be white, but rather wants to explore how being Black in late nineteenth-century Russia can impact his character's choices and behaviors.

Students want agency over which roles they will accept – and which they won't – often basing their decisions on issues of representation. Actors may be reluctant to take a role that is outside their race or culture for fear of taking a role away from someone whose voice and experience are aligned with that culture. An able-bodied actor may resist taking a role written for a character who is disabled. A student actor may look Latinx, but may actually be a Pacific Islander and might baulk at being cast in a Latinx production because it is not their culture.

A central premise of theatre is that everything we do is imagined – from the stories we tell (even those based on fact) to the characters who inhabit those stories. No one would argue that you have to be a murderer to authentically play a murderer, but where is the barrier between identity and imagination? Actors aren't literally their characters, but they bring their identities into the audition room. When preparing students to participate in the profession, how do we encourage them to embrace who they are while expanding their conception of what they can be cast as?

Training vs Professional Practice

The academic environment provides opportunities for growth that aren't possible in the professional world. Students often play roles that are outside their age range, "type," and experience – roles for which they would never be considered in the professional world. These opportunities can result in growth that would otherwise be impossible to achieve. The development of empathy is extremely important to the training of the actor, and exploring what it is like to live as a person with physical disabilities, neurodivergent, or from extreme poverty helps with this process. Can we extend these opportunities to explorations of different cultures without offending students or audiences? What choices in casting can we make in the name of training and student growth?

A Professional's Perspective

Amber Snead, actor and Southern California Regional Theatre casting director, has a unique perspective both as an actor of color and from the casting perspective in the professional setting:

Conscious casting has not been a thing because a lot of times, I think, people cast shows and they just cast them. They are not actually really paying attention to or thinking about diversity. They are just casting a show, business as usual, and you'll see an ensemble that all looks the same. They are all 20-somethings, predominately White college students. Unless there is a specific need for older character actors in the ensemble, it tends to be younger. Unless there is a specific need for an ensemble with actors of color, the ensemble tends to skew less diverse. I don't think that when people are casting a show, they actually think about who they are casting and who they are not casting. It's not until the cast announcement goes out and other people call it to their attention that they notice. And it's usually the people in the minority that are calling out the lack of diversity. But I don't think it's conscious at all, and that's part of the problem. It's a sort of unconscious bias. And a lot of times it's unintentional, they're not even thinking about it. And then there are the times when it is very intentional and in response to backlash, they [producers] are like *we need diversity* and it's one or two people and they say, *look we did it!* Diversity is such a huge issue that we're only scraping the surface of in theatre. There are a lot of people from many different groups that are ready to see themselves represented on stage.

People need to be mindful in general. There's a long history for us [people of color] not getting cast in things and so when companies say they want to cast diverse, we think it's all talk. But then as someone behind the table, when you know that you really are trying to cast more diversely, and don't get the turn out you were hoping for and you don't get as diverse a cast as you hoped it would be, it's also challenging because again, people look at the cast announcement and they say, *so much for diversity*. They don't know what's going on behind the scenes and the efforts that have been made, they only see the end results, and that is everything. That end result is really all that ends up mattering. Unfortunately, there's been a lot of *not worth my time to go to the audition because I know they're not going to cast me*, so they don't go anymore. I completely understand that because I've been there as an actor. When you see how things are cast over and over again, and it doesn't include your type/people that look like you, why would you keep putting yourself through that? So we [behind the table] have a lot of making up to do to draw people back in and show actors that we're serious about making a change.

It's being more aware of who is brought in – who makes it in the room. Making sure we [casting] are doing our due diligence and casting our net wider.

I also see that diversity is okay for certain shows and not for others. For some shows, people [audience and casting] don't care about it and for some shows, they very much care. A show like *Shrek*, every production is different. No one really cares who plays who overall … in the ensemble. Then there's Shrek himself. *Shrek* is GREEN! He could be absolutely anyone. Fiona is an ogre and a princess. But always a White princess, right? Same goes for Elphaba in Wicked. Also GREEN! And yet, how many have we seen that weren't White? Maybe a handful probably. I think people feel safe having diversity in supporting characters and don't/won't make a big fuss about it. It's usually with the leads. Like the show *Grease*, which I love the music but I hate the moral – *don't be who you are but change everything and start smoking and he'll love you*. People love to cast *Frenchie* and *Rizzo* and anyone else "diversely." But to see a Danny and Sandy of color? *Danny* and *Sandy*, that's like pushing it.

Navigating the Casting Process

Understanding and confronting these complex challenges of casting is paramount if the goal of academic theatre and training programs is to eventually make the professional theatre at large more diverse and accessible. As we have said before, we have a lot of questions, but no answers; these will be discovered through trial and error as we find our way through these challenging times. However, we can look to the guiding principles for ideas on how to begin to approach these problems.

Guiding principle #1: Practice trust, respect, and inclusivity

There are many voices to include in the season selection conversation. What stories need to be told is a first step. But also: Who in the department is right for the role and do they have the training to support the role? The most important question to ask: Does the department have the actors to support the plays chosen? As with the professional world, choosing a season based on actor availability can be tricky; actors get better-paying offers and students quit programs or transfer to other schools. But you can only make your decisions based on the information you have at the time; the rest is out of your hands.

Guiding principle #2: Maintain constant and open communication

The topic of casting is clouded with emotion: emotion to get it right; emotions to be heard, seen and included. There is a frustration among so many in the theatre community who have tried to access opportunities, and over time it happens again and again. Complicated feelings accompany these individuals. There might be a lack of trust, a guardedness. This is understandable. If we listen – really listen – and offer concrete choices that serve the mission of inclusivity, then change is possible. Having many points of view in the conversation will light up the path to change. It can also make it difficult, but difficult is better than the alternative. Changing decades of policies requires communicating in collaboration and compromise from all those involved. It requires having the uncomfortable conversations and the humility to say 'yes' to change.

Guiding principle #3: Encourage generosity in yourself and others

Active and real listening requires the generosity to hear all points of view. Engaging students, staff, and faculty is important and helpful to gain perspective, but so is knowing that everyone won't be 100 per cent happy with the final decisions. You will never make everyone happy – and to try is a fool's errand – but if the decisions are made with equitable consideration within the division of responsibilities, then we have done our best. Even then, if we are not all 100 per cent on board, we can find a compromising 80 per cent or even 60 per cent to move the needle forward.

Guiding principle #4: Pursue a clear, unified vision

Any policy that has been held over from the past and is no longer useful can be removed. Nothing is forever. We are ever-changing vessels because we are dependent on the human condition, which is constantly changing and evolving. As long as we look towards our goals of inclusivity, we will continue to evolve in the casting process that supports the community with respect to each person's race, gender, identity, sexual orientation, socioeconomic background, and abilities.

Theatre is for everyone. If we include everyone in the conversation and foster everyone's story, then we will finally have a theatre that truly holds up a mirror to our society, which is what theatre has done since its inception.

Over the years I've intentionally built an extensive and inclusive casting database of talented actors. Many of whom have previously not been well represented, or misrepresented, onstage in theatre productions. It is important to me that we cast theatre, film and television with the people who actually represent the story truthfully. So, when I see it come to life with the actors, I've cast… well, it's just one of the great thrills in life!

– Jackie Diamond, fortheactor.net

Note

1   Mary McColl, Executive Director of Actor's Equity Association. Accessed April 17, 2021 from www.actorsequity.org/news/PR/DandIReport2020.

Appendix 3
Seeing the Student and Encouraging them to Work from their Cultural Point of View[1]

Authors' note: What follows is a reprint of an article written by Rufus and published in the *Musical Theatre Educators Alliance Journal*. Rufus has been experimenting with teaching culture in the acting classroom at Syracuse University, breaking the boundaries of race to expand students' empathy, compassion and understanding of cultures different from their own. We felt it would be a valuable part of this book to share his ideas and practices.

In DRAMA 261: Musical Theater Practicum – Acting the Song, a course offered at Syracuse University, investigating culture is used as a vehicle to acknowledge the student's ancestral heritage. On the first day, the students share with the class the culture of their families. As they share, the students recognize their classmates' various ethnicities ranging from German to Irish to Australian to Nigerian.

The students are always encouraged to bring themselves and their culture to their work. For the first unit, The Song You Know, the students sing a selection of their choice. We discuss why they selected the song and how it represents them. This unit continues the idea of seeing the student. The second song in this cycle, "Something's Coming," from *West Side Story*, reminds the students to dream.

After the student sings the lyric, "with a click, with a shock, door will jingle, door will knock, open the latch," the following questions are posed to the student: "Using those lyrics, what could happen right now in your life that would set you on fire?" and "What dream do you see coming true?" With these questions, the students come alive, place themselves in the situation, and the moment is activated. The next song, "Who Can I Turn to When Nobody Needs Me?" from The *Roar of the Greasepaint the Smell of the Crowd*, guides the students to the opposite end of their emotional life. The assignment requires the vulnerability of the students as they reveal their most painful moment. These two songs provide a space for the students to be seen while giving them the freedom to reveal themselves in their work.

The final unit, Breaking the Box, uses *Once on This Island* as the vehicle to investigate culture. Students read *My Love My Love* by Rosa Guy – the book that provides the cultural and historical foundation on which the musical is based. Research begins on the history, historical timeline of the play, and the people of Haiti. We discuss the racial and economic divide between the characters to understand one of the play's themes. We compare and contrast the storyline and characters' intent between the book and the musical. Once students compile their findings, the songs are assigned.

One semester, as I began to assign the songs, a very talented young lady approached me and stated that she did not feel comfortable singing material that was not from her culture. I replied, "If I thought that way, I would not have a career. For my entire education and most moments in the business, I did not sing material from my culture." After class, she expressed that she understood and thanked me for hearing her. I also spoke to her and the class, explaining that this would not be material to sing out in the world, but it was a moment to learn about another culture and sing beautiful music. I continued to reiterate that one cannot sing from another culture until you understand its voice. In that quick moment between the young lady and me, space developed for me to speak about the inequity of the musical theatre canon, the system of racism, and the fight I encounter as a Black man.

We must see our students. When a student feels invisible and as if nothing about who they are culturally exists in their work, they feel unwanted and sense that they are viewed as less than. In this cry of invisibility, the student believes their training expects them to assimilate and blend in while leaving themselves behind. We must begin to truly see our students from all walks of life and teach them to investigate the world as a whole. When this happens, not only will the classroom shift, but also concurrently, a change for humanity will emerge.

Note

1   Rufus Bonds Jr., "Race, Equity, and Inclusion in Musical Theatre Education," *MTEA Musical Theatre Educators Alliance*, 4 (2021), 8.

Appendix 4
What Would We Do?
(The Scenarios)

Looking back at our past challenges is often painful, but we felt that to do this book justice it was important to be honest with ourselves about both our successes and our mistakes. We would share our most personal horror stories so to speak but protect the privacy of others. In fact, that was where this book began. We would commiserate about our collaborations and wonder how might we do better. After all, it has to be about the students.

The scenarios became an important way to spark conversation about how to become better collaborators. We thought it might be interesting to share what we might have done and what we actually did. Whether what we did was right or wrong is not the point. We want to look at collaboration from all angles to learn about how we might handle ourselves better and become more collaborative in the future. If we don't learn from the past, we can't change the future.

Chapter 1, Scenario 1: Building Trust – A Summer Production

What Mark did

This was the one scenario where I provided what happened. Honestly, I wouldn't change a thing because it turned out so well and I learned so much. The play had won the Pulitzer Prize and the author came up to see the production. He was thrilled and later mentioned it in his preface to a new edition to the play. He had begun to question the play's relevance, but this production proved to him that the play wasn't dated – that it still had something important to say. If I had replaced this actress because we didn't get along, or if I had tried to impose my need for involvement in the process on her, we never would have arrived at this production *together*. I've never worked with this actress again – the opportunity never arose – but I would in a heartbeat and without hesitation. And I have every reason to believe she feels the same.

Maria's take on the scenario

My default is trust with caution. If you fool me once, shame on me. If you fool me twice, shame on me again. No longer will I give you my trust if that trust has been betrayed more than once. I believe in second chances, but I don't play the fool. I will proceed at a distance in collaborating to protect myself and my work, and I will choose not to collaborate again.

I once had a student who brought hostile energy to the class, which made it difficult to give the student feedback. When I side coached the student, the student displayed an emotional outburst that startled everyone in the room. The student negated exercises and made it difficult to teach and learn. I found myself tiptoeing around notes as I didn't want to set the individual off. When the behavior disrupted the flow of an exercise and completely halted the learning of other students, I offered the door and said, "You do not need to participate in this exercise if you choose not to, but other students would like to participate. There's the door." The actor complied but the disruption impacted the lesson and the entire trust in the room was gone. The entire creative atmosphere was damaged. No one felt safe. More incidents occurred and I met with the student outside class with support and discussed solutions. Although we came up with a plan, I backed off and just got through the semester without conflict, but trust was severed and it never returned.

Once trust is broken, it is a process to regain it and sometimes it never happens. Trust is earned when you know someone cares enough to not put you down in order to bring themselves up. When they see you struggling and they support you rather than celebrating your bad review or misfortune. There is a generosity and humility in trustworthy people. It's decent human kindness. Working with untrustworthy people takes the oxygen out of the room. I know the signs because I feel as if I have to watch my back and I can't breathe.

Trust is earned. It is not a given. This is why collaborators choose to work with proven collaborators again. They can get right to creating the work and dodge establishing the trust. It is already there because there is an understanding that there will be follow-through and respect for one another's work and individuality. Trust is the foundation upon which everything is built. When there is trust in the relationship, the work can flow and there is joy in a collaboration. When I make a suggestion to a collaborator who I trust, I do so freely, knowing they won't dismiss it, mock it, or demean it. They may not agree but they will hear it. Trust within the creative process prevents feelings from being bruised because the idea is about the work not about our feelings or egos.

Trust requires vulnerability and safety. Trust will not survive in an atmosphere of fear. The main reason I don't believe in cut programs (junior barrier programs) is because it breeds fear and it makes people distrust each other. It is the antithesis of ensemble. We build trust in our collaborations by celebrating each other's contributions, supporting them, uniting with them in service to the story and the art. We don't always have to agree but trust allows us to disagree with respect.

Gossip, dishonesty, and revenge are barriers to trust, and destroy trust and the creative environment. This does not serve anyone, especially the person who is initiating these actions. Their reputation will follow them because often they are transparent. When trust is lost due to a misunderstanding, playing games such as silent treatment or talking about someone disparagingly behind their back only perpetuates mistrust. Talking and clearing the air with the person and apologizing, honoring feelings, is the process towards healing. An honest apology is not, "I'm sorry your feelings got hurt" or "I'm sorry you feel that I hurt you." That's putting the responsibility on the person who was hurt. A real apology is "I'm sorry my words or actions hurt you. I will be careful to be more considerate in the future." Practicing the guiding principles will support trust in collaborative relationships.

Rufus's take on the scenario

Trust is essential to building a relationship between the actor and director. As the director, I consistently assess the situation before proceeding. In the actor Brooke's case, I would grant her the time to explore, especially if the work was getting done. Perhaps a few conversations during the breaks, nothing about the show for her to see another side of me. As Mark stated, she needed my assistance, and I would welcome the opportunity for us to discover together.

Chapter 1, Scenario 2: How do you Maintain Unity?

What Rufus did

The goal was to create an environment of joy that would strengthen the bonds of the cast. The result was accomplished by leading with generosity and respect while fostering acceptance.

Realizing that there was a conflict brewing in the company, I decided to create a ritual. Singers from another country created a song to represent the welcoming of a new soul. Various cast members were given slogans. While guiding the actor down a path, the cast began to whisper, "You are enough"; "Thank you for bringing us your gift"; "We have been waiting for you"; "You are the one." The ritual began just before the final performance of the actor departing the show. The chanting commenced. The new cast member was blindfolded and slowly guided through the group surrounded by a tunnel of soft chants. Various actors began to whisper the slogans into their ears. At the end of the line stood the person leaving the show. As the new member approached the end of the line, the singing increased. Once the actor reached the end, the blindfold was removed, and the person leaving the show embraced and welcomed the new soul. Everyone erupted in tribal shouts and screams as they applauded. The ritual is a beautiful moment that still happens today.

Mark's take on the scenario

I will admit that this is a situation that I've never come close to experiencing and have never given any thought. I love how Rufus solved it – it's a beautiful way to make the new member feel a part of the team immediately, and for the outcoming member to understand on a deep level just how important they were to the ensemble. It would be a wonderful ritual for any long-running production.

Maria's take on the scenario

Unity in a production is so important, especially in a long-running show. It can make coming to the theatre a joy or dread. How we establish unity is an important goal to achieve. When in rehearsal, I find I am so fixated on moving through the process to stay on task so we don't get behind that

I often don't take the time to unify. This scenario is a beautiful example of how singing, communing, and acknowledgment can support unifying a cast.

I believe we all come to the theatre for love and acceptance of who we are and the stories we want to tell. I can't think of anything more perfect than a ritual like the one Rufus created to ensure community, generosity, trust, and inclusivity.

If I were in this situation, I would definitely use his solution and adapt it to the circumstance.

Chapter 2, Scenario 1: Changing the Schedule

What Maria did

This has happened before, both on the day of and not on the day of the change. While I understand emergencies, in these two cases there was no emergency. When the stage manager notified me on the day of the change, I was not as apt to oblige as quickly. I said, "The dialect coach should be called and notified so as to not waste their time. Have them come at the end of the rehearsal. I will be working with two of the actors who do not have dialects after I stage the bows. We will divide and conquer. Next time, you need to consult me before changing the schedule." When I realized the schedule was changed by the stage manager before the day of the change, I told them to change the schedule back to what we had discussed or what I had planned. I said, "Please do not change the schedule without consulting me, after we have discussed it. If you have an idea of how to use our time better, share it with me first and we will collaborate on the change." Professional stage managers are very good with timelines and budgeting time. They often see things before the director. However, consulting with the director is important. No one wants to waste anyone's time and sometimes things take longer than expected. Remaining flexible is key in collaboration. This is an issue of not staying within your lane. Suggestions are always beneficial to a director. The stage manager might suggest, "If we do this first, this will save time and we can let these actors go." That is helpful, but changing the schedule without consulting is not staying in your lane.

Rufus's take on the scenario

WHAT DO YOU DO IF YOU ARE THE DIRECTOR?

The stage manager must honor the schedule for the day. At no point should a decision be made without the director. A director prepares for the rehearsal and is on a timeline. Any interruption to that timeline could delay work that needs to be accomplished before tech. I would allow the dialect coach to proceed because they are not at fault. I would converse with the stage manager to agree that this would never happen again.

WHAT DO YOU DO IF YOU ARE THE STAGE MANAGER, AND THE DIALECT COACH ASKS FOR THE CHANGE?

The stage manager needs to inform the dialect coach that they must check with the director to approve the change.

WHAT GUIDING PRINCIPLES COULD HAVE BEEN UTILIZED?

Using guiding principle #2 (maintain constant and open communication) could have prevented the confusion and the disruption of the rehearsal process. Using this principle will also solidify the director–stage manager relationship.

Mark's take on the scenario

I think Maria handled it very well, with tremendous respect. I would then add it to my list of expectations for my next stage manager. This is the list of items that I go over with new stage managers to make sure expectations are clear and that we are on the same page.

It may be helpful to understand *why* the stage manager didn't communicate the schedule change. They may have believed the schedule was their responsibility, giving them the right to change it on their own without notice. They may not have wanted to bother the director with a change they felt could easily be accommodated. They may have felt the pressure of trying to please two people – the director and the dialect coach – with very little time to communicate. When you understand the stage manager's reasons for making the change without consulting you, you can more easily guide them into avoiding the problem in the future.

Chapter 2, Scenario 3: Staying in your Lane

What Rufus did

As the actor, it became clear that the artistic director was determined to undermine the production and my performance. In the last week of the show, I asked the sound designer (who also served as the production's board operator) if they wanted me to speak the lines. I informed him that I was very aware that my voice was being compressed, and because of this action I was losing my instrument. I then asked whether everyone was happy that they were successful in undermining my ability to tell the story? After that conversation, for the last week of the show he restored the original sound design. I will never work there again. The only person who had my back in this situation, the director, was no longer at the theatre.

The principles of collaboration were destroyed when the artistic director decided to hold a grudge against the actor and director. There was no respect, no generosity, communication, or openness. The artistic director's actions and his team would face unforeseen consequences because of their lack of support for the production.

Mark's take on the scenario

The actor did the right thing in securing permission from the director before engaging with the sound designer. I would also have encouraged the actor to keep the stage manager apprised of what was happening. Once the artistic director began to interfere (after the director's departure), the actor should have communicated with the stage manager before re-engaging with the sound operator. The sound op, after all, works for the theatre, whose artistic head is the artistic director. By trying to go around the artistic director and dealing directly with the sound op, the actor is putting the sound op in a very tough place, and of course they will always side with the artistic director, no matter how much they might believe the artistic director to be wrong. Engaging the stage manager, then, becomes the best option for securing the proper solution. It is part of the stage manager's job to navigate such tricky waters, so involving them early can save tensions from escalating – and it keeps everyone in their lane.

If the stage manager proves ineffective, there are protections for the actor outside of the artistic collaboration. Assuming that this is a union show (AEA), the actor can go to the Equity deputy, the cast's representative when dealing with conflicts with management – that is, the artistic director. The deputy can communicate directly with the stage manager and the artistic director and/or contact the union. If the actor's concerns still aren't addressed, he can directly call the union to lodge a formal complaint. In my experience, this usually gets quick results. Ultimately, it does no good for the actor to butt heads with the artistic director; the chances of *anyone* coming out well in such a confrontation are very, very slim.

Maria's take on the scenario

The relationship between sound design and actors is complicated, especially for singers. What an actor hears on stage and what is heard in the house are two very different experiences. When a voice is over compressed, an actor may have to work harder because too much compression makes the voice sound unnatural. It might cause an actor to not hear themselves with the same kind of release coming back.

In this scenario, the actor knew what worked in the past to protect the health of his voice. That alone should be enough for all collaborators to sit up and listen. When the producer hires someone with expertise it behooves them to listen to them. The sound designer was collaborative and willing to listen and work with the actor to solve the problem. The actor went through the proper channels by informing the director, to whom he answers.

Why did the artistic director feel threatened by this collaboration? The only explanation I can come up with is that the artistic director felt the actor did not stay in his lane. Perhaps he saw it is the actor telling the sound designer what to do. From the point of view of the producer/artistic director, actors are sometimes thought of as the lowest on the hierarchy. Often this hierarchy can create dismissal of the actor's input. Why would an artistic director sabotage their own production as a power move and put their lead's health in jeopardy? Was it an aesthetic difference or a power move?

Humans do strange things to teach people lessons or to prove a point. I mean, I would rather have a great-sounding lead actor, happy and in vocal health, than win an argument – but then again, I am not a producer. Staying in your lane is a complicated concept. There is crossover and compromise. When offered with respect and trust, suggestions can support collaboration, which is what occurred between the actor and the sound designer. In this scenario, collaboration seems to have suffered due to lack of generosity and trust, and fear that somehow power was being taken away because an actor wanted input and a say in how his voice was going to be mixed.

Chapter 2, Scenario 2: Colliding roles – the Artistic Director's Dilemma

What Mark did

The artistic director left the rehearsal at the end of a long week of techs, culminating in the run-through at the end of our second ten-out-of-12 tech rehearsal. We were exhausted, so I went to the design team after the artistic director left (I had watched all of this unfold separated from my team), thanked them for their hard work, asked them to think about how to solve the problem, and then let them go. I felt I had been emasculated in front of my team and didn't know how I was going to regain their trust.

I couldn't sleep that night, unable to think – only to feel rage, humiliation, and a crippling sense of failure. The next morning, I walked into the artistic director's office – my boss's office – and let them have it. "Don't ever do that to a director in front of his design team again," was how I began, and I only got louder and angrier from there. When I finally finished – it was a rant, not a conversation, the artistic director apologized and said they would leave me and my team to work it out – and didn't show up again until performances, rarely offering any notes.

We got through to opening night with a solution that worked as well as it could, but was never what the playwright had envisioned, which was my deepest disappointment. I think to this day he blames me for his play not being a big hit, and I will shoulder that blame because that's what directors do. The buck stops here.

I am not proud of how I dealt with this, and I would never offer up what I did as a collaborative way of righting the ship. I have yelled (okay, screamed) at a boss twice in my life (for very different reasons), and remain surprised to this day that neither of them fired me. It was well within their rights to do so. As an artistic director myself, I once had a director tell me to "f*** off" at a dress rehearsal after giving her a note she didn't like. I didn't fire her, but it took time for our longtime personal relationship to heal. It's not fun for either side. It's also never a good solution to a problem because it only creates distance between the people involved. Although I kept the artistic director from damaging me further, I lost a collaborator and a valuable perspective as I tried to sharpen the production to its ultimate performance level. Worse, the relationship I had with the artistic director – which had been very good for several years – was severely damaged by the way I reacted and it never quite recovered. (In the second case, we worked through it and remain very good friends to this day – and probably for the rest of our lives – but I still wouldn't have blamed him, or held it against him, if he had fired me.)

If you ever think we make collaboration look easy, reread this scenario and understand that it is very difficult. So many factors come into play, and theatre artists can be highly volatile and emotional people. We are also extremely opinionated people, and most of us – theatre or non-theatre – don't cope particularly well when our opinions and beliefs are challenged.

Rufus's take on the scenario

FROM MARY'S PERSPECTIVE

From Mary's perspective: How should she move forward with her design team? Or should she withdraw from the production?

I'm sure Mary has allies on her team. First, she should have a conversation with the team to understand what was discussed. Mary knew there was a problem, and collectively the team was unable to solve it. Mary needs to have a conversation with the artistic director to assure them she is capable and open to their suggestions to fix the issues. If she cannot provide what the show and the artistic director require, she knows she will be released.

FROM THE DESIGN TEAM'S PERSPECTIVE

How do they move forward to a solution that will make Rob happy? He is, after all, the person who will most likely hire them again at this theatre; he is their boss. How do they move forward with Mary? Do they include her in the conversations about the problems?

All must make sure Rob is pleased. The team needs to converse with Mary unless Rob requests that they do not. This situation is difficult for everyone. The most crucial issue is getting the show ready, and that takes precedence over everything.

FROM ROB'S PERSPECTIVE

He is responsible for ensuring the production works. The first performance is in two days. Does he replace the director with one of his company directors? Does he ask the director to step aside and ask one of the designers to lead the search for a solution? Or does Rob ask Mary to meet with him the next day with a list of solutions? What if Rob thinks none of them will work?

Excluding Mary from the meeting indicates that Rob is looking to find a different solution. If he were interested in having Mary fix the issue, he would have included her in the conversation. Rob will find someone either on the creative team or one of his company directors. Rob's only concern is to fix the show at all costs. Rob will make it work. I would assess the problem, have a conversation with Mary and the team, and quickly figure out a path forward.

Maria's take on the scenario

I can certainly understand the feeling of betrayal after the power play of the artistic director towards Mary. After reading the scenario again more carefully, I ask: was it a power play or a time issue? The artistic director waited until the last minute to see where the production was at and since it was a design issue, he wanted to hear from them. He absolutely should have come around to include the director. That was disrespectful.

Collaboration is a two-way street and while the buck stops at the director, it really begins and ends with who hired who –and that is the artistic director. Two days of tech time is a lot of time to solve something and often endings don't come together until the very end when all the elements coalesce – that is, if emotions are kept in check and professionalism prevails.

It is easy for me to say this because when we aren't in the situation our lens is more objective. I have been in a similar situation where I was trumped by a colleague of higher rank in a rehearsal in front of actors. It was humiliating. Deflating. I walked the person out after their display. I went to work to solve the problems. Everyone in the room felt betrayed by me. It was a similar situation, but I never regained the respect of the actors.

In Mary's situation, the artistic director undermined her authority as leader of the production by not including her voice in the conversation. He initially trusted she would be able to complete her job. I suppose that's why he didn't show up until two days prior. However, if he had attended earlier in the process, this is where the crisis might have been prevented. Mary absolutely should have been part of the conversation. That's how problems get solved. Collaboration. Putting minds together to identify the problem (as Rob said to the designers) and coming up with solutions together where everyone involved weighs in.

In my opinion, Mary did the right thing. If I was in her situation, I might have instinctually chimed in if I saw an opportunity during the post-rehearsal production meeting. Walking into the artistic director's office and sharing that she felt disrespected and establishing boundaries was absolutely the right thing to do.

I admire the self-respect to stand up to the boss. It takes guts. No one should disrespect anyone, no matter what position they hold, not matter what position they are in.

Theatre is problem-solving. Things can go from awful to not bad to solved in a day, but if egos and power play get involved, it damages relationships and the creative spirit – sometimes to a point where they are unrepairable.

Chapter 3 Scenario: Parting Company

What Mark did

This scenario and the scenario from Chapter 5 (Intimacy in the Rehearsal Room) are from a production I directed in New York City. The events of these two scenarios dovetailed with one another. The problem of the kiss was never solved because it was interrupted by the explosion – the "fit" – mentioned in this scenario. At the cast meeting that occurred immediately following this interruption, the actors were almost evenly divided into two factions: one side hated the process and wanted it changed; the other side had no problem with the process and believed the director determined process. Interestingly, those in this latter group were all members of the theatre company, while those in the former group were "guest artists" at the theatre. These three actors were also represented by the same, very powerful agency.

At this meeting, which occurred on the last day of rehearsal for that week, I listened to both sides. Eventually, I said something close to this:

> It's very clear to me that there are unhappy people here. I don't want to work with unhappy people, so here's what I'm going to do: tomorrow is the day off. If you're unhappy, you have a choice to make: you can leave the production without penalties or repercussions (they were under contract); if you decide to stay, then the complaining, negativity and resistance stop and we continue forward. I want a decision from you by Monday at noon.

That Monday, the three actors withdrew from the production. I found out later that their agent – one of the most powerful in the industry at that point – tried to get the artistic director (my boss) to fire me. I will be forever grateful that she stood by me. (She was on vacation in Florida when all of this happened, and I made the offer to the actors without consulting her, although I called her immediately after the meeting to let her know what had happened.)

We were a week away from techs, so we had to scramble to replace the three actors. One of the cast members – who has gone on to win two Tony Awards as a director – immediately put me in touch with two of his classmates, who were perfect for the roles and signed on almost immediately. The third actor was a little harder to replace, and I went back into auditions. We landed on a woman who this past year (2020) got her first Tony Award nomination.

The difference was astonishing. The tension completely left the rehearsal room. Everyone was focused on the work, and everyone loved the play and gave it their all. As I mentioned in the scenario, the first three weeks were the hardest of my career; the second three weeks were the easiest.

The problem with the intimacy (Chapter 5 scenario) was no longer a problem. Neither actor – one gay (a replacement), one straight (original cast member) – had any problem executing the intimacy between the two men required by the script.

I have, of course, thought about this process many times over the years and have often asked myself what I would have done differently. My honest answer is that I would have replaced the two actors (the male actor was also the actor in the Chapter 5 scenario) after the first day. The issue with the woman was one that I couldn't have foreseen. She was cast several months before rehearsals and began her research on the role – a transgender role – almost immediately. It was that research that led her to believe that the role wasn't truthful and it was why she demanded changes in the script. It was clear from that first day that she could no longer embrace the role or the script, and that should have determined immediately that we needed to part company. She wouldn't be convinced, and the playwright couldn't have met her demands without abandoning the whole reason he wrote the play. The actor was a completely different issue. I should have been more alert in casting him. There were warning bells, but he nailed the role in auditions and there really wasn't anyone that the playwright and I wanted more.

In terms of the Chapter 5 scenario, we didn't have intimacy directors back then. It was more cut and dried: actors simply executed the script as written. After all, they knew what they were getting into when they signed the contract. They had read the play and knew what was required of them. The resistance completely caught me by surprise. Since then, when casting a play that required physical intimacy, I've made sure in the audition process that the actors understood the demands of the script and made sure they were comfortable with them. I have never had a problem since. I will say that, in today's climate, I would absolutely avail myself of an intimacy coach. I have spoken with a number of actors who have worked with one, and they say it makes a huge difference to their level of comfort and confidence.

Rufus's take on the scenario

1. WHAT WERE MY OPTIONS? NOTHING IS OFF THE TABLE.

There are many options; the question is which consequence are you willing to face?

It is so important to unify the company. When camps begin to form, problems arise that may have nothing to do with rehearsal, the play, or you. These issues must be addressed immediately. Find out what the cast needs. Determine the point and seek a resolution. If the problem cannot be solved, you can fire people. Contact their agent to see whether there is an issue. Have open conversations. Call around and ask about the actors. Recast all the actors.

2. SHOULD WE (THE PLAYWRIGHT AND I) HAVE FIRED ONE OR BOTH OF THE ACTORS AFTER THE FIRST
REHEARSAL?

No. You cast them, and you need to figure out a way to make it work. I would investigate the casting process and see what was missed concerning their personalities. Were they so great that the talent overshadowed seeing who they were?

3. SHARED VISION BECAME AN ISSUE HERE: THE ACTRESS HAD A VISION THAT WAS DIFFERENT FROM THAT
OF THE PLAYWRIGHT, SHOULD THE PLAY CHANGE IN THE SPIRIT OF COLLABORATION? WHY OR WHY NOT?

No, the actress did not write the play, and she cannot determine how to change the vision to suit her character's needs. If there exists unclear dialogue, of course discuss the matter to seek understanding. The whole of the piece is greater than the one part.

4. WHAT COULD HAVE OCCURRED THAT FIRST DAY OF REHEARSALS THAT MIGHT HAVE GOTTEN OFF TO A
BETTER START? WHAT ABOUT THE SECOND DAY?

On the first day, one must establish boundaries. I would confront the actress with the understanding that the change she was requesting was not going to occur, and if she could not accept this, perhaps this was not the right project for her. On the second day, a meeting with the cast must occur to establish the process going forward. An individual encounter during the day might be beneficial.

5. COULD SOMETHING HAVE BEEN DONE IN CASTING TO ENSURE A MORE COLLABORATIVE COMPANY?

It is always good to seek information from people who have worked with the actors. No matter how great the actor may be, it is essential to look for clues about their personality. Yet sometimes issues are not revealed until you begin the work.

6. IF WE WERE GOING TO REPLACE ONE OR MORE OF THE ACTORS, WHAT ARE THE CRITERIA FOR WHO
GOES AND WHO STAYS?

If an actor is destructive, violent and disrespectful, constantly late, and unprepared, then you may be able to find grounds for dismissal. If the actor pushes back trying to support their work or shuts down, it would be difficult to release them. This is a huge problem for the director, but one they must manage.

It all depends on the situation. If the actress acknowledges that she cannot get past the text and will not be able to work, the organization should come to an agreement and release her from her contract: "I am really sorry this is not working for you. The playwright is positive; this is the story they want to tell. Is there a way we can work through this? (No), Okay, I don't want you to be unhappy. You're wonderful in the role, but your wellbeing is more important." Hopefully, this is at the beginning of the rehearsal process. The decision must be united: the director, the writer and, the artistic director all must be on board.

Maria's take on the scenario

Mercutio's line, "A plague o' both your houses," comes to mind. Original works provide different challenges to collaboration. The script is being developed and it is a challenging process, which requires everyone to collaborate with a unified vision that begins with the playwright, supported by the director and buy-in from the actors. If none of that happens, the result will be ego, turf wars, and tantrums.

Like Mercutio says, it's death when there is fight. Creating a play is dependent upon creativity and this requires generosity from everyone. It may not be right … yet. Allowing the process to unfold with patience and trust in one another is the only way it can happen.

I think the goal to communicate was fruitful. It seemed to work. That is where I would have started as well. Firing people is a last resort, and when it is the first thing to be brought up, it is seen as hyperbole and dramatics caused by ego.

I think a conversation at the beginning of the rehearsal might have prevented the factions. Listening to everyone's thoughts about the play – not what they think the play should be, but what it is right now, what is clear and what is unclear – may have prevented the crisis. Everyone wants to rewrite someone else's play because they are reading it from their own point of view. That's not the gig. The gig is to put the playwright's play up on its feet so they can see whether it is what they visualized in their head. Then they can go into rewrites based on the information they get from the playing of it. Rewrites by committee are not play development. That is devised theatre. And that's a different genre.

Letting actors know what the project is and what the process will be before casting may help to prevent misunderstandings. Letting actors know what they are getting into will help the director and playwright choose the best actors willing to participate in the process chosen for this particular project.

Casting is everything. There is nothing worse than taking the short-cut and casting someone sight unseen with no meeting and no conversation. It is not only talent that is required but a willingness to collaborate and to be of service to the play rather than oneself.

Chapter 3 Scenario: The Rogue Artist

What Mark did

In this scenario, I was the associate producer. The director was a young director I had worked with when I was an artistic director at another theatre. He is – still – a brilliant director, but focus was an issue. Nevertheless, I was deeply invested in the success of this production, both as the theatre's associate producer and as the mentor to a very promising director. (He has since worked on Broadway.)

I spent the entire day of the new production stage manager's first day in techs in the theatre, observing the process. I watched the tension between the new production stage manager – who was trying to keep rehearsals moving – and the lighting designer – who was resisting any attempts to move her more quickly. The director completely avoided getting in the middle of it. Finally, the lighting designer snapped, basically telling the production stage manager to "back off." I felt I could no longer watch without acting, so in a very loud voice from across the audience, I said, "Let him do his job." A few minutes later, the lighting designer appeared by my side, furious, and said very quietly, "You only get to do that once." But the stalemate had been broken, and from that point forward the production stage manager – who was very good at his job – ran the rehearsals without interference. The next day, the lighting designer took me to lunch and apologized. I want to make really clear that I adored this lighting designer and consider her to be one of the best in the business with a ton of Broadway productions under her belt. She's in demand – and for a very good reason: she's good. We've worked together a couple of times since, and there has never been a problem.

I have to lay a lot of this at the director's feet and acknowledge that he was completely intimidated by her, due in part to his lack of experience. This threw the collaboration out of balance. In an ideal world, the original production stage manager would have controlled the rehearsal. I believe he too was intimidated by the lighting designer. (By the way, she intimidated the hell out of me as well.) The decision to fire the original production stage manager was in an effort to restore the balance of the collaboration, but without the director's support, the second production stage manager was being set up for failure. I had to step in to make sure he succeeded; I would much rather have had the director be the one to step in. But we don't live in ideal worlds, so we have to do what we feel is best to make sure the production succeeds.

Rufus's take on the scenario

1. THE DIRECTOR

You are a young director working with a Broadway lighting designer – that you have chosen. You are on stage and in techs, so you have in fact staged the show. What do you do now? Do you re-block the scene? Fight it out with the lighting designer? How do you feel about being called out in front of the entire company?

Being called out on stage in front of anyone is a horrible feeling. It is disrespectful and leads to more discord. As the director, I need to figure it out immediately. Hopefully, I have another eye in the room to assist me. If not, you look at the work and determine what is not working and adjust. If re-blocking will fix the scene, yes. The lighting designer is already mad, and may need to adjust the lights, but they want it to work at the end of the day. You do not fight it out with the lighting designer. You need them.

2. THE PRODUCTION STAGE MANAGER

You've just replaced the previous production stage manager. You've never worked with this company before, but you want to continue working with them in the future. You know you were hired because the previous production stage manager couldn't keep the rehearsal moving. What do you do?
You place your presence in the room, reassuring the cast and the creative team that you are there to support them, keep everyone on task, and get the work done. You cannot be passive or aggressive. You must be a supporting force moving the process along. Moving the process involves establishing conversations with everyone on the team at some point.

3. THE LIGHTING DESIGNER

You've designed hundreds of shows in your career. You know when a scene isn't working. You also know the amount of time you have to get the show up and running, and you know how to get there; experience has taught you this. Do you push on for excellence, or do you settle for mediocrity and move on?

Yes, you push on for excellence – what better way is there for a young director to learn?

4. THE ASSOCIATE PRODUCER

As the producer's representative, you have to make sure this production – the company's big money-maker – makes it to opening night a week away. You know the dilemma the production stage manager faces, and you want to support this person. You don't want to interfere in the artistic collaboration, but you are also responsible for keeping things moving. What do you do?

Understanding the climate in the room, I would check in with the director first and see how he needs to be supported. I picked the director first because if you go to the lighting designer, the director will feel the conversations are about him. I would then check in with the lighting designer to assure him things will be managed and see what he needs. I would then speak with the production stage manager to reiterate the importance of moving the process and making sure they felt supported.

Maria's take on the scenario

1. THE DIRECTOR

You are a young director working with a Broadway lighting designer – that you have chosen. You are on stage and in techs, so you have in fact staged the show. What do you do now? Do you re-block the scene? Fight it out with the lighting designer? How do you feel about being called out in front of the entire company?

The LD crossed the line. This should have been said in private and it should have been a conversation, not an accusation. It is also not the lighting designer's role to call the director out. However, I would admit that the staging needs clarifying and ask for a half hour to clarify. Doing this in front of everyone shows that I can think on my feet, I admit my downfalls, and I can solve the problem.

2. THE PRODUCTION STAGE MANAGER

You've just replaced the previous production stage manager. You've never worked with this company before, but you want to continue working with them in the future. You know you were hired because the previous production stage manager couldn't keep the rehearsal moving. What do you do?

I'd be sensitive to the needs of the moment. If the director needs a half hour to solve something, then I make the time. If it goes beyond that, then I would try to push things along. Every area needs their time to problem-solve, within reason. I might ask the director, "How long do you need" and start there. Give others a break to take the pressure off. Order pizza to keep morale up. Problem-solving doesn't happen when feet are held to the fire, especially with younger directors. It is helpful to keep the atmosphere positive and acknowledge that we are in this together and our work involves patience and respect.

3. THE LIGHTING DESIGNER

You've designed hundreds of shows in your career. You know when a scene isn't working. You also know the amount of time you have to get the show up and running, and you know how to get there; experience has taught you this. Do you push on for excellence, or do you settle for mediocrity and move on?

I think the lighting designer could have addressed the problem with more generosity. The lighting designer might have had a conversation with the director, starting with questions: What's important? Who's leading the scene? What's the highest point of conflict in the scene? Here's a hot spot, I can light them really well here if you want to make an adjustment. Suggest, but berating only distances our collaborators.

4. THE ASSOCIATE PRODUCER

As the producer's representative, you have to make sure this production – the company's big money-maker – makes it to opening night a week away. You know the dilemma the production stage manager faces, and you want to support this person. You don't want to interfere in the artistic collaboration, but you are also responsible for keeping things moving. What do you do?

Watch and look for opportunities. Ask: "How much time do you need for this so we can plan?" Let the others know your job is to watch the clock. Stay present and don't take your focus away. Sometimes a problem can get solved and then there is no leader to move on. Keep everyone abreast of the time-line, but allow for creative problems to be solved without pressure.

Chapter 5, Scenario 1: Intimacy in the Rehearsal Room – an Awkward Stage Kiss

What Mark did

See Chapter 3 scenario: Parting Company. The two scenarios are from the same production and the events are tightly connected.

Rufus's take on the scenario

1. I WAS OBVIOUSLY BLINDSIDED IN REHEARSALS. WHAT COULD I HAVE DONE TO BETTER PREPARE THE ACTORS FOR THIS SCENE?

It would have been great to discuss the scene with the actors in the audition. Since Bruce was selected by the playwright at the last moment, a conversation still needed to happen about the issue. In the room, perhaps the two actors dance to explore each other physically.

2. IS THERE SOMETHING I COULD HAVE DONE IN CASTING THAT WOULD HAVE ALERTED ME TO POTENTIAL CHALLENGES WITH INTIMACY? SHOULD THOSE *POTENTIAL* PROBLEMS BE TAKEN INTO ACCOUNT WHEN CASTING?

If the actor cannot fulfill the playwright's action of kissing, they should not be cast.

3. IS REPLACING (FIRING) BRUCE AN OPTION? UNDER WHAT CIRCUMSTANCES WOULD YOU/WOULDN'T YOU TAKE ADVANTAGE OF THIS OPTION?

Bruce should not be fired. If there is a point where Bruce becomes homophobic, dangerous, violent, or refuses to perform the kiss, a dismissal should be considered. If Bruce is replaced, the problem of casting the role still exists.

4. *WEIRD STAGE KISS* IS A NEW PLAY. IS IT AN OPTION TO GO TO THE PLAYWRIGHT – A COLLABORATOR IN THIS PRODUCTION – AND ASK THEM TO REWRITE THE SCENE AND OMIT THE SEXUAL ACTIVITY? WHY OR WHY NOT?

To omit the kiss will alter the story. The play no longer provides the stakes necessary for the scene or the through-line of the play.

5. WHAT RESPONSIBILITY DOES THE ACTOR HAVE FOR ALERTING THE DIRECTOR TO POTENTIAL PROBLEMS BEFORE THEY GET TO THE SCENE? WHAT REASONS WOULD AN ACTOR HAVE FOR NOT DISCLOSING ISSUES THEY MAY HAVE WITH THE SCENE–OR OTHER SCENES OF A SIMILAR NATURE?

It is the responsibility of the actor to express their discomfort with the material. The actor can communicate to the director that he may need assistance exploring the kiss. The actor may not have disclosed this information to save their job. They may also believe that when the moment arrives, they will be able to meet the challenge.

6. HOW MIGHT THIS SCENARIO INHIBIT OR INSPIRE COLLABORATION? WHAT EFFECT – POSITIVE OR NEGATIVE – MIGHT THIS CAST MEMBER'S "PROBLEM" HAVE ON THE OTHER COLLABORATORS IN THE COMPANY?

How the situation is handled will determine the attitude of the cast. If the director can help Bruce through the moment, collaboration occurs and the room will relax. If Bruce is combative, tensions will arise, inhibiting the work and the relationship between the director and Josh. Everyone will wonder why Bruce accepted the job knowing the kiss was a key component of the scene. His reaction could cause resentment and a toxic environment.

Maria's take on the scenario

1. I WAS OBVIOUSLY BLINDSIDED IN REHEARSALS. WHAT COULD I HAVE DONE TO BETTER PREPARE THE ACTORS FOR THIS SCENE?

I am never surprised that some actors feel uncomfortable with intimacy. As an actor, I was excited about tackling this challenge, but appreciated it when directors approached it as choreography and shared exactly the kind of kiss it would be. I think most actors are curious about how the intimacy is going to be handled and directed. When there is no explanation, our imaginations can confuse us.

A conversation would have been a great place to start. Which character do you think might initiate the kiss? Start there. Do you think your character would resist the kiss at first or not resist? How long do we think the kiss is? Here is a count of five. Shall we start there? Okay, so Josh, your character initiates it and Bruce, you hesitate and then allow it. Let's practice the timing before you two actually make contact. This is how I have approached it in the past. Now with a bit more intimacy education, I would start with addressing boundaries. But a conversation is always a great place to start.

Sure – some actors just go for it. In the past, that was accepted. When I taught at USC School of Cinema and Television, I brought actors in for the first-year directors to direct in scenes from *Thelma and Louise*. The first time through the scene both actors did not know each other and immediately just made out. No preparation. So, that was the expectation 20 years ago. Actors have been taken advantage of and I believe that is why it is different today. Boundaries must be acknowledged and honored. We now have language and a process.

2. IS THERE SOMETHING I COULD HAVE DONE IN CASTING THAT WOULD HAVE ALERTED ME TO POTENTIAL CHALLENGES WITH INTIMACY? SHOULD THOSE *POTENTIAL* PROBLEMS BE TAKEN INTO ACCOUNT WHEN CASTING?

Yes. I think you could ask a question about intimacy onstage and what is within the actor's boundaries and what is not. Clearly back in those days, less material was intimate and it was unknown territory. Anything unknown is terrifying and expectations were different.

3. IS REPLACING (FIRING) BRUCE AN OPTION? UNDER WHAT CIRCUMSTANCES WOULD YOU/WOULDN'T YOU TAKE ADVANTAGE OF THIS OPTION?

I think Bruce just needed a step-by-step process; with any choreography, an actor relies on the specifics. A fight is choreographed for physical safety, so why is a kiss expected to be any different? A kiss can hurt someone – it can cross a line and be psychologically upsetting. It is time we acknowledge that these behaviors are intimate and intimacy takes vulnerability. When someone crosses a line, it's a violation just like if someone is slapped. It can hurt but in a different way. If after there is conversation about how the intimacy might go and the actor still cannot take part in the activity, then I would consider replacing the actor.

4. *WEIRD STAGE KISS* IS A NEW PLAY. IS IT AN OPTION TO GO TO THE PLAYWRIGHT – A COLLABORATOR IN THIS PRODUCTION – AND ASK THEM TO REWRITE THE SCENE AND OMIT THE SEXUAL ACTIVITY? WHY OR WHY NOT?

I would not use this option. A playwright wrote the scene in a certain way. Handled with professionalism and being specific, the playwright can have his play and the actors can feel safe. It is very possible, especially now.

5. WHAT RESPONSIBILITY DOES THE ACTOR HAVE FOR ALERTING THE DIRECTOR TO POTENTIAL PROBLEMS BEFORE THEY GET TO THE SCENE? WHAT REASONS WOULD AN ACTOR HAVE FOR NOT DISCLOSING ISSUES THEY MAY HAVE WITH THE SCENE–OR OTHER SCENES OF A SIMILAR NATURE?

It is important that all collaborators discuss the needs for the play and expectations within professional protocol.

I don't see Bruce's anxiety as a problem unless he was still resistant after care was taken to walk through the steps. Actors respond emotionally because that is how we are wired. It is part of who we are. With care, patience, and a process, we can find the solution. Bruce had not been in this situation. Bruce may not have known he was going to have this kind of response. Looking back, his response to Josh's delay coming to rehearsal was a sign of anxiety with the role. Discussion and understanding of what the intimacy is going to be and what it will entail might have prevented the surprise.

Chapter 5, Scenario 2: Exercises to Make the Actor Feel Safe in a Sexually Driven Play

What Rufus did

Entering this process, having had no intimacy training, I needed to determine how I would approach the students with this material. The process of developing a brave space began during the audition. In the audition, it is significant to find actors who are comfortable with their bodies and willing to make bold choices around the theme of sex.

As an exercise, the women were divided into two groups on opposite sides of the room. The center of the room represented the sexual climax. As the ladies moved closer to the center, they would physically display a sexual climax as an animal. They screamed animal sounds, convulsed physically, crawled, jumped, displayed physical ticks, all to express their state of being. As the ladies crossed the room to the other side, the climax subsided. Watching the ladies gave me a clear indication of who was open and willing to be daring.

I wanted to create a moment displaying excessive lust, without using those words. I felt the word "lust" would hinder the actors' imaginations. *Lysistrata* is a comedy, and the actors could create extreme, bold physical actions grounded in their immediate needs. In one scene, the women would smell a man in the distance. They were asked to investigate the act of being vampires and zombies in heat. They took this idea and ran with it, creating a bold, sexually driven moment free of self-consciousness.

It was important for the actors not to feel that they were being asked to have sex on stage.

We explored choreography, lighting, and sound to simulate sexual acts. The actors played the game of creating a machine to establish some of the choreography. The actors added mechanical sounds to support the action further. The audience would witness illusions of comedic sex acts while the actors remained safe and committed.

The women's goal in the play was to drive the men crazy by not having sex. Using the cat and mouse game, constantly teasing and enticing the men, created the energy of sexual play.

The physical life of the play was established using these tools. Placing the sexual actions in the world of animals released the actors' inhibitions. Using choreography allowed the actors to feel safe, knowing the actions would be consistent every night. Throughout the entire process, the actors were in control of their bodies and how they desired to use them. Following guiding principles #1 (trust, respect, and inclusivity) and #2 (communication) successfully protected everyone's boundaries.

Maria's take on the scenario

Without formal intimacy training, what language would you develop for everyone in the room to feel safe?

I would begin with Chelsea Pace and Laura Rikard's boundaries work. What are each actor's gates and fences? I would establish the language so everyone is utilizing it and it is part of the culture in the work.

How would you approach a show with sexual content requiring sexual actions by the actors?

Pace and Rikard give us specific terms with respect to how much pressure, how far and how close, what the count and shape of the movement is. I would approach it as choreography, utilizing the language these experts provide.

How would you make the actors feel safe?

Safety comes from knowing and trusting that everyone respects the boundaries established in the process. Individuals feel unsafe when they don't know
what to expect. I would make sure everyone knows what to expect all of the
time, and at any time we have a process to stop what might be considered
crossing a boundary.

How would you aid in releasing their inhibitions?

If an actor has resistance to something intimate or sexual on stage, there is
a reason, and I must respect it. It is not ordinary that we simulate sex with
people with whom we are not in an intimate relationship. This is a professional relationship and imaginary circumstances. Inhibitions are part of it. It
is the actor's responsibility to express what choreography/behavior supports
their instrument and what does not. It is not my job to challenge their boundaries. I can help to build trust and create a safe and trusting environment so
they feel they can access their truthful boundaries. If their boundaries cannot
serve the story, that is when a conversation about replacing the actor takes
place. Sometimes that is the only solution to honoring boundaries.

I would develop the intimate choreography around their gates/fences. I might
explore a warm-up where movement and their spirit are free and relaxed,
and where joy rather than fear is at the core of the exploration. A warmed-
up instrument is more expansive and actors love to move. Most of them.
I would certainly take my time and cues off them and not rush the process
or impose an expectation for them to "just do it." In my experience, when
there is trust there is a willingness to play and explore and actors often want
to expand into it. I think if we give them room to expand where it is safe,
they will release inhibitions on their own and they don't need me to enforce
it. I can assist by holding the creative space for them where permission is an
agreement, giving them freedom to express themselves in an intimate way.

When I was directing *Baby* with students, the actors who played Lizzie and
Danny were both shy about the kiss. Looking back, they were shy because
they were attracted to each other. It was palpable from the beginning and
one of the reasons they were cast. Chemistry. When we got to the kiss after *I
Chose Right*, they were looking at me with a frozen stare that implied, "Now
what?", knowing they were supposed to kiss. I hadn't officially staged it. It
was before I learned about intimacy education, but my instincts were right.

I stepped in, which you're not supposed to, and said, "May I help?" They both nodded. I touched both of them on the back of their heads and gently pushed them towards each other. I gave the nudge. They did the rest. I also counted for them how long I thought the kiss would be. I believe I said, "Did the length feel right?" They smiled and said "Yes." I gave them a count of eight for the kiss and said, "The return from the kiss begins on the sixth count, ending with you two looking into each other's eyes."

The fireworks continued between them. It scared them both. Love can be scary and when working on a love story the feelings can be confusing. They would hold back in rehearsal. So I asked them to come to see me during my office hours so I could do a little Michael Chekhov work with them. We used the archetypal gesture of "reach." I had Lizzie reach to Danny without him looking at her and then reversed it. We did this for five minutes and then I said, "When you feel the energy of your partner, turn to them and receive them."

They took each other in on a whole other level and permission was established. They brought this connection on stage with them. It's not surprising that the two fell in love during *Baby*. After graduation they moved to New York City, married, and had a baby of their own. A love story from the theatre that grew out of intimacy on stage. It happens. It's beautiful. Boundaries don't mean we don't have to connect in life. We just have to know the difference. *Lizzie and Danny, what could be better than that?*[1]

Mark's take on the scenario

It is important to remember that this scenario is set in an academic environment. In the current climate, I simply wouldn't undertake a play of this nature in a university without an intimacy coach or director – and I would want the coach in the auditions if possible. I agree completely with Rufus that a level of comfort has to be ascertained in the audition process. Without that, you risk casting actors who will freeze up and make a joyful collaborative process nearly impossible.

In a professional setting, I would probably also ask for a choreographer, one hopefully experienced in the processes of creating intimacy on stage. The exercises and creative methods used by Rufus would probably also work quite well in a professional production. In both cases, professional and academic, I would consider an intimacy coach to be essential.

Chapter 6 Scenario: A Harmful Demand by the Producer

What Rufus did

When the producer asked the director to give the lead actress the gorilla doll to carry on stage as her baby, the director responded, "Absolutely not!" The producer stated that he had invested over $300 in the gorilla doll and demanded that the actress carry it. The director began to explain the historical implications of his request – how White people have called Black people jungle bunnies, beasts, and gorillas; he refused to make the actress carry the doll. Rehearsal came to a halt and the stage manager called for a 10-minute break as the producer stormed out of the room.

The following day, the producer and the director communicated and agreed to eliminate the doll. The director realized that being combative would not yield a favorable resolution. Through open dialogue, we were able to move forward while maintaining our relationship. When a situation goes against your person, you have choices. You must always be aware that with those choices come consequences. Fortunately, in this case the director successfully protected both his actor and his integrity, a clear example of using guiding principle #2 (maintain constant and open communication).

Maria's take on the scenario

If I were in this situation and knew the historical implications the prop would have for an audience, I would ask, "Why?" I would communicate by engaging in questions. Why do you find it important to use this prop? The cost of a prop is not a good enough reason. Objects hold relevance. They hold sensory power and trigger memories. They symbolically support the story. What story are you telling with this doll? What are you implying by using this doll?

If the producer pushed back and said the prop must stay, I would ask the actor who was using the prop whether they were comfortable with the prop. One person is not telling the story: everyone in the company is invested in the collective vision. If the object/prop does not support the collective vision the director has established and the implications of using it are racist, then it would be important that the producer support this request to remove it. If the producer decides not to cut the prop, we are only led to believe the producer is okay with racist behavior. Then, I would walk.

Mark's take on the scenario

The problem here strikes me not as one of racist insensitivity – although that's certainly a layer of it – but of poor communication, particularly on the part of the artistic director. The challenge for any artistic director is how and when to communicate their expectations of a director. As with most of these situations, early and honest is better – and assumptions will only lead to tensions and animosity. If the artistic director wants approval over every aspect of the show – which is their right, as foolish and as intrusive as it may be – then they need to create the mechanism for that to occur, and the earlier the better. If the artistic director wants a particular prop used, then that needs to be communicated to the director before rehearsals begin. And if the artistic director plans on behaving like a co-director, then they need to say to the director up front: "I will wander in and out of rehearsals and if I ask for something, I expect it to be done; you work for me." If that expectation is articulated up front – before the director is hired – then by accepting employment, the director accepts those terms. Otherwise, they should decline the assignment.

Directors, for better or for worse, make an assumption that they have all the control – and that's a bad assumption on their part. The smart directors, just like smart artistic directors, communicate their expectations up front. Jerry Zaks was once being courted to take over the direction of a Broadway-bound musical. He made it clear to the producers and everyone involved – before he accepted the assignment – that he was the director and the input of producers and writers was not welcome. He had final say, and what he said was what would go. The producers accepted that, and Jerry agreed.

Of course, not every director has the power of a Jerry Zaks, so they must make their position known in other ways. In this case, the director needed to work with the artistic director as a collaborator, walking them through the conceptual and design choices and allowing them to voice objections and concerns before rehearsals could even begin. The director could also have said, "You're welcome at rehearsal anytime, but I need all of your notes to go directly through me outside of rehearsal" – that is, never in the moment. If the artistic director doesn't agree to that, then you negotiate; if they do, then the director can remind them if/when the director oversteps the bounds.

Chapter 6 Scenario: Perpetuating Stereotypes

What Maria did

John and I talked about the problem of perpetuating stereotypes. He told me that time and time again he has been asked to play the same clichéd characters from the point of view of a White person because the color of his skin. We talked for weeks about it. He schooled me on micro-aggressions. How trust is not easily restored after being misunderstood so many times over and over again.

Out of the event, John created Multicultural Arts Council, a place for students to talk and share their thoughts about unsafe places and to explore the racial divide through art. He was my first teacher on institutional racism. He helped me see the problem, which I had not previously seen, and I listened.

The last line of X is "Don't none of you think I'm gonna change." And I asked John, "What if X did change and the audience sees this?" John found a song about forgiveness that supplied the moment for the sound cue and in his physical action he made a transformation of contrition and redemption, showing X in his transition to the afterlife to be one of healing, not of judgement.

Mark's take on the scenario

This was a project without a costume designer, which exacerbates it a bit. In a setting where there is a costume designer, I encourage the designer to work with the actor to develop the look of the character together. It is counterproductive to make the actor wear something they aren't comfortable with; if the actor is uncomfortable, it shows and it damages the performance. If I'm not working with a costume designer, I rely heavily on the actor to bring in options of clothing and we work from there. To be honest, I always tell my costume designers that I have "clothes blindness" – something similar to colorblindness. I know when an actor isn't wearing clothes, but other than that, clothes just don't impact me – unless they're clearly "wrong." A blessing and a curse.

In other ways, this scenario does set off certain alarms in general. We are so sensitized to images that we make decisions that aren't always for the right reason. It calls to mind a quote from Luca Guadagnino, the director of the film *Call Me by Your Name*: "We could judge a friend's behavior and help a friend, but do we need to judge a character? If we start sanitizing our characters from provocativeness of ethical questions, we'd just better stop doing what we do." The point here, in my view, is that the first consideration for these kinds of choices is the demands of the story as determined by the playwright. Sometimes playwrights write stereotypes for very specific and valid reasons, and to fight against that can work against the story. As with so many aspects of dramatic storytelling, there is no "one size fits all." What keeps a scenario like this from spiraling out of control is communication: early and often, and from all parties. Moving forward on assumptions rather than knowledge will harm all parties.

Rufus's take on the scenario

If I were John, I would challenge the director to fight against presenting an image that has flooded the television and film industry, depicting Black men as dangerous and violent. Although John speaks of killing, can we think of how people judge a person based on their appearance with something cultural, such as hair? How do you feel about torn jeans, an oversized shirt, and dreadlocks?

As the director, I would take full responsibility for insulting John. I would then ask for us to investigate the juxtaposition of John's two statements: the moment when John talks about killing people, and his last line, "Don't none of you think I'm gonna change." Let's go to the last line and see what develops if the character is in a polo shirt, slacks, and sneakers. Let's physically see the opposite of how people believe the character would appear. What are your thoughts?

Chapter 7 Scenario: Communication is a Two-Way Street

What Maria did

Disrespect of this kind has happened more than just a few times and not with only one person. This was a combination of scenarios to illustrate communication and respect. Disrespect in production meetings happens. People sometimes do not listen, they have sidebar meetings, some get bored when it does not apply to them. I'm sure I am guilty of this too. If I am directing, I leave it up to the production manager to bring everyone back to one conversation. If it is during my presentation and it is not being addressed, I ignore it. It will reoccur. If more than one individual is getting restless, I cut my presentation short because I know I have lost my audience. I have also learned that it is not my job to be the tone police. I cannot make someone respect me. I can ask them how they would like to contribute, but I can't make them like the concept or agree or not feel bored. I listen. I hear them. And I move forward with my job. It is not necessarily what I would have done in the past, but the past is the past. I have gotten upset in the past, which did not serve me at all. I have learned that people behave for different reasons. The new technical director was operating from anxiety and not knowing the protocol, and chose usurping control as the solution. I understand this. I don't adhere to it, but I get it. I actually stopped directing because of these challenges and lack of solutions on how to solve them. If a process does not promise to bring me joy, I choose to pass. I go elsewhere to work. It is my goal to end meetings on a positive note, and some colleagues enjoy throwing a wet rag on progress. How I try to counteract this negativity is to toss out a solution even if it is just for a second. This happened recently when someone sucked up the last two minutes of the meeting on how nothing had been achieved, nothing was being done. After an hour and a half of progress, albeit small, this statement seemed untrue in my perspective. I tossed out a solution to add to the meeting notes. It was merely to just end the meeting with everyone understanding that communication is a two-way street. If we are to end it on the problem, this deflates morale, joy, and progress. If we end it on one possible solution (perhaps one that may not work), then it might inspire other solutions that will work. Communication either breeds creativity or it kills it. In the case of the new technical director, it was killing it. And in the future, I will still bring cookies because the majority of the people enjoyed them. All it takes is one sour apple to spoil the environment. All we can do is do our part to not be that person.

Mark's take on the scenario

I find this one of the hardest scenarios to find a solution to. There are some people who will always be resistant, and there is not a lot you can ultimately do about it. That represents a real challenge to a collaborative team, because the resistant team member is always a drag on the spirit of collaboration. I think Chris made the right move in trying to make the new hire feel welcome, but it obviously didn't do much to change Aaron's attitude or willingness to participate.

There are clues in Aaron's remarks in terms of what his needs are, and you can see connection and control coming into play. Essentially, he is asking for more involvement in the process from the early stages and feels he has the power to determine the feasibility of a choice, giving him a lot of power and control.

I think it is always a good idea to sit down with a new hire over a cup of coffee to get to know them and figure out what makes them tick. If you do this, it should be done as early as possible, before you work together on a production. If your fundamental values and sense of how the world works are at odds, this ultimately won't solve the problem, but it can provide you with insights.

In Chris's shoes, I have two choices: one is to let it slide; the other is to engage. Letting it slide is the easier path, and if you have no recourse because this person is here to stay, it may be the wisest choice. However, it means things will stay the same, and the tendency with the status quo is that it mostly deteriorates, rarely improves, and never stays constant. The better, harder choice would be for Chris to request a meeting with Aaron. In that meeting, I would explain my perception of their behavior. In this case, I would say something along the lines of, "Aaron, I noticed you were disengaged in the meeting and I found your comments afterwards aggressive and hostile. Is this accurate?" Often, we are unaware of how we come off to others. (This is why actors need directors.) If my perceptions were correct, the next question is, "What can I do to make the situation better for you?" If the requests are reasonable and rational, then you can take steps towards improving the relationship. If they are not, and if Aaron says something like, "I just don't like the way you handle things," then your last step is to set expectations. I, being aggressive by nature, would say, "Okay, I understand you're unhappy and I'm not going to be able to do anything about that. When you're in a meeting, I expect – and need – you to behave like a professional, which means I need your attention, I need you to participate in the conversations in a positive way, and if you have any problems other than those being discussed in the moment, I need you to keep them to yourself until after the meeting, when you can feel free to say anything to me that you like."

Yes, it is *much* easier to let it slide …

Rufus's take on the scenario

1. WHAT SHOULD CHRIS DO?

Chris must have a conversation with Aaron and address the issue. He must also inform Aaron that he will provide the ground plans for him once the concept becomes clear and his input is welcomed.

2. DO YOU SEE ANY OF THE PRINCIPLES OF GOOD COLLABORATION AT WORK IN THIS SCENARIO?

Amy embracing Chris's action to share a part of his culture is an example of guiding principles #1 and #2. Amy is offering respect and inclusivity as well as generosity.

3. WHICH OF THE PRINCIPLES OF GOOD COLLABORATION WERE VIOLATED – AND AT WHICH POINT(S) ALONG THE WAY?

Aaron and one of the student designers violated the first three guiding principles immediately. By laughing and Aaron rolling his eyes, they are both disrespectful, emitting a lack of trust for Chris's vision, showing no generosity, and not being open to communication.

4. WHERE DID THE COLLABORATION GET OFF TRACK?

The collaboration continued to be challenged by Aaron when he asked about the ground plans.

5. WAS THE DIRECTOR SENSITIVE TO THE ROOM OR DID HE GIVE UP HIS POWER?

The director was very sensitive to the room. He offered the cookies as a way into the world of his concept. When he recognized that Aaron was detached from the meeting, he shifted gears and attempted to bring him into the world. Not being discouraged, Chris continued the discussion, focusing on the other designer's work.

6. HOW DO YOU THINK THIS COMMUNICATION BREAKDOWN COULD HAVE BEEN PREVENTED?

Aaron was on a mission, and collaboration was not a part of his plan.

7. WHAT ACTIONS COULD HAVE BEEN TAKEN TO RESOLVE THE CONFLICT EARLIER IN THE PROCESS?

Chris could have called Aaron in. Rather than allowing Aaron to poison the meeting without taking ownership of his action, Chris could question his disrespectful action towards his family's traditions.

8. WHAT WOULD YOU HAVE DONE DIFFERENTLY TO RESOLVE THE CONFLICT IN YOUR FAVOR HAD YOU BEEN THE DIRECTOR? THE NEW STAFF MEMBER?

As the director, I would ask Aaron out for coffee to have a conversation away from watching eyes. As Aaron, I could have been more sensitive to Chris and the tradition he was sharing. I could have been attentive and not rolled my eyes. I could have apologized.

9. WHAT ARE SOME WAYS IN WHICH COMMUNICATION AND PROFESSIONALISM COULD HAVE IMPROVED?

If everyone in the room had followed all four of the guiding principles, the meeting would have been both successful and respectful.

Chapter 7 Scenario: Exploring Culture in Context

What Maria did

Students are provided with a comprehensive list of plays, including diverse characters with regard to race and LGBTQ+ identifying individuals and playwrights that are BIPOC and also White. Students are free to choose roles they want to work on and who they work with. Because everyone must participate in the class discussions, students are required to read all plays, whether they are in them or not. This promotes learning about characters unlike themselves and encourages discussion beyond their limited experience.

No White student has ever asked to play a Black character. If they did, I would question why. If the "why" served a purpose and it was only for class and about learning about the Black culture, I would ask the people of color in the class how they felt about it. The discussion would inevitably provide both pros and cons. If the consensus was about learning and stepping into someone else's shoes, I might consider it, but I would want the larger community to understand why we were doing this in this class and avoid misunderstandings that this scenario might imply casting White people in Black roles. If the involved community impacted by this experience saw the educational value in learning about others through working on material outside their race, I would consider it.

Education is about expanding one's perspective and psyche, and that happens in a class where fear is not present but trust exists between the people and in the process. In that, the entire class, including myself, would research the culture to fully understand the world of the play and to seek how to play the role from the character's point of view. We have learned that the Black experience has been one of oppression, highly misunderstood and lived in an inequitable world. If we can do a small part in class about viewing the world from a Black person's lens by working on a scene from the canon of Black plays, perhaps this might be one step toward change. It must be done with the utmost detail, care, and respect. There will be mistakes, but if we work from always questioning and asking whether this remains true to the culture with respect and curiosity, and without judgement, then we might be contributing a small part of growth towards understanding and change.

Mark's take on the scenario

There are no easy answers to this scenario. We are working through a minefield and what we need from each other is patience as we work this out. Unfortunately, there doesn't seem to be a lot of patience or room for error, and someone who makes an honest mistake can find themselves shamed on social media, "erased," or worse. Yet we can't get to the best answers without being allowed to fail along the way.

Rufus has suggested that, in the performance classroom situation, we need to require students to explore and experience cultures different from their own. It should be okay for students of one race to act a role that is of a different race. White actors should be required to perform a scene from an August Wilson play. This scares the s**t out of me. I would love for my White directors to direct a scene from an August Wilson play with a mixed-race cast that includes White actors. When I floated this with my students, they said, "Please don't do this, Mark; you will lose your job." Rufus's response: "Black actors have always been asked to perform roles that are not Black. What's the difference?" He acknowledges that it will take time to lay a foundation for this kind of exploration, but the payoff will be incredible. I agree with him 100 per cent. So I will begin conversations with my colleagues, my chair, my dean and ultimately my students. I will approach it as an experiment – one that could very well fail, but one we need to try. There is no forward movement without failure, and if we are ever going to really get to the heart of the challenge of race that currently consumes us, all ideas must be on the table – and we must be allowed to fail. Perhaps this is a new principle of collaboration: everyone in the "collaborative bubble" must be allowed to fail without judgment.

Rufus's take on the scenario

HOW DO YOU THINK THIS SCENARIO MIGHT MAKE YOU FEEL IF YOU WERE THE BLACK STUDENT?
As a Black student, I would welcome the opportunity to work on material from my culture. To exclude the work does not prepare me for the profession. I will seek roles based on the human conditions unrelated to race, although I will still be viewed as Black to many.

HOW DO YOU THINK THIS SCENARIO MIGHT MAKE YOU FEEL IF YOU WERE THE WHITE STUDENT?
Not being White, I can imagine there will be some discomfort. Because our educational system does not require White students to investigate roles of color, push-back might occur. This push-back could stem from many

reasons: "I will never be cast as Black, so how does this prepare me for the industry?" "I find the request offensive." "I don't want to offend the Black student in the room." Then maybe I will because it will be informative to view the world through someone else's eyes.

SHOULD THE TEACHER HAVE SINGLED OUT THE BLACK STUDENT?

Yes. Not to ask the student would be excluding him from the rest of the class. At that point, he would feel left out and invisible.

HOW MIGHT THE TEACHER AND THE STUDENTS HANDLE INCLUSIVITY IN SCENE SELECTION? WHAT IF A WHITE STUDENT WANTED TO PLAY A ROLE WRITTEN FOR A BLACK INDIVIDUAL BECAUSE THEY WANTED TO LEARN WHAT IT FELT LIKE TO STEP INTO SOMEONE ELSE'S SHOES?

We should select scenes for learning objectives, cultural identification, and human exploration. I believe each student should experience all of these in the classroom. Learning objectives should be structured for the skills necessary to understand the craft. Work involving cultural identification must give opportunities for students to explore text familiar to their own lives: human exploration that encompasses work across racial lines to investigate people's lives and languages they would never consider examining.

Chapter 7 Scenario: A question of Generosity – *The Play Ablunt the Cat*

What Mark did

I don't like to interfere in a situation that may become a valuable learning moment for a graduate director. We all work with difficult people under less than ideal circumstances, so we all need to learn how to work through them. Sometimes, however, the power dynamic makes it necessary for me to step in as one faculty member to another – and this was the case here. I essentially put an end to the problem by saying, 'This is how this is going to happen; the director is going to get what she wants because she's done everything right, met all of your demands, and now it's time for you to get out of the way.' And I said this in front of the whole production team. I also knew that I had the backing of the chair/producer because I had kept her apprised of the situation throughout. Problem solved.

But there was a great problem here – a problem of departmental culture. This was early in my time at the university and I had come with expectations instilled in me from my time in professional theatre. What I experienced was a culture where production personnel (faculty, staff, and students) created problems for the director and designers. This was the exact opposite of professional practice, where production personnel are always the first ones with a solution and their primary goal is to realize the vision of the creative team. I was so surprised by this that it took me a long time to figure out how to deal with it.

One person can't change a culture, but they can make choices that can mitigate the damage or the tensions. The best way I've found is to set expectations as early as possible. Now, when I'm directing, at the first production meeting I state that I need the production team to help me and my designers solve the problems of the play and that I expect them to bring solutions, not problems, to the table. If they do feel the need to present a problem, I also insist that they bring a solution. It doesn't have to be a perfect solution – or even the one that we eventually decide on – but I need to know that they've investigated the problem enough to understand a possible solutions to the problem. I encourage my grad students to pursue this same process. Over time, personnel changes have resulted in policies that have moved us towards more professional practice, but occasionally the old culture rears its head. One thing that will not change for me is the practice of establishing expectations from day one.

Rufus's take on the scenario

1. DO YOU SEE ANY OF THE PRINCIPLES OF GOOD COLLABORATION AT WORK IN THIS SCENARIO?

Yes, the collaboration between the director and her mentor is excellent. The director feels supported, there is trust, and the mentor continues to support her vision. The director collaborated with the production manager, maintaining constant and open communication.

2. WHICH OF THE PRINCIPLES OF GOOD COLLABORATION WERE VIOLATED – AND AT WHICH POINT(S) ALONG THE WAY?

The production manager violated guiding principles #1, #2, and #3. By not reading the play, he was disrespectful, and he couldn't understand the vision. For weeks, he was not open to communicating from the director's point of view, only his own.

3. WHERE DID THE COLLABORATION GET OFF TRACK?

Collaboration got off track at the very beginning when the production manager had not read the play to understand a cat was essential to the story.

4. WHAT REASONS COULD THE DIRECTOR HAVE FOR INSISTING ON THE CAT? WHAT REASONS COULD THE PRODUCTION MANAGER HAVE HAD FOR NOT WANTING THE CAT IN THE SHOW? WHAT ROLE SHOULD I, THE MENTOR, HAVE PLAYED? IS THERE A POINT WHERE I SHOULD HAVE INTERVENED? WAS IT MY PLACE TO INTERVENE? WAS THERE ANYONE ELSE WHO SHOULD HAVE BEEN INVOLVED IN THE DECISION-MAKING PROCESS?

The director insisted on the cat because it was vital to the conclusion of the story. The production manager was uncomfortable with the logistics of using the cat. The mentor should support the director and encourage her through the experience. It is essential to allow the director to go through the process to learn. Yes, the director was a student and the production manager a member of the faculty, so a significant power imbalance exists. I believe bringing more voices into the conversation would only complicate the matter.

5. HOW DO YOU THINK WE ARRIVED AT THE FINAL CONSENSUS – TO ALLOW THE CAT TO APPEAR ON STAGE? DO YOU THINK WE WERE ABLE TO REACH CONSENSUS?

The director had provided the production manager with everything he asked her to do. There was no legal reason the cat could not happen. I believe the production manager realized this and conceded.

6. WHAT ACTIONS COULD HAVE BEEN TAKEN TO RESOLVE THE CONFLICT EARLIER IN THE PROCESS?

Early at the play selection committee meeting, someone should have addressed the point that a live cat was mandatory.

7. WHAT WOULD YOU HAVE DONE DIFFERENTLY TO RESOLVE THE CONFLICT IN YOUR FAVOR HAD YOU BEEN THE DIRECTOR? THE PRODUCTION MANAGER? THE MENTOR?

I agree with the actions of the director and the mentor. As the production manager, I would have read the play. If there were concerns around the cat, the issue could have been addressed in the play selection committee meeting.

8. HOW AND WHEN COULD GENEROSITY HAVE COME INTO PLAY IN THIS SCENARIO?

The production manager, realizing his mistake, could have addressed the issue supportively. He should have assisted the director in troubleshooting the problem, rather than delegating, and once the case found its resolution, he should have accepted the outcome.

Maria's take on the scenario

This seems like a power struggle. It seems the production manager wanted to solve it their way and was not interested in supporting the director's vision. I was curious to hear the reasoning behind the production manager's refusal to use a live cat and what were the production manager's solutions – and whether they had merit. Because the director dismissed them, I'm going to assume they did not support the director's vision.

When a problem goes in circles without any real solutions, it has been my experience that the road blocker is not seeking solutions, but rather a fight. To show dominance. The question I ask is was the production manager heard? Indeed, they were. The research was done to see whether there were rules prohibiting the use of the animal. Once the facts were revealed about the school not having a policy (good news) on using a live animal on stage, I would have done the same thing: moved forward with securing the cat and sharing the details of who and how the cat would be cared for during the show (wrangler). After all, isn't that what production managers want? What is best for the production, and contingency plans in place for everyone (including the cat) to be safe?

I think communication is a big guiding principle here that may have been missed. Listening to the complaint and understanding the reasoning is the first step toward solving a problem without a fight. Some people want the fight. My strategy is to not engage in a fight. Back off. Cool off and go solve it. I don't see any other way that this could have been solved than the way it was.

Create your Own Scenarios

We hope you have enjoyed discussing these real-life experiences. You can turn your own challenges into learning opportunities by creating scenarios based on the bumps in the road you encounter in your own collaborative experiences and sharing them with your classmates or colleagues. Here are some things to think about when creating your scenarios:

1. First, allow some distance (time) between the events in your professional or educational life and creating your scenario. Time provides perspective. You also don't want to open up an ongoing process to outside scrutiny. For dealing with problems more immediately, it is best to enter private discussions with your faculty mentors.
2. Respect your colleagues' identities by altering specific names, productions, roles, etc. so you don't damage your relationships.
3. Articulate the key participants and the roles they play in the scenario. Identify the "protagonist" and clearly state the problem that they are facing.

4. DON'T SOLVE THE PROBLEM, but prepare questions for your colleagues that will allow for the widest variety of possible responses.
5. Try to be as fair in your presentation of the facts as you can possibly be, and strive to present as balanced a point of view as you can. A fair articulation of the situation will provide you with the best chance to get good advice from those discussing the scenario.
6. Once the scenario has been presented to your class or group, listen. Approach the conversation as openly and as full of curiosity as you can. You may hear things you don't like, but that's okay – that's part of the learning process. As we say in the rehearsal room, "take the note." Write it down and give it your full consideration. It is your best chance to actually learn something that will help you the next time you encounter a similar problem.

ENJOY!

Note

1   Richard Maltby, "What Could Be Better?", *Baby*, original lyric.

Appendix 5
Contributor Biographies

LYNN AHRENS and STEPHEN FLAHERTY are considered the foremost theatrical writing team of their generation, and are members of the Theater Hall of Fame. They won Tony, Drama Desk, and Outer Critics Circle Awards for *Ragtime*, and were nominated for two Academy Awards and two Golden Globes for *Anastasia*, Twentieth Century Fox's animated feature film. *Anastasia* is also now a long- running hit on Broadway. Last season, their *Once on This Island* won Broadway's 2018 Tony Award for Best Revival of a Musical. In 2019, Ahrens and Flaherty were nominated for their fourth Grammy Award, as well as for the Songwriters' Hall of Fame. Other theatre credits include *Seussical* (one of the most produced shows in America); *Rocky*; *My Favorite Year*; *Chita Rivera – The Dancer's Life*; *Dessa Rose*; *A Man of No Importance*; *The Glorious Ones*; *Lucky Stiff* and two upcoming shows, *Knoxville* and *Marie* are due to premiere at the Asolo Repertory Theater in Sarasota, Florida and Seattle's Fifth Avenue Theater respectively. They are on the Council of the Dramatists Guild of America and are co-founders of the Dramatists Guild Fellows Program. See AhrensandFlaherty.com.

ALEXANDRA BILLINGS is Professor of Acting at the USC School of Dramatic Arts, as well as an actress, singer, author, teacher, and activist. Her television credits include: *The Connors, Transparent, How To Get Away With Murder, Grey's Anatomy* and *Goliath*. On Broadway credits include *Wicked* and *The Nap*. She is an activist and Viewpoints teacher. Awards include the TPA award and the Rainbow Spirit Award, five Dark Awards and the Joseph Jefferson Award.

BROOKE ASTON HARPER is a graduate of California State University, Fullerton's Musical Theater program, and an alumna and current faculty of The Young Americans. She began traveling as a performer at the age of 16. She sings in bands and directs theatre. She also directs, writes, and produces variety shows, including her own headliner shows. She recently directed *The Wizard of Oz*, *All Shook Up*, and *The Young Americans: Rise*. Some of her favorite roles include Armelia in *Ain't Misbehavin'*, Brenda in *Smokey Joe's Café*, and Sylvia in *All Shook Up*. As an educator, she has dedicated herself to the empowerment of young theatre-makers to create with equity and inclusion in mind.

DAVID BRIDEL's work in the performing arts has been seen in theatres, opera houses and festivals across the world. He is the winner of multiple awards for his groundbreaking fusion of text, movement, music, clowning, and story. His original plays, *Lunatics and Actors*, *I Gelosi* and *Sublimity*, are all published by Original Works Press. He is the Founding Director of The Clown School in Los Angeles, a studio devoted to the pursuit of all aspects of clowning, and he co-edited the book *Clowns – in Conversation* (Routledge, 2nd ed. 2022). He sits on the board of the National Alliance of Acting Teachers.

JILL GOLD has been an Equity stage manager since 1984, with over 250 show and event credits since then. Primarily based in Los Angeles, she toured the United States with *Les Miserables*, *The Unsinkable Molly Brown*, *City of Angels* and *Wicked*, as well as Germany and Austria with *Sisterella*. Jill teaches stage management at Occidental College and advanced stage management at UCLA, and co-authored *Stage Management* by Lawrence Stern and Jill Gold, which celebrates its 12th edition in Fall 2021.

JOHN GROMADA composed his first professional theatre score at the age of 22 for Jonathan Miller's Broadway production of *Long Day's Journey into Night*, starring Jack Lemmon, Kevin Spacey and Peter Gallagher. In the 22 years since, he has become one of the most sought-after composer/sound designers working in the theatre today. On Broadway, he has written original scores for *Next Fall*, *A Bronx Tale*, *Prelude to a Kiss*, *Heartbreak House*, *Rabbit Hole*, *Twelve Angry Men*, *Well*, the Tony Award-winning *Proof*, *Sight Unseen*, *Enchanted April*, *The Retreat From Moscow*; revivals of *A Streetcar Named Desire*, *Summer and Smoke*, and *Twelve Angry Men* at the Roundabout; and *Holiday* at Circle in the Square. Gromada's music was also featured in the Broadway and road productions of the long-running *A Few Good Men*. His awards include the Lucille Lortel Award, the Drama Desk Award, the Village Voice Obie award, a 1993 LA Drama-logue award, and Connecticut Critics

Circle Awards. For 22 consecutive years, he has received ASCAP special awards for his theatrical composition work.

KIMBERLY HARRIS made her Broadway debut as an original cast member of *The Color Purple*. She originated the role of Church Lady Doris and went on to recreate her role on the first national/international tour. Other production highlights include: *The Full Monty* (first national tour), *Bubblin' Brown Sugar* (European tour), *Sophisticated Ladies* (European tour), *Blues in the Night* (South American tour) *Ain't Misbehavin'* (National tour), *Little Shop of Horrors*, *Carmen Jones*, *The Apple Tree*, *The Sisters of Rosewall High*, *The Color Purple* (world premiere – Alliance Theatre, Atlanta), *Play On!* (Crossroads), *Once on This Island* (Actors Theatre) and many, many more. TV appearances include *Law and Order*, *One Life to Live*, *Third Watch* and much more to come. Ms. Harris has written a musical and 3 TV pilots. See KimberlyannHarris.com

KARI HAYTER was nominated for the 28th Annual LA Stage Alliance Ovation Award Best Direction of a Musical for both *Parade* at the Chance Theatre and *Urinetown: The Musical* for Coeurage Theatre Company. She was also nominated for the Los Angeles Drama Critics Circle Award for theatrical excellence in 2016 for Direction of *Urinetown: The Musical*. Current and future projects include SDCF Observership – *The Unsinkable Molly Brown* (directed and choreographed by Kathleen Marshall/Transport Group at Abrons Art Center, New York City). Her directing credits include: South Coast Repertory, Cerritos Center for the Performing Arts for 3-D Theatricals and The Chance Theatre. She is currently a professor at the American Musical and Dramatic Academy in Los Angeles.

CELISE HICKS is a Creative development/artistic director/assistant choreographer/dance therapist. She was a member of Ailey II, where she performed works from Alvin Ailey, Lar Lubovitch, Avila/Weeks, Jose Limon, and Shen Wei. She was a principal dancer with Ronald K. Brown/ Evidence. She worked and performed for choreographers Talley Beatty, Eleo Pomare, Donald Byrd, Mercedes Ellington, Matthew Rushing, Earl Mosley, Brian Brooks, and Hope Boykin. Her theatre credits include *Black Nativity* (US tour), *Harlem Nutcracker* (US tour), *Notre Dame de Paris* (Las Vegas), and *The Lion King* (Los Angeles), where she was also was dance captain. Television credits include *Saturday Night Live*, *The Oprah Show*, *Jay Leno*, *Dancing with the Stars*, and the *Daytime Emmys*.

Celise has appeared in commercials and music videos with artists such as James Brown, Jill Scott, and TLC, and performed in Nike and Adidas industrials. She was the resident dance supervisor for *The Lion King* for two US tours and the Las Vegas and Taipei productions. Celise teaches in universities and is currently the resident dance supervisor of *The Lion King London*, the assistant choreographer of *The Lion King Worldwide* and co-director of Bennu Creative House, based in London.

ARIANNA HUHN is an anthropologist and director of the Anthropology Museum at Cal State San Bernardino, where she has developed collaborative curatorial projects such as "Re | Collect" and "In | Dignity" with the surrounding community and with faculty in the social sciences and creative arts.

TONI-LESLIE JAMES has designed costumes nationally and internationally for every entertainment venue: feature film, television, opera, dance, industrials, regional theatre, and Broadway. For Broadway, she has designed *Birthday Candles*, *Flying Over Sunset*, *Bernhardt/Hamlet* (Drama Desk Award, Tony nomination) *Come From Away* (Hewes Design Award, Drama Desk nomination), *August Wilson's Jitney* (Tony and Drama Desk nominations), *Lucky Guy*, *The Scottsboro Boys*, *Finian's Rainbow*, *Chita Rivera: The Dancer's Life*, *Ma Rainey's Black Bottom*, *King Hedley II*, *One Mo' Time*, *The Wild Party*, *Marie Christine*, *Footloose*, *The Tempest*, *Twilight Los Angeles 1992*, *Angels in America: Millennium Approaches & Perestroika*, *Chronicle of a Death Foretold*, and *Jelly's Last Jam* (Hewes Design Award, Tony and Drama Desk nominations). Ms. James received a BFA in Theatre from Ohio State University. She is currently an Assistant Professor of Design at the Yale School of Drama and Yale Repertory Theatre's resident costume designer.

JOHN KAUFMANN is a theatre teacher, director and performer. He worked as planetarium supervisor at Pacific Science Center and developed original programs including the improvised astronomy musical *Starball*. In Seattle, he worked with Seattle Children's Theatre, was on the development team for several *Cranium* board games and facilitated improvisation training for chaplains at Harborview Medical Center. As "Interactive Host" for the 2018 TEDx Seattle Conference, he helped 2800 attendees engage intimately with each other. Kaufmann earned his MFA in theatre directing from the University of Iowa and currently teaches theatre at Evergreen Valley College in San Jose, California.

RON KELLUM is a seasoned director and producer with experience ranging from sports entertainment to circus, theatre, film and television. Ron was the artistic director of Cirque du Soleil's show *Volta* from 2018 to 2020 and the company's acclaimed *Kooza*. His directing and choreography credits include *Iron Man 2*, starring Robert Downey Jr. as well as the musicals *Ain't Misbehavin*, *Chicago*, *A Chorus Line*, *The Color Purple*, *Dreamgirls*, *Jesus Christ Superstar*, *Once on This Island*, *Rent*, *Smokey Joe's Cafe* and *5 Guys Named Moe*. As a performer, Ron has appeared on Broadway in *Joseph and the Amazing Technicolor Dreamcoat* and *Chicago*, and toured nationally *in Aida*, *Dreamgirls*, *Fosse*, and *Chicago*.

BEN KRYWOSZ, dramaturg/director/producer, has served as co-founder and artistic director of Nautilus Music-Theater, based in St Paul, Minnesota since 1986. Nautilus develops writers, composers, and performers interested in telling stories through music, whether with opera, musicals, or alternative work. Nautilus offers performer training in integrated singing-acting, composer-librettist studios, works-in-progress developmental sessions, and fully staged productions. Ben also serves as a stage director, group facilitator, administrative consultant, and community organizer, and teaches master classes in singing-acting and collaboration for academic institutions around the country.

KECIA LEWIS made her Broadway debut at 18 years of age in the original company of *Dreamgirls*, directed by Michael Bennett. Broadway credits include: *The Gospel* at Colonus (with Morgan Freeman), *Big River*, *Ain't Misbehavin'* (standby for Nell Carter), *Once on This Island* (OBC), *The Drowsy Chaperone* (OBC), *Chicago*, *Leap of Faith* (OBC), *Cinderella* (as Marie/Fairy Godmother) and most recently *Children of a Lesser God* (directed by Kenny Leon). Off Broadway, she starred in the title role of *Mother Courage*, in *The Skin of Our Teeth* (Obie Award), *Dessa Rose* at Lincoln Center (Drama Desk award nomination), and *Marie and Rosetta* (Lortel & Drama League nominations/ Obie Award winner). Her television credits include *Law & Order*, *Law & Order SVU* (recurring), *Madam Secretary*, *Royal Pains*, *Limitless*, *Conviction*, *Unbreakable Kimmy Schmidt*, *Blue Bloods*, *SMILF*, *The Blacklist* (recurring), *The Passage* (recurring), *Mad About You* (recurring), and the Hulu series *Wu-Tang: An American Saga* (recurring). As a vocalist, Kecia has performed in Canada, Switzerland, Hong Kong, New Zealand, and Russia.

STANLEY WAYNE MATHIS is a native Washingtonian who now hails from New York City. He was last seen in the first national tour of *The Book of Mormon*. Broadway credits include: *The Book of Mormon*, *Nice Work If You Can Get It*, *Wonderful Town*, *Kiss Me Kate!*, *You're a Good Man Charlie Brown*, *The Lion King*, *Jelly's Last Jam*, and *Oh Kay!* His film and TV credits include: *Dark Streets*, *Santa Baby*, *Brother to Brother*, and *Shame* by Steve McQueen, as well as *Law & Order*, *Criminal Intent*, *20/20*, *Gossip Girls*, and NBC's *Rise*, as principal Evan Ward. National and international productions include *Gem of the Ocean* (Seattle Rep), *Ruined* (Florida Studio Theatre), *Death of a Salesman* (Yale Rep), *Spunk* (Royal Court Theater London), and most recently Regina Taylor's *Oo-Bla-Dee* (Two Rivers Theater New Jersey), directed by Ruben Santiago-Hudson. Stanley has recently written his own multimedia play titled *Preachin' to the Choir/An Inconvenient Truth: A Blacklivesmatter Odyssey*. See Smathis0155@aol.com

HEATHER McDONALD's plays include *Masterpieces of the Oral, Intangible Heritage of Humanity*, *An Almost Holy Picture*, *When Grace Comes In*, *Dream of a Common Language*, *Available Light*, *The Rivers and Ravines*, *Faulkner's Bicycle*, *The Two Marys*, *Rain and Darkness*, and the upcoming *The Suppressed-Desire Ball* (developed at Sundance–Ucross Writer's Retreat). Her work has been produced on Broadway (starring Kevin Bacon) and off Broadway, and at such theatres as The Roundabout Theatre, Arena Stage, The McCarter Theatre, Center Stage, Berkeley Repertory Theatre, Seattle Repertory Theatre, Indiana Rep, California Shakespeare Theatre, Round House Theatre, Signature Theatre, Yale Repertory Theatre, The Actors Theatre of Louisville – Humana Festival of New Plays, the La Jolla Playhouse and internationally in Italy, Spain, Portugal, England, and Mexico.

TRACEY MOORE is a full professor and Chair of Music Theatre in the Hartt School's Theatre Division. National Broadway Tours include *Camelot* with Richard Harris and the role of Emma Goldman in *Ragtime*. Her books, *Acting the Song* and the new *Student Companion to ATS*, are available through Allworth Press, and she has published articles in the *Chronicle of Higher Ed*, *The New York Times*, *Teaching Theatre*, and several journals. Before coming to academia, Tracey was known for her work on new musical theatre. She holds an MFA in acting from Brooklyn College, an MA in dramatic literature from Southern Illinois University, and a BM in voice from Indiana University.

MARIEL MULET is a labor and employment lawyer and senior investigator at Public Interest Investigations, Inc. She has extensive experience conducting investigations of sexual misconduct and discrimination for both public and private universities. She served as the Title IX Coordinator and Discrimination, Harassment and Retaliation Administrator for California State University, Los Angeles, where she implemented and enforced legislation and policies related to civil rights and Title IX, investigated cases, and designed and delivered related training. Mariel also investigated complaints of discrimination, harassment, and sexual misconduct at the University of Southern California, including complaints involving faculty, students, and staff. Before becoming an investigator, Mariel litigated cases of harassment, discrimination, and retaliation in California for nine years.

CRICKET S. MYERS earned a Tony Nomination and a Drama Desk Award on Broadway for her design of *Bengal Tiger at the Baghdad Zoo*. Regional designs include La Jolla Playhouse, The Ahmanson, The Mark Taper Forum, Kansas City Rep, South Coast Rep, Shakespeare Theater Company in Washington, DC, The Kirk Douglas Theater, Pasadena Playhouse, The Wallis Annenberg, and the Geffen Theater. She has earned 24 Ovation nominations, as well as winning The League of Professional Theater Woman's Ruth Morley Award and The Kinetic Award for Outstanding Achievement in Theatrical Design. See www.cricketsmyers.com.

CHELSEA PACE (SDC, MFA Arizona State University) is an intimacy choreographer, intimacy coordinator for film, and movement specialist. She is an assistant professor at the University of Maryland, Baltimore County and she choreographs and consult on best practice for staging intimacy for professional and educational theatre and film across the country. Chelsea is co-founder and head of the Faculty of Theatrical Intimacy Education and President of the Association of Theatre Movement Educators. See www.chelseapace.com and www.theatricalintimacyed.com.

MICHELE PATSAKIS received her Doctorate of Musical Arts from the USC Thornton School of Music and an MM from the New England Conservatory. In demand as an adjudicator, presenter, and masterclass technician, her work in the areas of vocal pedagogy and music education has been featured with the National Association of Teachers of Singing, the Performing Arts Medicine Association, and the California

Music Educators Conferences. Acclaimed as an operatic soprano with companies such as De Munt in Brussels and the New York City Opera, she won awards from the Metropolitan Opera National Council Auditions and the Loren L. Zachary National Vocal Competition.

DANNY PELZIG is a director, choreographer, educator, and producer. Credits include *33 Variations* and *A Year with Frog and Toad* on Broadway; and the Manhattan Theatre Club, New York Theatre Workshop, City Center *Encores!* and Roundabout Theatre Opera off Broadway. Opera credits include the Metropolitan Opera, Seattle Opera, Houston Grand Opera, La Scala, Lyric Opera of Chicago, and Santa Fe Opera. Regional theatre credits include the Huntington Theatre, The Guthrie, Oregon Shakespeare Theatre, Goodman Theatre, La Jolla Playhouse, Alliance Theatre, Arena Stage, Old Globe, Ahmanson Theatre, Shakespeare Theatre Company, Shaw Festival, Musical Theatre West and the Kennedy Center *Sondheim Celebration*. He served as resident choreographer for the Boston Ballet, and is currently a full professor at Boston Conservatory at Berklee.

JIM PENTECOST was involved in the theatre as a producer, director and stage manager, ranging from Broadway productions to national touring companies. His credits include the Broadway productions of *Crimes of the Heart, La Cage Aux Folles, Romance, Romance, Gypsy* with Tyne Daly, and the musical, *Nick and Nora.* He made his motion picture debut as the producer of the Disney animated feature, *Pocahontas.* He was the executive producer for the Stephen Schwartz musical *Geppetto* on the *Wonderful World of Disney.* Jim taught drama at Santee Education Complex in Los Angeles from 2006 to 2019.

LORA K. POWELL is a faculty member at UC San Diego, where she teaches stage management in the department of Theatre & Dance. Stage management credits include the national tours of *Blithe Spirit* and *Wicked.* Broadway productions include *Chicago, The Life, Annie Get Your Gun.* In Los Angeles, she has worked on *The Lion King, The Producers, Wicked, Amélie, Harmony, The Scottsboro Boys, Backbeat, Seminar, Follies,* Bill Irwin's *On Beckett, Parfumerie, Maurice Hines' Tappin' Thru Life, Satchmo at the Waldorf, Carrie the Killer Musical Experience* and *The Christopher Boy's Reunion* (written and directed by David Mamet). Regional credits include the South Coast Repertory, The Wallis Annenberg Center, The Alliance Theatre and the Paper Mill Playhouse.

CLINT RAMOS is a designer, educator, activist, and producer. He is the recipient of a Tony Award for Best Costume Design of a Play (the first person of color to win in his category) and has also been nominated twice for his designs for *Once on This Island* and *Torch Song*. He has designed sets and/or costumes for over 200 theatre, opera, and dance productions. Film credits include production design for *Lingua Franca* by Isabel Sandoval for Netflix, and costume design for *RESPECT*, the Aretha Franklin biopic starring Jennifer Hudson for MGM. Clint is the producing creative director for Encores! at New York City Center, is professor of design and head of design and production at Fordham University, and serves on the American Theater Wing's advisory committee. His lifelong advocacy is for an equitable landscape in theatre and film for Black and Indigenous people, and people of color, and for the rights of immigrants.

KELVIN "KJ" RHODES is a 2017 graduate of the MFA Acting program at California State University Fullerton. Since graduating, he has worked on over 20 projects, ranging from plays and musicals to podcasts and round-table discussions on diversity in theatre. He is currently working on a book of his poetry, which he aims to have published by the end of the year.

LAURA RIKARD is an assistant professor at the University of South Carolina Upstate, and co-founder and head of the Faculty of Theatrical Intimacy Education. She is a director, actor, educator, and an intimacy choreographer and coordinator. She is a member of AEA, SAG-AFTRA, and the SDC. She most recently served as an intimacy coordinator with NBC Universal. She has taught workshops on theatrical intimacy at the Kennedy Center, and many universities and training programs, and contributed to the book *Staging Sex* by Chelsea Pace.

RUI RITA (lighting designer) has worked on numerous Broadway productions, including *Trip to Bountiful, Velocity of Autumn, Present Laughter, Dividing the Estate, Old Acquaintance, Enchanted April, The Price*. Off Broadway productions include: Atlantic Theatre – *Skeleton Crew*; Second Stage – *Happiest Song Plays Last*; Roundabout – *Just Jim Dale, Talley's Folly, Milk Train Doesn't Stop Here Anymore*; Signature-NY – *Piano Lesson*, Horton Foote's *The Orphans' Home Cycle*; TFANA – *Engaged* (Obie Award), *All's Well That Ends Well*; Manhattan Theatre Club – *Nightingale, Moonlight and Magnolias*; Lincoln Center – *Big Bill*,

The Carpetbagger's Children. Regional theatre work has included Alley, American Conservatory Theatre, Arena Stage, Center Stage, Center Theatre Group, Ford's Theatre, Guthrie Theater, Hartford Stage, Huntington Theatre, Kennedy Center, Old Globe, Oregon Shakespeare Festival, Shakespeare Theatre Company, Two River Theatre, and the Williamstown Theatre Festival.

SUSAN SAMPLINER has been the company manager for the Broadway production of *Wicked* since it began rehearsals in March 2003. She has been company managing for almost 40 years, dividing her time between the commercial and not-for-profit theatre in New York, both on and off Broadway. She was the associate general manager for *Grease*, *Chicago*, and *Damn Yankees*, as well as for the New York Shakespeare Festival for four years. Susan is a graduate of Brown University and holds a certificate in arts management from SUNY Purchase, where she also taught for two years.

ANN SHEFFIELD previously taught set design at Cal State Fullerton, before joining the Department of Theater and Dance at the University of California, Santa Barbara in 2019 as head of design and director of performance. Concurrently, Ann continues her work with regional theatres across the country, including Indiana Repertory Theatre, Laguna Playhouse, La Jolla Playhouse, Goodspeed Opera House, Philadelphia's Walnut Street Theatre, Washington, DC's Ford's Theatre, Arizona Theatre Company, Oklahoma Festival Ballet, Children's Theatre Company of Minneapolis, and South Coast Repertory Theatre. Ann continues a long association with award-winning designer Tony Walton, having assisted him on major Broadway productions in her early professional life. Ann is a graduate of the Yale School of Drama.

AMBER SNEAD is a performer turned casting director. She has been working in casting in regional Southern California theatre for seven years. She predominantly casts shows for 3D theatricals. When not behind the table, she still loves the thrill of being on stage, and can frequently be seen in *Miscast: Right Singer, Wrong Song* at the Federal Bar in NoHo. Select casting credits include: *Kinky Boots*, *Once on This Island*, and *Million Dollar Quartet*. Select acting credits include *Disney's Aladdin: A Musical Spectacular*, *Mary Poppins*, *Hair*, *Ragtime*, and *Seussical*.

CHERYL THOMAS is an award-winning professional makeup artist and a native of Atlanta, GA. She is a proud member of Hair and Makeup Unions 706 and 798. She is the current worldwide hair and makeup supervisor of *Aladdin* and *Aladdin on Broadway*. She was the assistant hair and makeup designer for *Lion King Worldwide*, and has worked on numerous award-winning Broadway productions. She has been guest lecturer at North Carolina School of the Arts and University of Texas in Austin for Theater, Design and Production and Film. She has worked at CNN, CNN International, Headline News, ABC World of Sports, the Netherlands Olympic TV, HBO, and E! Fashion Emergency. Her career has allowed her to work with many celebrities, designers, and icons, but she maintains the belief that all things are possible if you believe and that she was created to create.

SALISHA THOMAS is a California native and a former Miss California. She graduated from CSU Fullerton with a BA in theatre, is a former vocalist for Disneyland, has performed regionally throughout California, and toured with *Beautiful: The Carole King Musical* and eventually joined the cast on Broadway. Before Broadway shut down, Salisha was in rehearsals for the Britney Spears musical *Once Upon a One More Time*. She currently resides in New York City. Follow her blog at www.salishathomas.com.

DARYL WATERS has composed, arranged, orchestrated, music supervised, and conducted various Broadway musicals, including *Bring in 'da Noise, Bring in 'da Funk* (Tony nomination-original music) and *Memphis* (Tony Award-best orchestrations), the *Cher Show*, *Shuffle Along or the Making of the Musical Sensation of 1921*, and *All That Followed*. In addition to his theatrical accomplishments, Waters became Eartha Kitt's music director in 1986, performing concerts with her on six continents over 22 years. He also conducted and arranged for many other stars, including Leslie Uggams, Sammy Davis Jr., Gregory Hines, Cab Calloway, Nell Carter, Patti Austin, and Jennifer Holliday.

RALPH ZITO is a professor in the Department of Drama at Syracuse University. Currently on administrative assignment from the dean, he served as chair of the department from July 2010 through December 2020, and will return to the chair in July 2022. He has served as a voice, text, or dialect consultant for numerous professional productions, both on and off Broadway, and at regional theatres around the country.

Previous positions include: chair, Voice and Speech Department, Juilliard School Drama Division; The Acting Company; artistic associate of The Chautauqua Theater Company; and board of directors of The American Society for the Alexander Technique (AmSAT). He is a graduate of Harvard University, The Juilliard School, and The American Center for the Alexander Technique.

Index